TOP 10 OF EVERYTHING 2017

Portable Press
An imprint of Printers Row Publishing Group
10350 Barnes Canyon Road, Suite 100,
San Diego, CA 92121
www.portablepress.com

Written and researched by Paul Terry

Top 10 Of Everything was devised and created by Russell Ash

Copyright © 2016 Octopus Publishing Group

All notations of errors or omissions should be addressed to
Portable Press, Editorial Department, at the above address.
All other correspondence (author inquiries, permissions)
concerning the content of this book should be addressed
to Octopus Publishing Group Ltd, Carmelite House,
50 Victoria Embankment, London EC4Y 0DZ
www.octopusbooks.co.uk

Portable Press
Publisher: Peter Norton
Publishing Team: Gordon Javna, JoAnn Padgett, Melinda
Allman, Brian Boone, Trina Janssen, J. Carroll, Aaron Guzman

Octopus
Editorial Director Trevor Davies
Editor Pollyanna Poulter
Designers Jack Storey and Paul Shubrook
Production Controller Sarah Kulasek-Boyd

Library of Congress Cataloging-in-Publication Data available
on request.
ISBN: 978-1-62686-846-5

Printed in China

20 19 18 17 16 1 2 3 4 5

TOP 10

OF EVERYTHING

2017

BY
PAUL TERRY

AUTHOR'S INTRO

Love Batman? But do you know what the biggest bats on Earth are? Adore BB-8? But can you guess which *Star Wars* movies are the biggest hits? That's where we come in. Other books are obsessed with weird "number 1s," but we're all about the Top 10s. Of *everything*.

Inside these pages you're gonna find a bit of everything. With music streaming more popular than ever, we've got the stats that matter the most from the music world. Fan of outer space? We've got the lowdown on planet Mars and humanity's plans to colonize it. Olympic and Paralympic champions, massive wolves, the most popular art galleries, the largest lakes...*Top 10 of Everything 2017* has over 10,000 facts for you to pore over.

If, like me, you also love sci-fi, you'll find tons of genre TV and movie facts in this tome. Yes, for the first time, our Movie zone now covers TV from around the world, too. Maybe you'll find something in here that will inspire you to write a novel or a screenplay? And if it features giant bats, remember us when you're famous.

ABOUT THE AUTHOR

PAUL TERRY has written and edited official publications for Bad Robot's TV shows *Alias*, *Lost*, and *Fringe*, as well as for LEGO, Disney, *Star Wars*, *The Simpsons*, and *Futurama*. He coauthored (with frequent collaborator Tara Bennett) *The Blacklist: Elizabeth Keen's Dossier*; *Sleepy Hollow: Creating Heroes, Demons & Monsters*; *Lost Encyclopedia*; and *Fringe: September's Notebook*.

Paul is also the author of the Top 10 book series. His eighth, the *Top 10 of Everything 2017*, combines his love of comic books, creatures, and pop culture. Paul was also the designer and editor for Anneke van Giersbergen's book *The Road to Drive*.

When he's not writing books, Paul writes music. His film scores include *Emily* (starring Oscar-nominee Felicity Jones and Emmy-winner Christopher Eccleston) and the award-winning chiller *Care*. Under his solo moniker of Cellarscape, his records include *Exo Echo* and the award-winning album *The Act of Letting Go*.

CONTENTS

ANIMAL KINGDOM

ZONE **1**

Standing on its hind legs, a Polar Bear can be up to **11.1** FT. tall

BIGGEST CARNIVORES

If an organism eats another organism, it has made the criteria for this Top 10...

	TYPE	NAME	WEIGHT (LB)	(KG)
1	WHALE	BLUE WHALE	418,877	189,999
2	SHARK	WHALE SHARK	47,000	21,318
3	DOLPHIN	ORCA WHALE	22,000	9,979
4	SEAL	SOUTHERN ELEPHANT SEAL	11,000	4,990
5	CROCODILE	SALTWATER CROCODILE	4,409	2,000
6	WALRUS	PACIFIC WALRUS	4,151	1,883
7	BEAR	POLAR BEAR	2,209	1,002
8	STINGRAY	GIANT FRESHWATER STINGRAY	1,320	600
9	SQUID	COLOSSAL SQUID	1,091	495
10	BIG CAT	SIBERIAN TIGER	1,025	465

BLUE WHALE

1 As far as our current knowledge of life on Earth goes, this oceanic mammal is the heaviest organism ever to have lived. It grows to up to 110 feet (33.5 m) in length, with flippers 13 feet (4 m) long.

SALTWATER CROCODILE

5 This ambush predator strikes its prey seemingly from nowhere. Growing to 23.3 feet (7.1 m) in length, this Australian and Asian resident attacks the likes of water buffalo and wild boar.

ZERO CONTENDERS

This illustrates just how big the Blue Whale is...

BLUE WHALE 418,877 LB

WHALE SHARK 47,000 LB

ORCA WHALE 22,000 LB

SOUTHERN ELEPHANT SEAL 11,000 LB

SALTWATER CROCODILE 4,409 LB

TOP 10

HEAVIEST HERBIVORES

Animals that live off of vegetation, instead of hunting and eating other animals or fish, can be found here...

	TYPE	NAME	AVERAGE WEIGHT (LB)	(KG)
1	ELEPHANT	AFRICAN BUSH ELEPHANT	26,455	12,000
2	HIPPOPOTAMUS	COMMON HIPPOPOTAMUS	9,921	4,500
3	RHINOCEROS	SOUTHERN WHITE RHINOCEROS	8,819	4,000
4	GIRAFFE	ROTHSCHILD GIRAFFE	4,255	1,930
5	BOVINE	CHIANINA	3,924	1,780
6	HORSE	SHIRE HORSE	3,307	1,500
7	DEER	CHUKOTKA MOOSE	1,598	725
8	TORTOISE	GALÁPAGOS TORTOISE	919	417
9	GORILLA	EASTERN LOWLAND GORILLA	595	270
10	KANGAROO	RED KANGAROO	201	91

A Chianina's height can reach

6.6
FEET

SOUTHERN WHITE RHINOCEROS

3 This African giant grows to a height of more than 6 feet (1.8 m). Its name comes from a general description of its light gray skin color (which can also be a muddy yellow hue).

LARGEST REPTILES

Taking into account all of the different families of reptiles, these are the biggest you'll find in each...

	REPTILE FAMILY	NAME	WEIGHT (LB)	(KG)
1	**CROCODYLIDAE**	SALTWATER CROCODILE	4,409.2	2,000
2	**ALLIGATORIDAE**	BLACK CAIMAN	2,900	1,310
3	**GAVIALIDAE**	GHARIAL	2,150	977
4	**DERMOCHELYIDAE**	LEATHERBACK SEA TURTLE	2,120	961.1
5	**TESTUDINIDAE**	GALÁPAGOS TORTOISE	919	417
6	**BOIDAE**	GREEN ANACONDA	550	249.5
7	**VARANIDAE**	KOMODO DRAGON	366	166
8	**PYTHONIDAE**	RETICULATED PYTHON	350.1	158.8
9	**VIPERIDAE**	GABOON VIPER	44	20
10	**ELAPIDAE**	KING COBRA	28	12.7

LEATHERBACK SEA TURTLE

4 Although the female lays its eggs (often more than 100) on beaches, this sea turtle spends most of its life in the open ocean.

GABOON VIPER

9 Measuring up to 6.8 feet (2.1 m) in length, this is the heaviest viper. Its two front fangs can grow up to 1.9 inches (5 cm) in length.

Gharial have **110** teeth

TOP 10

BIGGEST PREHISTORIC BIPEDAL CARNIVORES

Of the fossils we've uncovered so far, these ancient meat-eating beasts were the largest...

	DINOSAUR	LENGTH (FEET)	(M)
1	SPINOSAURUS	59	18
▶ 2	CARCHARODONTOSAURUS	43.3	13.2
=	GIGANOTOSAURUS	43.3	13.2
4	CHILANTAISAURUS	42.7	13
5	TYRANNOSAURUS REX	40.4	12.3
6	TYRANNOTITAN	40	12.2
▶ 7	TORVOSAURUS	39.4	12
=	ALLOSAURUS	39.4	12
9	ACROCANTHOSAURUS	37.7	11.5
10	DELTADROMEUS	36.1	11

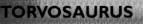

TORVOSAURUS

7 This dinosaur was officially named in 1979. Similar in appearance to *Tyrannosaurus rex*, *Torvosaurus* also had two very short arms.

The largest *T. rex* tooth discovered to date is

12 INCHES long

CARCHARODONTOSAURUS

2 Scientists estimate this meat-eating dinosaur weighed up to 33,290 pounds (15,100 kg). Its teeth were serrated like steak knives, with the longest measuring 8 inches (20.3 cm).

11

GIANT WATER BUG

7 A fearless predator, the Giant Water Bug attacks prey much larger than itself, including small snakes, amphibians, and even young turtles.

TOP 5 INSECTS COMPARED

Side by side, the 5 largest would look like this...

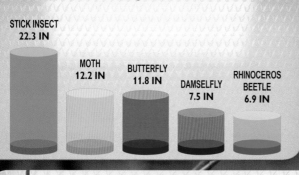

STICK INSECT
22.3 IN

MOTH
12.2 IN

BUTTERFLY
11.8 IN

DAMSELFLY
7.5 IN

RHINOCEROS BEETLE
6.9 IN

BIGGEST INSECTS

TOP 10

Comparing the different kinds of critters from the insect kingdom, these are the largest...

	TYPE	INSECT	SIZE (LENGTH) (IN)	(CM)
1	STICK INSECT	CHAN'S MEGASTICK	22.3	56.7
2	MOTH	WHITE WITCH MOTH	12.2	31 *
3	BUTTERFLY	QUEEN ALEXANDRA'S BIRDWING	11.8	30 *
4	DAMSELFLY	MEGALOPREPUS CAERULATUS	7.5	19 *
5	RHINOCEROS BEETLE	HERCULES BEETLE	6.9	17.5
6	LONGHORN BEETLE	TITAN BEETLE	6.6	16.7
7	WATER BUG	GIANT WATER BUG	4.75	12
8	FLY	MYDAS FLY	3.9	10 *
9	MANTID	GIANT AFRICAN MANTIS	3.1	8
10	WASP	TARANTULA HAWK SPIDER WASP	2	5

* Wingspan. The rest are lengths.

MYDAS FLY

8 Resembling a mutant hornet much more than a housefly, the Mydas Fly could be compared to something out of a sci-fi movie. There are more than 400 species in existence in hot climates all over the world.

The stinger of a Tarantula Hawk Spider Wasp is **0.3** IN. long

BAT HIDEOUTS

Bats don't just hang out in caves. Some tiny South American bats make tentlike shelters out of palm tree leaves.

BONIN FLYING FOX

6 This kind of fruit bat lives exclusively on the Ogasawara Islands, south of Japan. Deforestation threatens to wipe out this species.

The Canary Big-eared Bat lives in places as high as **7,546** FT. above sea level

MOST ENDANGERED BATS

TOP 10

Many species of bats are in danger of becoming extinct, especially the following 10...

	BAT	APPROXIMATE POPULATION REMAINING
1	CHRISTMAS ISLAND PIPISTRELLE	4
2	CUBAN GREATER FUNNEL-EARED BAT	100
=	SEYCHELLES SHEATH-TAILED BAT	100
4	BULMER'S FRUIT BAT	160
5	FLAT-HEADED MYOTIS	250
▶ 6	BONIN FLYING FOX	300
=	ARNHEM LEAF-NOSED BAT	300
8	NEW GEORGIAN MONKEY-FACED BAT	500
9	THAILAND ROUNDLEAF BAT	1,200
10	CANARY BIG-EARED BAT	1,250

A Cheetah can accelerate from **0-64** MPH in 3 seconds

CENTRAL BEARDED DRAGON

10 Growing to 2 feet (0.6 m) long, this lizard displays its beard and opens its yellow-colored mouth whenever it feels threatened.

PEREGRINE FALCON

1 This, the fastest animal on Earth, is also highly celebrated. Revered by many Native American tribes, it is also the national animal of the United Arab Emirates.

TOP 10

FASTEST ANIMAL SPECIES

Among all of the different species, these are the fastest of them all...

	TYPE	ANIMAL	AVG. SPEED (MPH)	(KMH)
1	RAPTOR	PEREGRINE FALCON	242	389
2	BONY FISH	BLACK MARLIN	80	128.7
3	BIG CAT	CHEETAH	75	120.7
4	ARTIODACTYL MAMMAL	PRONGHORN	60.9	98
5	BAT	MEXICAN FREE-TAILED BAT	60	96.6
=	FLIGHTLESS BIRD	OSTRICH	60	96.6
7	SHARK	MAKO SHARK	59	95
8	HORSE	AMERICAN QUARTER HORSE	53.4	86
9	DOLPHIN	ORCA WHALE	40.1	65
10	REPTILE	CENTRAL BEARDED DRAGON	24.9	40

Cape Buffalo
weigh up to

2,000
POUNDS

TOP 10

MOST **DEADLY**

From spreading dangerous diseases to inflicting fatal
bites, these are the creatures that are deadliest to us...

	CREATURE	HUMAN FATALITIES
1	MOSQUITO	DISEASES IT SPREADS KILL 2 MILLION PER YEAR
2	TSETSE FLY	DISEASES IT SPREADS KILL 250,000–300,000 PER YEAR
3	INDIAN COBRA	RESPONSIBLE FOR MOST OF INDIA'S 50,000 ANNUAL SNAKEBITE DEATHS
4	BUTHIDAE FAMILY OF SCORPIONS	3,250 DEATHS PER YEAR
5	AUSTRALIAN SALTWATER CROCODILE	1,000+ DEATHS PER YEAR
6	HIPPOPOTAMUS	500+ DEATHS PER YEAR
7	ELEPHANT	APPROXIMATELY 500 DEATHS PER YEAR
8	CAPE BUFFALO	200+ DEATHS PER YEAR
9	AFRICAN LION	APPROXIMATELY 150 DEATHS PER YEAR
10	AUSTRALIAN BOX JELLYFISH	APPROXIMATELY 90 DEATHS PER YEAR

TSETSE FLY

2 Most of the African
countries affected
by the Tsetse
Fly struggle with
poverty and famine,
making eradicating
this fly, and the
diseases it spreads,
very difficult.

AUSTRALIAN BOX JELLYFISH

10 Four distinctive sides give this
deadly sea creature its name.
Thousands of sting-inflicting cells
called nematocysts are located in
the 15 tentacles at each corner.

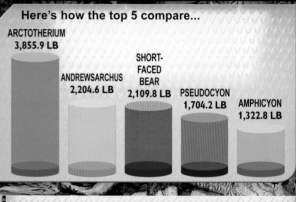

Prehistoric herbivore the Woolly Mammoth weighed **12,000** LB.

MASSIVE MAMMALS

Here's how the top 5 compare...

ARCTOTHERIUM
3,855.9 LB

ANDREWSARCHUS
2,204.6 LB

SHORT-FACED BEAR
2,109.8 LB

PSEUDOCYON
1,704.2 LB

AMPHICYON
1,322.8 LB

DIRE WOLF

9 Dire Wolves are famously part of George R. R. Martin's *Game of Thrones* world. Far from fictional, this prehistoric canine fed mainly on ancient horses and bison.

AMPHICYON

5 Living more than 18 million years ago, these mammals resembled a cross between a bear and a large dog. Their mass was similar to the largest of the big cats that exist today.

TOP 10

BIGGEST PREHISTORIC CARNIVOROUS MAMMALS

The word "prehistory" usually brings dinosaurs to mind, but this list shows that prehistoric mammals were colossal too...

	CREATURE	AVG. WEIGHT (LB)	(KG)
1	ARCTOTHERIUM	3,855.9	1,749
2	ANDREWSARCHUS	2,204.6	1,000
3	SHORT-FACED BEAR	2,109.8	957
4	PSEUDOCYON	1,704.2	773
▶ 5	AMPHICYON	1,322.8	600
6	SMILODON	1,036.2	470
7	THYLACOSMILUS	264.6	120
8	PACHYCROCUTA	242.5	110
▶ 9	DIRE WOLF	174.2	79
10	EPICYON	150	68

SAUROPOSEIDON

4 Appropriately for its ground-shaking dimensions, this dinosaur's name comes from the Greek god Poseidon, who was the god of earthquakes, storms, and the ocean.

TOP 10

LARGEST PREHISTORIC HERBIVORES

From the knowledge we currently have, these titans are the largest plant-eaters ever to have walked the Earth...

	DINOSAUR	LENGTH (FEET)	(M)
1	AMPHICOELIAS	196.8	60
2	ARGENTINOSAURUS	118.1	36
▶ 3	MAMENCHISAURUS	114.8	35
4	FUTALOGNKOSAURUS	111.5	34
▶ =	SAUROPOSEIDON	111.5	34
6	DIPLODOCUS	108.3	33
7	XINJIANGTITAN	105	32
8	PUERTASAURUS	98.4	30
=	TURIASAURUS	98.4	30
10	DREADNOUGHTUS	85.3	26

MAMENCHISAURUS

3 Current paleontological studies put this plant-eating sauropod at a length of 114.8 feet (35 m). It lived 160 million years ago, and part of its skeletal fossil was first discovered in 1952.

A baby *Argentinosaurus* had to grow

25,000

times its size by adulthood

EURASIAN WOLF

1 This canine has been steeped in mythology for centuries. Several cultures view wolves as spiritual beings, with some also believing in the werewolf, a creature that can transform from a man into a wolf during a full moon.

Tundra Wolf's length:
54 INCHES

ARCTIC WOLF

3 Feeding on a diet that includes Arctic Hares and Muskoxen, these white-coated wolves have been known to approach humans out of curiosity.

TOP 10

BIGGEST WILD CANINES

Even the smallest domesticated dogs share genes with canines that roam in the wild and howl at the moon...

	NAME	WEIGHT (LB)	(KG)
1	EURASIAN WOLF	190	86.2
2	NORTHWESTERN WOLF	175	79.4
3	ARCTIC WOLF	155	70.3
4	GREAT PLAINS WOLF	150	68
5	TUNDRA WOLF	115	52.2
6	INDIAN WOLF	90	40.8
=	RED WOLF	90	40.8
8	STEPPE WOLF	88	39.9
9	MEXICAN WOLF	80	36.3
10	DINGO	77	34.9

BONUS WOLF PACK

Here are the next 10 largest wild canines...

- DEER WOLF — 67 LB
- AFRICAN WILD DOG — 66 LB
- ARABIAN WOLF — 55 LB
- MANED WOLF — 51 LB
- ETHIOPIAN WOLF — 43 LB
- DHOLE — 40 LB.
- EUROPEAN JACKAL — 33 LB
- SIDE-STRIPED JACKAL — 31 LB
- BLACK-BACKED JACKAL — 29 LB
- SYRIAN JACKAL — 27 LB

BIGGEST RODENTS

You may think of mice and rats when you hear the word "rodent," but there are much bigger types of this order of mammals...

	NAME	WEIGHT (LB)	(KG)
▶ 1	CAPYBARA	201	91.2
2	NORTH AMERICAN BEAVER	110	49.9
3	LESSER CAPYBARA	100	45.4
4	EURASIAN BEAVER	88	39.9
5	CAPE PORCUPINE	66	29.9
6	CRESTED PORCUPINE	60	27.2
▶ 7	NORTH AMERICAN PORCUPINE	39.7	18
=	INDIAN CRESTED PORCUPINE	39.7	18
9	COYPU	37	16.8
10	PHILIPPINE PORCUPINE	11.9	5.4

NORTH AMERICAN PORCUPINE

7 A tool of defense, more than 30,000 quills cover this animal's body. The North American Porcupine also has a potent odor it secretes to discourage predators from getting too close.

CAPYBARA

1 A highly sociable South American native, Capybara commonly live in groups of 20 to 100. Adults stand at 2 feet (0.6 m) in height and grow to more than 4 feet (1.2 m) in length.

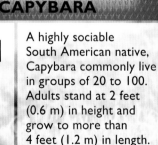

Including their long tail, Coypu are

42 INCHES in length

HEAVIEST ON LAND

This is a list of the largest known weights of animals that dwell on land...

NAME	WEIGHT (LB)	(KG)
1 AFRICAN BUSH ELEPHANT	26,455	12,000
2 ASIAN ELEPHANT	11,464	5,200
3 SOUTHERN ELEPHANT SEAL	11,000	5,000
4 COMMON HIPPOPOTAMUS	9,920.8	4,500
5 SOUTHERN WHITE RHINOCEROS	8,818.5	4,000
6 PACIFIC WALRUS	5,000	2,268
7 SALTWATER CROCODILE	4,409.2	2,000
8 ROTHSCHILD GIRAFFE	4,254.9	1,930
9 CHIANINA	3,924.2	1,780
10 SHIRE HORSE	3,306.9	1,500

ROTHSCHILD GIRAFFE

8

Reduced to only hundreds in their number, this highly endangered mammal towers over the African plains at a height of 20 feet (6.1 m).

ASIAN ELEPHANT

2

Living to more than 60 years of age, the Asian Elephant can be recognized by its ears, which are smaller and rounder than the ears of the African Elephant.

Pacific Walrus's tusk:

3.3 FEET long

EASTERN GREY KANGAROO

9 The heaviest Australian marsupial at 145 pounds (65.8 kg), this animal, also known as the Great Grey Kangaroo, reaches a length of over 9 feet (2.7 m).

A cross between a male lion and a tigress is a

LIGER

PRONGHORN

2 With its muscular and lean 150-pound (68-kg) build, the Pronghorn is able to evade such predators as bobcats, wolves, and coyotes. Within a few days of being born, a baby pronghorn can sprint faster than a human.

TOP 10

FASTEST ON LAND

Some sprint on two legs, and others engage all four. These are the 10 fastest animals on land...

	NAME	SPEED (MPH)	(KPH)
1	CHEETAH	75	120.7
2	PRONGHORN	60.9	98
3	SPRINGBOK	60.3	97
4	OSTRICH	60	96.6
5	AMERICAN QUARTER HORSE	53.4	86
6	LION	49.7	80
7	AFRICAN WILD DOG	44.7	72
=	ELK	44.7	72
9	EASTERN GREY KANGAROO	43.5	70
10	COYOTE	42.9	69

SNOW LEOPARD

5

An endangered species, the Snow Leopard's record length is 8.2 feet (2.5 m) including its tail, which accounted for more than 3 feet (0.9 m) of that figure.

Eurasian Lynx's height:

30
INCHES

TIGER, THE TOP CAT

This emphasizes how big the number 1 is...

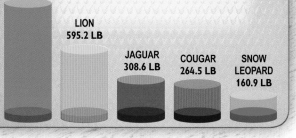

SIBERIAN TIGER
1,025.2 LB

LION
595.2 LB

JAGUAR
308.6 LB

COUGAR
264.5 LB

SNOW LEOPARD
160.9 LB

TOP 10

BIGGEST BIG CATS

The next time you look at a domesticated cat, think about the sizes of these, the largest felines in the world...

	CAT	WEIGHT (LB)	(KG)
1	SIBERIAN TIGER	1,025.2	465
2	LION	595.2	270
3	JAGUAR	308.6	140
4	COUGAR	264.5	120
5	SNOW LEOPARD	160.9	73
6	LEOPARD	141.1	64
7	CHEETAH	121.2	55
8	EURASIAN LYNX	77.2	35
9	CLOUDED LEOPARD	55.1	25
10	CARACAL	44.1	20

SIBERIAN TIGER

1

The king of the big cats can eat up to 88 pounds (39.9 kg) of meat at any one time, which is comparable to the size of a 12-year-old human.

TOP 10

MOST POPULOUS CARNIVOROUS MAMMALS

Of all the different mammals on Earth, these species are the most numerous...

Number of recognized domesticated dog breeds:

332

	NAME	APPROXIMATE GLOBAL POPULATION
1	DOMESTICATED CAT	600,000,000
2	DOMESTICATED DOG	400,000,000
3	CRABEATER SEAL	12,000,000
4	HARP SEAL	8,000,000
5	BROWN FUR SEAL	2,092,000
6	NORTHERN FUR SEAL	1,100,000
7	AMERICAN BLACK BEAR	950,000
8	HOODED SEAL	662,000
9	SOUTHERN ELEPHANT SEAL	500,000
=	WEDDELL SEAL	500,000

CRABEATER SEAL

3 During its daily hunting session (which lasts up to 10 hours), this seal will make more than 100 dives to eat krill, not crabs, despite what its name suggests.

AMERICAN BLACK BEAR

7 Of the three bear species found in North America, the American Black Bear is the smallest. It lives on a diet mainly of insects, honey, plants, salmon, and small mammals.

Arambourgiania's standing height was comparable to a

GIRAFFE

PTERANODON

5 Of all the different pterosaurs, fossils of *Pteranodons* have been unearthed the most, to the sum of more than 1,200.

QUETZALCOATLUS

1 Scientists estimate that this colossal pterosaur weighed up to 500 pounds (226.8 kg). The first fossils of *Quetzalcoatlus* ever unearthed were found in Texas in 1971.

TOP 10

BIGGEST PREHISTORIC FLYERS

The wingspans of the creatures that soared across the skies of old were closer to the widths of aircraft...

	PTEROSAUR	WINGSPAN (FEET)	(M)
1	HATZEGOPTERYX	34.4	10.5
=	QUETZALCOATLUS	34.4	10.5
3	ARAMBOURGIANIA	32.8	10
4	ORNITHOCHEIRUS	23	7
5	PTERANODON	21.3	6.5
6	COLOBORHYNCHUS	19.7	6
7	MOGANOPTERUS	15.4	4.7
8	ISTIODACTYLUS	14.1	4.3
9	TUPUXUARA	13.1	4
10	ZHENYUANOPTERUS	11.5	3.5

TOP 10

SMALLEST PREHISTORIC FLYERS

Although the prehistoric skies were home to some terrifying giants, other flying creatures were a lot smaller...

	PTEROSAUR	WINGSPAN (IN)	(CM)
1	IBEROMESORNIS ROMERALI	7.9	20
2	NEMICOLOPTERUS CRYPTICUS	9.8	25
3	PALAEOCHIROPTERYX TUPAIODON	11.8	30
4	ANUROGNATHUS AMMONI	13.8	35
5	ICARONYCTERIS INDEX	14.6	37
6	PREONDACTYLUS BUFFARINII	17.7	45
7	PETEINOSAURUS ZAMBELLII	23.6	60
8	CONFUCIUSORNIS SP.	27.6	70
9	JEHOLOPTERUS NINCHENGENSIS	35.4	90
10	ARCHAEOPTERYX SP.	39.4	100

ANUROGNATHUS AMMONI

4

British sci-fi TV series *Primeval* (2007–11) featured this tiny flying pterosaur during its five season run. U.S. spin-off *Primeval: New World* aired in 2012.

Some experts believe *Iberomesornis romerali* lived

125
MILLION
years ago

ARCHAEOPTERYX SP.

10

This pterosaur, one of the most famous of all the prehistoric flyers, weighed 2.2 pounds (0.9 kg). A birdlike dinosaur, its name translated from Greek means "ancient feather."

GYRFALCON

3 These falcons prefer to nest on a cliff ledge, rather than build their nests from scratch. They are also known to reuse nests abandoned by other birds.

FASTEST FIVE

Here is how the top 5 compare visually...

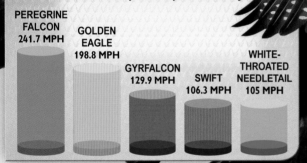

PEREGRINE FALCON 241.7 MPH

GOLDEN EAGLE 198.8 MPH

GYRFALCON 129.9 MPH

SWIFT 106.3 MPH

WHITE-THROATED NEEDLETAIL 105 MPH

Grey-headed Albatross's wingspan:

7.2 FEET

TOP 10

FASTEST IN THE AIR

New data is in, which means we have some new speed champions when it comes to the fastest birds in the world...

	BIRD	MAXIMUM KNOWN SPEED (MPH)	(KPH)
1	PEREGRINE FALCON	241.7	389
2	GOLDEN EAGLE	198.8	320
3	GYRFALCON	129.9	209
4	SWIFT	106.3	171
5	WHITE-THROATED NEEDLETAIL	105	169
6	EURASIAN HOBBY	100	161
7	FRIGATEBIRD	95.1	153
8	SPUR-WINGED GOOSE	88.2	142
9	RED-BREASTED MERGANSER	80.8	130
10	GREY-HEADED ALBATROSS	78.9	127

GOLDEN EAGLE

2 This bird of prey is chosen most often as a national animal. It has been adopted as such by Albania, Austria, Germany, Kazakhstan, and Mexico.

TOP 10

BIGGEST BATS

There are many different species of these flying mammals, but these are the largest...

	BAT	WIDTH (FEET)	(M)
1	LARGE FLYING FOX	7	2.1
2	BLACK FLYING FOX	6	1.8
3	GIANT GOLDEN-CROWNED FLYING FOX	5.6	1.7
4	PEMBA FLYING FOX	5.2	1.6
5	GREY-HEADED FLYING FOX	5	1.53
6	INDIAN FLYING FOX	4.9	1.5
=	GREAT FLYING FOX	4.9	1.5
8	LIVINGSTONE'S FRUIT BAT	4.6	1.4
9	MADAGASCAN FLYING FOX	4.1	1.25
10	LITTLE RED FLYING FOX	3.9	1.2

GREY-HEADED FLYING FOX

5 This bat is the largest found in Australia. Weighing up to 2 pounds (0.9 kg), they can live to approximately 15 years in the wild.

LARGE FLYING FOX

1 This species lives on a diet of nectar and fruit, so it doesn't possess the power of echolocation that many other bats are famous for using to hunt.

The Little Red Flying Fox weighs

18 OUNCES

27

King Penguin's height:

3.3 FEET

OSTRICH

1

This is the fastest flightless bird on Earth, achieving speeds of up to 60 mph (96.6 kph). Ostrich eggs weigh over 3 pounds (1.4 kg), the largest of any bird.

TOP 10

HEAVIEST BIRDS

Whether swimmers, runners, or flyers, these are the 10 birds that tip the scales the farthest...

	BIRD	WEIGHT (LB)	(KG)
1	OSTRICH	346	156.8
2	DOUBLE-WATTLED CASSOWARY	190	85
3	EMU	130	60
4	GOLD-NECK CASSOWARY	128	58
5	EMPEROR PENGUIN	100	45.4
6	GREATER RHEA	88	40
7	DARWIN'S RHEA	63	28.6
8	LITTLE CASSOWARY	57	26
9	KING PENGUIN	35	16
10	DALMATIAN PELICAN	33	15

DALMATIAN PELICAN

10

The largest of all pelicans, this bird has a wingspan of 11.3 feet (3.4 m). It favors a diet of fish. The large pouch located underneath its bill can be used to store prey to consume later.

Experts estimate there are over **10,000** bird species

CRIMSON CHAT

8 This Australian species weighs 0.4 ounces (10 g). Males have brighter red coloring to attract females. The Crimson Chat's egg incubation time is 14 days.

STRIATED PARDOLATE

3 This species is found in almost every territory of Australia, except some of the desert regions in the western part of the country. They tend to feed on insects in Eucalyptus trees.

TOP 10

SMALLEST BIRDS

Check out the internet to find the smallest species of bird where you live. Compare your findings to the list below...

	BIRD	LENGTH (IN)	(CM)
1	BEE HUMMINGBIRD	1.97	5
2	BANANAQUIT	2.96	7.5
3	WEEBILL	3.15	8
=	STRIATED PARDOLATE	3.15	8
5	GOLDCREST	3.35	8.5
6	BROWN GERYGONE	3.54	9
=	LESSER GOLDFINCH	3.54	9
8	CRIMSON CHAT	3.94	10
=	GOLDEN-HEADED CISTICOLA	3.94	10
10	TROPICAL PARULA	4.33	11

BIGGEST BUTTERFLIES

These delicate winged insects are so large that when seen in flight, they are often mistaken for birds...

	BUTTERFLY	WIDTH (IN)	(CM)
1	QUEEN ALEXANDRA'S BIRDWING	11.8	30
2	GOLIATH BIRDWING	11	28
3	GIANT AFRICAN SWALLOWTAIL	9.8	25
4	RIPPON'S BIRDWING	7.9	20
=	WALLACE'S GOLDEN BIRDWING	7.9	20
6	PALAWAN BIRDWING	7.5	19
=	PRIAM'S BIRDWING	7.5	19
8	MAGELLAN BIRDWING	7.1	18
9	RAJAH BROOKE'S BIRDWING	6.7	17
10	CHIMAERA BIRDWING	6.3	16

A Goliath Birdwing lays up to **20** eggs at a time

GOLIATH BIRDWING

2 Males are smaller but also brighter in color than females. They have green and yellow patterning, while the females are brown and yellow.

QUEEN ALEXANDRA'S BIRDWING

1 The largest butterfly in the world is an endangered species, and it's illegal to capture and sell one. The male's wingspan can be up to 3.5 inches (9 cm) smaller than the female's.

BUTTERFLIES VS. MOTHS

Here is how the top 5 from each chart measure up...

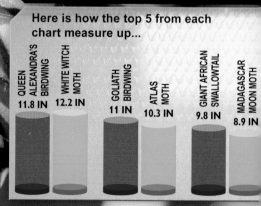

QUEEN ALEXANDRA'S BIRDWING 11.8 IN

WHITE WITCH MOTH 12.2 IN

GOLIATH BIRDWING 11 IN

ATLAS MOTH 10.3 IN

GIANT AFRICAN SWALLOWTAIL 9.8 IN

MADAGASCAR MOON MOTH 8.9 IN

DEATH'S-HEAD HAWKMOTH

Just missing out on a place in this Top 10 is the Death's-head Hawkmoth. Its wingspan measures 4.7 inches (12 cm). It was a key part of the case in the 1991 thriller *The Silence of the Lambs*.

WHITE WITCH MOTH

1 This huge species may also be known by its other names, such as the Great Owlet Moth, the Ghost Moth, or the Great Grey Witch Moth.

TOP 10

BIGGEST MOTHS

With more than 160,000 different kinds of moths, these are the 10 that come out on top when comparing wingspans...

	MOTH	WIDTH (IN)	(CM)
1	WHITE WITCH MOTH	12.2	31
2	ATLAS MOTH	10.3	26.2
3	MADAGASCAR MOON MOTH	8.9	22.6
4	CECROPIA MOTH	7	17.8
5	IMPERIAL MOTH	6.9	17.4
6	BLACK WITCH MOTH	6.7	17
7	EMPEROR GUM MOTH	5.9	15
=	POLYPHEMUS MOTH	5.9	15
9	OWL MOTH	5.5	14
10	LUNA MOTH	5	12.7

Atlas Moth caterpillar's length:

4.5 INCHES

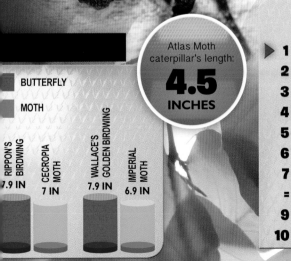

BUTTERFLY

MOTH

RIPPON'S BIRDWING
7.9 IN

CECROPIA MOTH
7 IN

WALLACE'S GOLDEN BIRDWING
7.9 IN

IMPERIAL MOTH
6.9 IN

LARGEST PREHISTORIC FISH

A school bus is around 45 feet (13.7 m) long, and many of these entries are at least half that length...

	NAME	LENGTH (FEET)	(M)
1	MEGALODON	52.5	16
2	DUNKLEOSTEUS	32.8	10
=	LEEDSICHTHYS	32.8	10
4	ONCHOPRISTIS	26.2	8
5	RHIZODUS	23	7
6	CRETOXYRHINA	20	6.1
7	ISURUS	19.7	6
=	XIPHACTINUS	19.7	6
9	MAWSONIA	13.1	4
=	ONYCHODUS	13.1	4

ONCHOPRISTIS

4 This prehistoric fish is related to the modern sawfish, and little has changed in its biology over millions of years. Its barbed snout grew to a length of nearly 9 feet (2.7 m).

DUNKLEOSTEUS

2 Scientists estimate that this huge bony-jawed fish weighed up to 8,000 pounds (3,628.7 kg). To date, fossils unearthed suggest there were 10 different kinds of *Dunkleosteus*.

Isurus, an ancient ancestor of the modern Mako Shark, had teeth **3.5 IN** long

TOP 10

BIGGEST PREHISTORIC OCEAN BEASTS

Combining reptiles, mammals, and fish, these were the largest creatures in prehistoric oceans...

	NAME	TYPE	LENGTH (FEET)	(M)
1	SHONISAURUS	REPTILE	66	21
2	BASILOSAURUS	MAMMAL	65.6	20
3	LIVYATAN	MAMMAL	57.4	17.5
4	MEGALODON	FISH	52.5	16
5	MOSASAURUS	REPTILE	49.9	15.2
=	HAINOSAURUS	REPTILE	49.9	15.2
7	ELASMOSAURUS	REPTILE	46	14
8	PLIOSAURUS	REPTILE	42	12.8
9	DUNKLEOSTEUS	FISH	32.8	10
=	LEEDSICHTHYS	FISH	32.8	10

SHONISAURUS

1 The name of this marine lizard was coined in the 1950s after a large number of its remains were successfully excavated in the Shoshone Mountains of Nevada.

Bones of *Pliosaurus* were first discovered in

1841

MOSASAURUS

5 On April 18, 2015, fossil enthusiast Lars Barten and his father Jos discovered the remains of a *Mosasaurus* in the North Brabant region of the Netherlands. *Jurassic World* (2015) features a *Mosasaurus* in a huge water tank.

Pacific Sleeper Sharks live at depths of

6,500 FEET

BIGGEST SHARKS

You've probably heard of the Great White, but there are even bigger sharks living in our planet's oceans...

	SHARK	LENGTH (FEET)	(M)
1	WHALE SHARK	41.7	12.7
2	BASKING SHARK	40.4	12.3
3	GREAT WHITE SHARK	26.2	8.0
4	PACIFIC SLEEPER SHARK	24.3	7.4
=	TIGER SHARK	24.3	7.4
6	GREENLAND SHARK	21	6.4
7	GREAT HAMMERHEAD SHARK	20	6.1
8	THRESHER SHARK	19.7	6.0
9	BLUNTNOSE SIXGILL SHARK	15.7	4.8
10	BIGEYE THRESHER SHARK	15.1	4.6

GREAT HAMMERHEAD SHARK

7 Females of this species (the biggest of the Hammerhead Sharks) can weigh up to 1,280 pounds (580.6 kg) when pregnant with a litter of 50+ young.

BLUNTNOSE SIXGILL SHARK

9 This shark's name comes from the fact that most sharks have only five gill slits. This deep-sea shark has been tracked at depths below 6,150 feet (1874.5 m).

SMALLEST SHARKS

At the opposite end of the shark scale, these sharks are so tiny that none of them exceed the length of a 12-inch (30-cm) ruler...

	SHARK	LENGTH (INCHES)	(CM)
1	DWARF LANTERNSHARK	8.3	21.2
2	PANAMA GHOST CATSHARK	9.1	23
3	PYGMY RIBBONTAIL CATSHARK	9.4	24
4	GREEN LANTERNSHARK	10.2	26
▷ 5	PYGMY SHARK	10.6	27
6	GRANULAR DOGFISH	11	28
=	LOLLIPOP CATSHARK	11	28
▷ =	SPINED PYGMY SHARK	11	28
9	BRISTLY CATSHARK	11.4	29
=	FRINGEFIN LANTERNSHARK	11.4	29

PYGMY SHARK

5 This tiny shark produces around eight pups in each litter. It hunts prey such as small fish and crustaceans at depths of 6,000 feet (1,829 m), but only during the daytime. At night, it stays near the surface.

Granular Dogfish have been caught only in waters off the Falkland Islands

GIANT VS. TINY

The biggest and smallest sharks side by side...

WHALE SHARK
41.7 FEET

DWARF LANTERNSHARK
8.3 INCHES

SPINED PYGMY SHARK

6 Like all of the sharks in this Top 10, the Spined Pygmy Shark is considered a rare fish that is seldom seen by divers. Its underside is bioluminescent, meaning it glows in the dark.

BELUGA STURGEON

2 This colossal fish is critically endangered due to overfishing, especially for its caviar (its eggs). Some believe that sightings of Scotland's Loch Ness Monster could be a misidentified sturgeon swimming near the surface.

TOP 10

LONGEST BONY FISH

This class of fish (called as such because they have a skeleton of bone, unlike sharks) includes the most species...

	NAME	LENGTH (FEET)	(M)
1	GIANT OARFISH	49.9	15.2
2	BELUGA STURGEON	24	7.3
3	WHITE STURGEON	20	6.1
4	EUROPEAN SEA STURGEON	19.7	6
5	KALUGA STURGEON	18.4	5.6
6	SLENDER OARFISH	18	5.4
7	ATLANTIC BLUE MARLIN	16.4	5
=	CHINESE STURGEON	16.4	5
9	BLACK MARLIN	15.3	4.65
10	OCEAN SUNFISH	15.1	4.6

NEXT WAVE OF FISH

Here is how the top 11–20 measure up...

SWORDFISH	14.9 FT
ARAPAIMA	14.8 FT
OARFISH	14 FT
SHARPTAIL MOLA	11.2 FT
SOUTHERN OCEAN SUNFISH	10.8 FT
STREAMER FISH	9.8 FT
WEST INDIAN OCEAN COELACANTH	6.6 FT
INDONESIAN COELACANTH	6.6 FT
SIBERIAN STURGEON	6.6 FT
SLENDER SUNFISH	3.3 FT

Black Marlin can weigh

1,650 POUNDS

GIANT OARFISH

1 Famously elusive, oarfish are rarely seen in the wild. Their giant length has made them a suspect for the tales of sea serpents recorded over the centuries.

OCEAN SUNFISH

1 This fish is also known as the Mola Mola. When born, hatchlings start life 0.09 inches (2 mm) long. This means that they must grow more than 2,000 times in length to reach adulthood.

WHITE STURGEON

8 Sturgeons look like prehistoric fish because they are! Their physical appearance has hardly changed over hundreds of millions of years. A sturgeon's lifespan can exceed 100 years.

Swordfish can be found in waters ranging from **41-81°F**

TOP 10

HEAVIEST BONY FISH

Switching from length to weight, these are the 10 bony fish that tip the scales the farthest...

	NAME	WEIGHT (LB)	(KG)
1	OCEAN SUNFISH	4,400	1,995.8
=	SHARPTAIL MOLA	4,400	1,995.8
=	SOUTHERN OCEAN SUNFISH	4,400	1,995.8
4	BELUGA STURGEON	3,463	1,570.8
5	KALUGA STURGEON	2,205	1,000.2
6	ATLANTIC BLUEFIN TUNA	2,010	911.7
7	ATLANTIC BLUE MARLIN	1,803	817.8
8	WHITE STURGEON	1,799	816
9	BLACK MARLIN	1,650	748.4
10	SWORDFISH	1,430	648.6

PAEDOPHRYNE AMAUENSIS

1 Due to their tiny size and excellent camouflage, these frogs are difficult to detect in their home environment. This is also because their calls resemble an insect's more than an amphibian's.

The tiny frogs in this chart live in Brazilian forests that are **2,230** FT. above sea level

BRACHYCEPHALUS DIDACTYLUS

6 Also called the Flea Frog, the future of this species (like the others in this chart) is under threat due to the destruction of rainforests by agriculture and industrial development.

TOP 10

SMALLEST AMPHIBIANS

The photographs on this page show just how tiny these critters are. All entries here are a kind of small frog...

	NAME	LENGTH (INCH)	(MM)
1	PAEDOPHRYNE AMAUENSIS	0.3	7.7
2	PAEDOCYPRIS PROGENETICA	0.31	7.9
3	PAEDOPHRYNE SWIFTORUM	0.34	8.6
4	PAEDOPHRYNE DEKOT	0.35	9
5	PAEDOPHRYNE VERRUCOSA	0.37	9.3
6	BRACHYCEPHALUS DIDACTYLUS	0.39	9.8
7	BRACHYCEPHALUS HERMOGENESI	0.41	10.5
8	PAEDOPHRYNE KATHISMAPHLOX	0.43	10.9
9	BRACHYCEPHALUS LEOPARDUS	0.47	11.9
10	BRACHYCEPHALUS FUSCOLINEATUS	0.49	12.4

TOP 10

LARGEST **SQUID/OCTOPUSES**

The subject of countless mariners' tales, these gigantic tentacled creatures are far from the stuff of myth...

NAME	TYPE	LENGTH (FT)	(M)
1	COLOSSAL SQUID	SQUID	45.9	14
2	GIANT SQUID	SQUID	42.7	13
3	BIGFIN SQUID	SQUID	26.2	8
4	GIANT PACIFIC OCTOPUS	OCTOPUS	20	6.1
5	ASPEROTEUTHIS ACANTHODERMA	SQUID	18	5.5
6	COCKATOO SQUID	GLASS SQUID	14.1	4.3
7	ROBUST CLUBHOOK SQUID	SQUID	13.2	4.02
8	SEVEN-ARM OCTOPUS	OCTOPUS	11	3.4
9	MEGALOCRANCHIA FISHERI	GLASS SQUID	8.9	2.7
10	DANA OCTOPUS SQUID	SQUID	7.5	2.3

TRULY COLOSSAL

Compared to the size of a diver, this shows just how colossal the squid is...

COCKATOO SQUID

6 Some Cockatoo Squid live more than 1 mile (1.6 km) below the surface. Although most people call them tentacles, the correct term for a squid's limbs is "arms."

The Seven-arm Octopus actually has **8** arms (one is just hard to see)

COLOSSAL SQUID

New Zealand $1

COLOSSAL SQUID

1 This species of squid was celebrated by New Zealand with a $1 stamp, issued on March 4, 2009. The extra-large stamp measures 2.05 inches (5.2 cm) wide by 1.48 inches (3.75 cm) high.

BIGGEST TURTLES

This Top 10 features true turtles and doesn't include tortoises, which are completely terrestrial...

	TURTLE	WEIGHT (LB)	(KG)
1	LEATHERBACK SEA TURTLE	2,120	961.1
2	LOGGERHEAD TURTLE	1,202	545.2
3	GREEN SEA TURTLE	871	395.1
4	YANGTZE GIANT SOFTSHELL TURTLE	550	249.5
5	HAWKSBILL TURTLE	280	127
6	INDIAN NARROW-HEADED SOFTSHELL TURTLE	260	117.9
7	ALLIGATOR SNAPPING TURTLE	236	107
8	CANTOR'S GIANT SOFTSHELL TURTLE	220	99.8
9	FLATBACK SEA TURTLE	198	89.8
10	KEMP'S RIDLEY SEA TURTLE	110	49.9

HAWKSBILL TURTLE

5 Favoring sponges as a food source, these turtles are most often found near coral reefs. They commonly live to around 50 years of age.

A Yangtze Giant Softshell Turtle's head can reach over

8 INCHES
in length

ALLIGATOR SNAPPING TURTLE

7 This turtle has no natural predators. Humans capture and kill them to sell their shells and meat. This has led to these turtles being protected and given the classification as an endangered species.

LONGEST EELS

In some parts of the world, these huge serpentine creatures are fished as a food source...

	EEL	LENGTH (FEET)	(M)
1	SLENDER GIANT MORAY EEL	13.1	4
2	EUROPEAN CONGER EEL	10	3.05
3	GIANT MORAY EEL	9.8	3
4	SERPENT EEL	8.2	2.5
5	DAGGERTOOTH PIKE CONGER EEL	6.6	2
=	NEW ZEALAND LONGFIN EEL	6.6	2
7	PIKE EEL	5.9	1.8
8	EUROPEAN EEL	4.9	1.5
=	JAPANESE EEL	4.9	1.5
10	AMERICAN EEL	4	1.2

ELECTRIC EEL

This 8.2-foot (2.5-m) fish was once mistaken for an eel (hence its name). It's actually a kind of knifefish. It discharges a 600-volt shock, which is strong enough to kill a human.

GIANT MORAY EEL

3 The Giant Moray may not triumph as the longest of all the eels, but in terms of mass it is the biggest, growing to nearly 70 pounds (32 kg) in weight.

Daggertooth Pike Conger Eels can live at depths of

330 FEET

HEAVIEST IN THE OCEAN

This chart doesn't just reflect the heaviest ocean-dwelling animals, these are also the heaviest organisms on Earth...

NAME	WEIGHT (LB)	(KG)
1 BLUE WHALE	418,877	189,999.4
2 BOWHEAD WHALE	219,999.3	99,790
3 NORTH ATLANTIC RIGHT WHALE	210,559.1	95,508
4 NORTH PACIFIC RIGHT WHALE	197,119.7	89,412
5 SOUTHERN RIGHT WHALE	190,400	86,364
6 FINBACK WHALE	165,760	75,187.5
7 SPERM WHALE	125,440	56,898.6
8 GRAY WHALE	88,184	39,999.6
9 HUMPBACK WHALE	88,050	39,938.8
10 SEI WHALE	62,720	28,449.3

The Finback Whale can reach over

89 FEET

in length

BOWHEAD WHALE

2 This species goes by many other names, including the Arctic, Polar, Russian, and Greenland Right Whale. Bowheads may be hunted by Orca Whales.

SPERM WHALE

7 It might be only the seventh-heaviest whale, but this mammal is the biggest predator on Earth that has teeth. It has up to 26 of them, and each tooth weighs more than 2 pounds (1 kg).

Indo-Pacific
Sailfish's length:
9.8
FEET

SHARK SPEEDS

Here's how the three sharks
in this chart compare...

MAKO
SHARK
59 MPH

GREAT
BLUE
SHARK
42.9 MPH

GREAT WHITE
SHARK
35 MPH

ORCA WHALE

7 Also called Blackfish and the Killer
Whale, Orcas were the subject of the
award-winning 2013 documentary
Blackfish, which alleged that sea parks
mistreat them in captivity.

SWORDFISH

8 Although they possess a spearlike
weapon, Swordfish do not skewer
their prey. Experts believe they swipe
creatures with it to slow them down.

TOP 10

FASTEST IN THE SEA
The aerodynamic body shape and powerful
musculature of these animals propel them at
speeds we travel at in cars...

	NAME	SPEED (MPH)	(KPH)
1	BLACK MARLIN	80	128.7
2	INDO-PACIFIC SAILFISH	68.3	110
3	MAKO SHARK	59	95
4	WAHOO	48.5	78
5	BLUEFIN TUNA	43.5	70
6	GREAT BLUE SHARK	42.9	69
7	ORCA WHALE	40.1	65
8	BONEFISH	39.8	64
=	SWORDFISH	39.8	64
10	GREAT WHITE SHARK	33	56.3

43

MECHANICAL
CREATIONS
ZONE 2

SCMaglev achieved its 375 mph speed on **APRIL 21, 2015**

NORTH AMERICAN X-15

3 The cockpit of this hypersonic rocket plane had room for just a single pilot. Only three of this experimental craft were built. Its debut flight was on June 8, 1959.

APOLLO 10

1 NASA's fourth manned space mission lasted a total of 8 days, 3 minutes, and 23 seconds. The Command Service Module's call sign was "Charlie Brown," and the Lunar Module's was "Snoopy."

TOP 10

FASTEST VEHICLES OF ALL

Comparing the different modes of transportation, these are the fastest of each...

	TYPE	NAME	COUNTRY	TOP SPEED (MPH)	(KPH)
1	ROCKET	APOLLO 10	U.S.	24,791	39,897
2	HYPERSONIC CRUISE VEHICLE	FALCON HTV-2	U.S.	13,000	20,921.47
3	ROCKET PLANE	NORTH AMERICAN X-15	U.S.	4,520	7,274.24
4	PLANE	LOCKHEED SR-71 BLACKBIRD	U.S.	2,193.2	3,529.6
5	JET-ENGINE CAR	THRUSTSSC	U.S.	763.04	1,227.98
6	UNMANNED AERIAL VEHICLE	BARRACUDA	GERMANY/SPAIN	647	1,041.3
7	CAR	BLUEBIRD CN7	AUSTRALIA	440	710
8	MOTORCYCLE	TOP 1 OIL-ACK ATTACK	U.S.	376.36	605.7
9	TRAIN	SCMAGLEV	JAPAN	375	603.5
10	BOAT	SPIRIT OF AUSTRALIA	AUSTRALIA	345	555.21

INTERNATIONAL SPACE STATION

7 The ISS's Expedition 49 (lasting from September to November 2016) comprised astronauts from Russian, American, and Japanese space agencies, led by Russia's Anatoli Ivanishin.

The ISS weighs almost **1 MILLION** pounds

TOP 10

BIGGEST VEHICLES OF ALL

By land, sea, sky, and beyond, these are the largest vehicles ever constructed...

	TYPE	NAME	COUNTRY	SIZE (FT)	(M)
1	TRAIN	BHP IRON ORE	AUSTRALIA	24,124	7,353
2	LAND TRANSPORTER	F60 OVERBURDEN CONVEYOR	GERMANY	1,647	502.01
3	SHIP	SEAWISE GIANT OIL TANKER	JAPAN	1,504.1	458.46
4	AIRCRAFT CARRIER	USS ENTERPRISE	U.S.	1,122	342
5	AIRSHIP	HINDENBURG & GRAF ZEPPELIN II	GERMANY	803.8	245
6	SUBMARINE	TYPHOON-CLASS	RUSSIA	574.15	175
7	SPACE STATION	INTERNATIONAL SPACE STATION	U.S./CANADA/RUSSIA/JAPAN/EUROPE	356*	108.5*
8	PLANE	HUGHES H4 HERCULES	U.S.	319.92**	97.51**
9	HELICOPTER	MIL V-12	RUSSIA (SOVIET UNION ERA)	121.39	37
10	TANK	CHAR 2C/FCM 2C	FRANCE	33.69	10.27

*All measurements are the vehicles' lengths except: *width and **wingspan.*

MIL V-12

9 Only two prototypes of this, the biggest helicopter ever, have been built. Including its rotor blades, it had a width of 219.82 feet (67 m).

TOP 5 LARGEST

This puts the number 1 in perspective...

BHP IRON ORE
24,124 FT

| F60 OVERBURDEN CONVEYOR **1,647 FT** | SEAWISE GIANT OIL TANKER **1,504.1 FT** | USS ENTERPRISE **1,122 FT** | HINDENBURG & GRAF ZEPPELIN II **803.8 FT** |

The hydrofoil craft HMCS *Bras d'Or* was **163.9** FT long

S 2000 SCORPION PEACEKEEPER

9 The top speed of this, the fastest tank in the world, was achieved in Chertsey, in the UK, on March 26, 2002. It weighs 17,800 pounds (8,074 kg) and has been in service since 1973.

DPV (DESERT PATROL VEHICLE)

8 These fast and agile vehicles have been in service in places such as Saudi Arabia since 1991. In the 2007 movie *Transformers*, you can see two DPVs helping to move the Allspark.

TOP 10

FASTEST MILITARY VEHICLES EVER

From piloted constructions to unmanned machines, these are the military's speediest vehicles...

	TYPE	NAME	COUNTRY	TOP SPEED (MPH)	(KPH)
1	HYPERSONIC CRUISE VEHICLE	FALCON HTV-2	U.S.	13,000	20,921.47
2	ROCKET PLANE	NORTH AMERICAN X-15	U.S.	4,520	7,274.24
3	PLANE	LOCKHEED SR-71 BLACKBIRD	U.S.	2,193.2	3,529.6
4	UNMANNED AERIAL VEHICLE	BARRACUDA	GERMANY/SPAIN	647	1,041.3
5	HELICOPTER	WESTLAND LYNX	UNITED KINGDOM	249.09	400.87
6	TRUCK	IFAV (INTERIM FAST ATTACK VEHICLE)	U.S.	97	156.11
7	SHIP	HMCS BRAS D'OR (FHE 400)	CANADA	72	117
8	LIGHT ATTACK VEHICLE	DPV (DESERT PATROL VEHICLE)	U.S.	60+	96.56+
9	TANK	S 2000 SCORPION PEACEKEEPER	UNITED KINGDOM	51.10	82.23
10	SUBMARINE	ALFA CLASS	RUSSIA	46	74

TOP 10

FASTEST MANNED VEHICLES (NON-SPACE)

If it requires a human to drive it, it had the chance of making it into this Top 10...

	TYPE	NAME	COUNTRY	TOP SPEED (MPH)	(KPH)
1	ROCKET PLANE	NORTH AMERICAN X-15	U.S.	4,520	7,274.24
2	PLANE	LOCKHEED SR-71 BLACKBIRD	U.S.	2,193.2	3,529.6
3	JET-ENGINE CAR	THRUSTSSC	U.S.	763.04	1,227.98
4	CAR	BLUEBIRD CN7	AUSTRALIA	440	710
5	MOTORCYCLE	TOP 1 OIL-ACK ATTACK	U.S.	376.36	605.7
6	TRAIN	SCMAGLEV	JAPAN	375	603.5
7	BOAT	SPIRIT OF AUSTRALIA	AUSTRALIA	345	555.21
8	HELICOPTER	EUROCOPTER X3	FRANCE	303	487.63
9	HOVERCRAFT	JENNY II	PORTUGAL	85.38	137.4
10	AIRSHIP	ZEPPELIN LUFTSCHIFFTECHNIK LZ N07-100	GERMANY	69.6	112

BLUEBIRD CN7

4 This is also known as the Proteus-Bluebird Campbell-Norris 7, named after its driver Donald Campbell and sibling designers Lewis and Ken Norris.

TOP 1 OIL-ACK ATTACK

5 The world's fastest motorcycle has 1,000 hp (horsepower) capacity, thanks to a Dual 1300cc Suzuki Hayabusa Sport Bike engine paired with an additional Garret turbo charger.

ThrustSSC's world speed record was set on **OCTOBER 15, 1997**

FORD

6 This motor company gets its name from its founder, American businessman Henry Ford (July 30, 1863–April 7, 1947). His Ford car firm was founded in Michigan June 16, 1903.

BMW has made in excess of **2.5** MILLION cars and motorcycles

VOLKSWAGEN

1 This word means "people's car," and Volkswagen was born out of a need to produce affordable cars for German citizens in the 1920s and 1930s.

TOP 10

HIGHEST GROSSING VEHICULAR COMPANIES

No matter what kind they produce, these are the manufacturers that profit the most from machines...

	COMPANY	HOME COUNTRY	REVENUE ($ BILLIONS)
1	VOLKSWAGEN	GERMANY	269
2	TOYOTA	JAPAN	248
3	DAIMLER	GERMANY	172
4	CHINA RAILWAY	CHINA	163
5	GENERAL MOTORS	U.S.	156
6	FORD	U.S.	144
7	HONDA	JAPAN	142
8	BMW	GERMANY	106
9	NISSAN MOTOR	JAPAN	103
10	SAIC MOTOR	JAPAN	102

SNOWMOBILE

6 Most high-spec snowmobiles can travel over 150 mph (241 kph). The Lamtrac G-force is the model that achieves more than 210 mph (338 kph).

TOP 10

FASTEST MACHINES IN SPORT

All of the different competitive sports that feature a vehicle have been studied for this chart...

	SPORT	TOP SPEED (MPH)	(KPH)
1	TOP FUEL DRAGSTER	332.18	534.59
2	AIRSHOW STUNT PLANE	264.7	426
3	INDY CAR	256.95	413.52
4	FORMULA ONE CAR	229.8	369.9
5	MOTOR RALLY (NASCAR, ETC.)	212.8	342.4
6	SNOWMOBILE	210.03	338
7	POWERBOAT	210	337.95
8	MOTORCYCLE (RACING)	193.24	310.99
9	JET SKI	112	180.24
10	MONSTER TRUCK	99.1	159.48

Early jet skis were called "water scooters" in the **1950s**

GO-KART

Just missing out on a place in the above Top 10 is the go-kart. The fastest models can attain speeds of more than 80 mph (128.7 kph).

FAST FIVE

Here's how the top 5 compare visually...

TOP FUEL DRAGSTER 332.18 MPH

AIRSHOW STUNT PLANE 264.7 MPH

INDY CAR 256.95 MPH

FORMULA ONE CAR 229.8 MPH

MOTOR RALLY 212.8 MPH

FASTEST COMMERCIAL MOTORCYCLES

If you're a fan of the world of motorcycling, this is the Top 10 for you...

	MODEL	TOP SPEED (MPH)	(KPH)
1	DUCATI DESMOSEDICI GP9	216.86	348
2	DUCATI DESMOSEDICI GP4	215.9	347.4
3	DUCATI DESMOSEDICI GP7	209.6	337.2
4	SUZUKI HAYABUSA GSX1300R (1999–2007 MODEL)	194	312
5	MV AGUSTA F4 R 312	193.24	310.99
6	BMW S1000RR	190	305
7	KAWASAKI ZX-12R	187	301
8	KAWASAKI NINJA ZX-14	186	299.3
9	HONDA CBR1100XX SUPER BLACKBIRD	178.5	287.3
10	KAWASAKI NINJA ZX-11	175	282

DUCATI DESMOSEDICI GP9

1 What sets this apart from other Ducatis is its carbon fiber chassis. Before this innovation, Ducati bikes were made of a steel trellis chassis.

Honda CBR1100XX Super Blackbird weighs

563 POUNDS

BMW S1000RR

6 Although now available for anyone to own, this model was initially created for the 2009 Superbike World Championship.

9ff GT9-R is
15.53
FEET
long

TOP 10

FASTEST CARS

Both production and concept cars are represented on this Top 10 of the speediest cars...

MODEL	TOP SPEED (MPH)	(KPH)
1 HENNESSEY VENOM GT	270.49	435.31
2 BUGATTI VEYRON 16.4 SUPER SPORT	269.86	431.07
3 KOENIGSEGG AGERA	260	418.42
4 SSC ULTIMATE AERO	257.44	414.31
5 9FF GT9-R	257	413.59
6 BUGATTI VEYRON GRAND SPORT VITESSE	254.04	408.84
7 SALEEN S7 TWIN-TURBO	248	399.11
8 KOENIGSEGG CCX	245	394.28
9 MCLAREN F1	243	391.06
10 KOENIGSEGG CCR	241.01	387.87

SALEEN S7 TWIN-TURBO

7 Twin turbos boost this car's power to 750 horsepower. The vehicle gets its name from Steve Saleen's namesake company, which since 1983 has specialized in making high-spec sports cars.

HENNESSEY VENOM GT

1 Models have been produced since 2011. Its record-setting speed was achieved on the Space Shuttle landing strip at Kennedy Space Center in Florida on February 14, 2014.

Afrosiyob's debut in Uzbekistan was on **OCT. 8, 2011**

HANVIT

4 In the past six years, a total of 46 trains have been produced. Hyundai Rotem (part of Hyundai Motor Group) manufactures this train.

TOP 10

FASTEST WHEEL-AND-TRACK TRAINS

Maglev (magnetic levitation) trains go even faster than these, but this list compares traditional trains...

	TYPE	FASTEST MODEL	COUNTRY	TOP SPEED (MPH)	(KPH)
1	SHINKANSEN	E6 SERIES SHINKANSEN	JAPAN	198.8	320
=	SIEMENS VELARO	EUROSTAR E320	FRANCE/UK/GERMANY	198.8	320
=	TGV	TGV RÉSEAU	FRANCE	198.8	320
4	HANVIT	KTX-SANCHEON	SOUTH KOREA	189.5	305
5	TALGO 350	AVE CLASS 102	SPAIN	186.4	300
=	ZEFIRO	CRH380D	CHINA	186.4	300
=	AGV	ETR 575	ITALY	186.4	300
8	ICE	ICE 2	GERMANY	173.9	280
9	TALGO 250	AFROSIYOB	UZBEKISTAN	155.3	250
=	PENDOLINO	AVANT CLASS 104	SPAIN	155.3	250

SHINKANSEN

1 The East Japan Railroad Company operates 24 full sets of this train. The train's length is 487.7 feet (148.7 m), and some cars measure up to 75.7 feet (23 m) long.

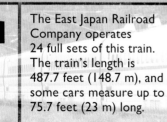

TOP 10

MOST SUCCESSFUL KARTING NATIONS

All of the countries that compete in the Karting World Championship have been compared...

COUNTRY	NUMBER OF WORLD CHAMPIONSHIP WINS
1 ITALY	21
2 UNITED KINGDOM	10
3 GERMANY	5
= NETHERLANDS	5
5 DENMARK	2
= FRANCE	2
= SWEDEN	2
8 SWITZERLAND	1
= BRAZIL	1
= NEW ZEALAND/U.S.	1

HISTORY OF KARTING

CIK-FIA is the central body for international karting. Founded in 1962 in Paris, France, CIK (Commission Internationale de Karting) merged with FIA (Fédération Internationale de l'Automobile) in 2000.

Go-karts (for public use or recreation) are limited to a top speed of

16 MPH

PLANET KARTING

This shows how much Italy dominates this sport...

- ITALY **21**
- UNITED KINGDOM **10**
- GERMANY **5**
- NETHERLANDS **5**
- DENMARK **2**

KARTING WORLD CHAMPIONSHIP

The first official world championship was held in Rome, Italy, in 1964. The 2009 competition was the first time it was held in Asia, in Macau, China. It also marked the first time Chinese drivers competed in an official CIK-FIA championship event.

CONVAIR B-36J-III

5 Also known as the "Peacekeeper," this aircraft was the first bomber constructed with the capability of carrying a nuclear weapon.

TOP 10

PLANES WITH LARGEST WINGSPANS

The average height of a human is 5.4 feet (1.6 m), which makes the width of these planes even more incredible...

	NAME	COUNTRY OF MANUFACTURE	DEBUT FLIGHT	WINGSPAN (FT)	(M)
1	HUGHES H-4 SPRUCE GOOSE	U.S.	NOV. 2, 1947	319.8	97.5
2	ANTONOV AN-225 MRIYA	RUSSIA (SOVIET UNION ERA)	NOV. 21, 1988	290	88.4
3	AIRBUS A380-800	EUROPE (VARIOUS)	APRIL 21, 2005	261.8	79.8
4	ANTONOV AN-124 RUSLAN	RUSSIA (SOVIET UNION ERA)	DEC. 26, 1982	240.5	73.3
5	CONVAIR B-36J-III	U.S.	AUGUST 8, 1946	230	70.1
=	CONVAIR XC-99	U.S.	NOV. 23, 1947	230	70.1
7	BOEING 747-8F	U.S.	FEB. 8, 2010	224.7	68.5
8	LOCKHEED C-5B	U.S.	JUNE 30, 1968	222.7	67.9
9	BOEING 747-400	U.S.	FEB. 9, 1969	211.3	64.4
=	ANTONOV AN-22 ANTEI	RUSSIA (SOVIET UNION ERA)	FEB. 27, 1965	211.3	64.4

AIRBUS A380-800

3 A total of 176 of these double-decker passenger planes have been built since April 27, 2005. With a length of 238.6 feet (72.72 m), it stands 79 feet (24.1 m) tall.

Number of Hughes H-4 Spruce Goose ever built:

1

FAIREY DELTA 2

9 Only two editions of this supersonic plane were ever built. It was designed by Scottish aeronautical engineer Sir Robert Lang Lickley (January 19, 1912– July 7, 1998).

Number of F-100C Super Sabre built:

2,294

TOP 10

FASTEST **MANNED PLANES**

Some supersonic craft are unmanned, but this Top 10 ranks the aircraft that require a human to control them...

	AIRCRAFT	PILOT(S)	DATE	TOP SPEED (MPH)	(KPH)
1	NORTH AMERICAN X-15	WILLIAM J. "PETE" KNIGHT	OCT. 3, 1967	4,520	7,274.24
2	LOCKHEED SR-71 BLACKBIRD	ELDON W. JOERSZ & GEORGE T. MORGAN	JULY 28, 1976	2,193.2	3,529.6
3	LOCKHEED YF-12A	ROBERT L. STEPHENS & DANIEL ANDRE	MAY 1, 1965	2,070.1	3,331.5
4	MIKOYAN GUREVICH YE-166	GEORGI MOSOLOV	JULY 7, 1962	1,665.9	2,681
5	MCDONNELL-DOUGLAS F-4 PHANTOM II	ROBERT G. ROBINSON	NOV. 22, 1961	1,606.3	2,585.1
6	CONVAIR F-106 DELTA DART	JOSEPH ROGERS	DEC. 15, 1959	1,525.9	2,455.7
7	LOCKHEED F-104A STARFIGHTER	W. W. IRWIN	MAY 16, 1958	1,404	2,259.5
8	MCDONNELL F-101A VOODOO	ADRIAN DREW	DEC. 12, 1957	1,207.6	1,943.5
9	FAIREY DELTA 2	PETER TWISS	MAR. 10, 1956	1,139.2	1,833.31
10	F-100C SUPER SABRE	HORACE A. HANES	AUGUST 20, 1955	822.1	1,323

LOCKHEED F-104A STARFIGHTER

7 After being in operation for almost 50 years, this Air Force fighter jet was retired in October 2004.

Sabrina Jackintell's world record for highest altitude by a female glider has stood since

1979

SABRINA JACKINTELL

6 Ohio-born glider Sabrina Jackintell (January 31, 1940–January 15, 2012) also set the women's land speed record in 1965. She appeared in *Soaring* magazine and on *The Merv Griffin Show*.

STEVE FOSSETT

1 Prior to his death in September 2007, adventurer Steve Fossett set records in a range of events and sports, including hot air ballooning, sailing, airship, aircraft, mountain climbing, skiing, and gliding.

TOP 10

HIGHEST GLIDERS

These glider pilots have achieved the highest altitudes in their engine-free aircraft...

	PILOT	DATE	ALTITUDE (FT)	(M)
1	STEVE FOSSETT	SEP 29, 2006	50,721.8	15,460
2	ROBERT R. HARRIS	FEB 17, 1986	49,009.2	14,938
3	PAUL F. BIKLE	FEB 25, 1961	46,266.4	14,102
4	LAURENCE R. EDGAR	MAR 19, 1952	44,255.2	13,489
5	WILLIAM S. IVANS JR.	DEC 30, 1950	42,099.7	12,832
6	SABRINA JACKINTELL	FEB 14, 1979	41,459.9	12,637
7	ROBERT F. SYMONS	MAR 5, 1951	38,305.1	11,675.4
8	HARLAND C. ROSS	JAN 27, 1950	36,000.7	10,973
9	MARY L. NUTT	MAR 5, 1975	35,462.6	10,809
10	GÜNTER CICHON	MAY 27, 1979	34,146.0	10,408

TOP 10

GLIDERS WITH THE LONGEST DURATION

The record times on this chart range from just hours to nearly two-and-a-half days spent gliding across the sky...

	PILOT	COUNTRY	DATE	DURATION GLIDING
1	CHARLES ATGER	FRANCE	APR 2, 1952	56 HRS. 15 MINS.
2	GUY MARCHAND	FRANCE	MAR 16, 1949	40 HRS. 51 MINS.
3	JACQUELINE MATHE	FRANCE	JAN 12, 1954	38 HRS. 41 MINS.
4	KURT SCHMIDT	GERMANY	AUG 3, 1933	35 HRS. 3 MINS.
5	MARCELLE CHOISNET	FRANCE	NOV 22, 1951	28 HRS. 41 MINS.
6	WANDA MODLIBOWSKA	POLAND	MAY 14, 1937	24 HRS. 14 MINS.
7	SUZANNE MELK	FRANCE	MAR 25, 1947	16 HRS. 3 MINS. 43 SECS.
8	FERDINAND SCHULZ	GERMANY	MAY 3, 1927	14 HRS. 7 MINS.
9	MADELEINE RENAUD	FRANCE	JUN 13, 1946	12 HRS. 53 MINS. 6 SECS.
10	E. ZELENKOVA	RUSSIA (SOVIET UNION ERA)	MAY 16, 1939	12 HRS. 30 MINS.

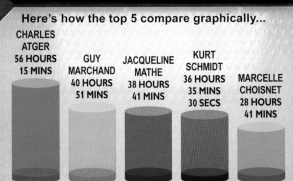

JACQUELINE MATHE

3 On January 13, 1954, 28-year-old Jacqueline Mathe and her 26-year-old copilot Marinette Gargarino set their gliding record of 38 hours and 41 minutes.

Wanda Modlibowska lived to the age of

91

GLIDING POWER

Here's how the top 5 compare graphically...

CHARLES ATGER
56 HOURS 15 MINS

GUY MARCHAND
40 HOURS 51 MINS

JACQUELINE MATHE
38 HOURS 41 MINS

KURT SCHMIDT
36 HOURS 35 MINS 30 SECS

MARCELLE CHOISNET
28 HOURS 41 MINS

FERDINAND SCHULZ

8 German glider Ferdinand Schulz achieved his record in May 1927, breaking the previous record set in 1925 of 10 hours, 29 minutes, and 43 seconds.

59

FLYING MACHINES

DAVID G. SIMMONS

2 Here is Simmons on the cover of the September 2, 1957, issue of *Life*. As part of Project Manhigh (a U.S. Air Force project sending men up into the Earth's stratosphere), he set his altitude record from inside a specially-made capsule suspended beneath a helium-filled balloon.

VIJAYPAT SINGHANIA

4 The Indian textile businessman set his ballooning record at age 67. During his ascent, air temperatures dropped to −135°F (−93°C).

TOP 10

HIGHEST BALLOONISTS

Imagine flying at more than 19 miles (30.5 km) above the ground in a balloon. That's what the top 2 entries in this chart did...

	NAME	COUNTRY	ALTITUDE (FT)	(M)
1	MALCOLM D. ROSS	U.S.	113,740.2	34,668
2	DAVID G. SIMMONS	U.S.	101,515.8	30,942
3	ORVIL ANDERSON	U.S.	72,395.01	22,066
4	VIJAYPAT SINGHANIA	INDIA	68,986.2	21,027
5	PER AXEL LINDSTRAND	UNITED KINGDOM	64,996.7	19,811
6	THOMAS G. W. SETTLE	U.S.	61,236.9	18,665
7	JULIAN R. P. NOTT	UNITED KINGDOM	55,134.5	16,805
8	AUGUSTE PICCARD	SWITZERLAND	53,152.9	16,201
9	CHAUNCEY M. DUNN	U.S.	52,998.7	16,154
10	JOSEF STARKBAUM	AUSTRIA	49,248.7	15,011

Malcolm D. Ross's total ballooning flight time was more than

100 hours

TOP 10

FIRST ZEPPELIN AIRSHIPS

These airships were once considered the most futuristic form of air travel...

	NAME	FIRST FLIGHT
1	LZ 1	JULY 2, 1900
2	LZ 2	JANUARY 17, 1906
3	LZ 3	OCTOBER 9, 1906
4	LZ 4	JUNE 20, 1908
5	LZ 5	MAY 26, 1909
6	LZ 6	AUGUST 25, 1909
7	LZ 7	JUNE 19, 1910
8	LZ 8	MARCH 30, 1911
9	LZ 10	JUNE 26, 1911
10	LZ 9	OCTOBER 2, 1911

LZ 1

1 In June 1898, German Count Ferdinand von Zeppelin started construction of the *LZ 1*. Completed in late 1899, it waited until the following summer to make its test flight.

LZ 4

4 This 446-foot (135.9-m) long airship could reach speeds up to 30 mph (48.3 kph). After a series of successful flights, it was ripped from its moorings and caught fire in 1908.

Length of the *LZ1*:

420 feet

JOHN LETHBRIDGE

1 The world's first deep-sea diving suit was 6 feet (1.8 m) long and about 2.5 ft (0.8 m) wide. Iron hoops inside and out prevented it from collapsing under pressure at depth.

TOP 10

FIRST ATMOSPHERIC DIVING-SUIT DIVERS

Deep-sea diving feels like something of a modern concept, but its roots go back centuries...

	NAME	YEAR OF FIRST DEEP-SEA DIVE
1	JOHN LETHBRIDGE	1715
2	JACOB ROWE	1720
3	WILLIAM TAYLOR	1838
4	LODNER D. PHILLIPS	1856
5	THOMAS CATO MCKEEN	1867
6	CHARLES WILSON	1870
7	LAFAYETTE	1875
8	STEPHEN TASKER	1881
9	CARMAGNOLLE BROTHERS	1882
10	OLIVER PELKEY	1889

A modern ADS (Atmospheric Diving Suit) can function at depths exceeding

2,000 FEET

MODERN DEEP-SEA DIVING

Nuytco Research Ltd.'s deep-sea diving suit called "Exosuit" is an evolution of their "Newtsuit." The suit can withstand a depth of 1,000 feet (304.8 m) and weighs up to 600 pounds (272.2 kg). The manufacturers plan to fit it with up to eight thrusters, and to give it a 1,250-foot (381-m) long "umbilical cord" to connect it to a ship (or base) at the surface.

TOP 10

MOST SUCCESSFUL WORLD CUP SAILING NATIONS

Sailing is a hugely popular sport and pastime all over the world, with these countries leading the way...

ISAF World Sailing Championships are held every

4 years

	COUNTRY	TOTAL GOLD	TOTAL SILVER	TOTAL BRONZE	TOTAL MEDALS
1	UNITED KINGDOM	87	82	68	237
2	AUSTRALIA	77	63	59	199
3	FRANCE	48	50	41	139
4	U.S.	33	29	43	105
5	NETHERLANDS	40	27	31	98
6	NEW ZEALAND	22	30	20	72
7	SPAIN	23	20	23	66
8	GERMANY	23	17	17	57
9	CHINA	20	15	15	50
10	CROATIA	13	18	17	48

2014 ISAF WORLD SAILING CHAMPIONSHIP

Success at this event, held in Santander, Spain, determined qualification for the 2016 Summer Olympics. France won the most events (three gold medals and one bronze medal).

TOP 5 BY GOLD MEDALS

Here are the nations with the most...

UNITED KINGDOM
87

AUSTRALIA
77

FRANCE
48

NETHERLANDS
40

U.S.
33

SAILING AT THE OLYMPICS

Sailing has been part of the Olympic Games since the first modern games took place in 1896. However, the inaugural games' event ended up being canceled due to a lack of competitors.

JULES FISHER

10 Belgian-born Fisher was more interested in competitive cycling in his youth. Prior to his 1924 flying record, he won the 1912 Hydroplane contest in Monaco.

TOP 10

FASTEST ON-WATER RECORD HOLDERS

Even with all of the advances in technology, the world record has not been beaten for nearly 40 years...

	SKIPPER(S)	VESSEL	COUNTRY	YEAR	BEST SPEED ACHIEVED (MPH)	(KPH)
1	KEN WARBY	SPIRIT OF AUSTRALIA	AUSTRALIA	1978	345	555.21
2	LEE TAYLOR	HUSTLER	U.S.	1967	285.22	459.02
3	DONALD CAMPBELL	BLUEBIRD K7	UK	1964	276.33	444.71
4	STANLEY SAYRES & ELMER LENINSCHMIDT	SLO-MO-SHUN IV	U.S.	1952	178.5	287.26
5	MALCOLM CAMPBELL	BLUEBIRD K4	UK	1939	141.74	228.11
6	GAR WOOD	MISS AMERICA X	U.S.	1932	124.86	200.94
7	KAYE DON	MISS ENGLAND III	ITALY	1932	119.81	192.82
8	HENRY SEGRAVE	MISS ENGLAND II	UK	1930	98.76	158.94
9	GEORGE WOOD	MISS AMERICA II	U.S.	1928	92.84	149.41
10	JULES FISHER	FARMAN HYDROGLIDER	BELGIUM	1924	87.39	140.64

KEN WARBY

1 Warby's fascination with the speed record came from his admiration of British speed-record maker Donald Campbell, who broke eight world speed records (on land and on water).

Number of World Records set by Donald Campbell between 1955 and 1964:

7

OHIO

2 This class of submarine can travel up to 23 mph (37 kph) under the waves. It's the largest sub constructed for the US Navy.

Number of Ohio-class submarines owned by the US Navy:

18

LONGEST SUBMARINES

These submersible military vehicles cost billions of dollars to develop and construct...

	CLASS	COUNTRY	LENGTH (FT)	(M)
1	TYPHOON	RUSSIA	574.14	175
2	BOREI	RUSSIA	557.74	170
=	OHIO	U.S.	557.74	170
4	DELTA III	RUSSIA	544.62	166
5	OSCAR II	RUSSIA	508.53	155
6	VANGUARD	UK	491.8	149.9
7	TRIOMPHANT	FRANCE	452.76	138
8	YASEN	RUSSIA	393.7	120
9	VIRGINIA	U.S.	377.3	115
10	SIERRA II	RUSSIA	364.17	111

TRIOMPHANT

7 There are four active submarines in this class currently serving the French Navy. Each holds 96 sailors and 15 officers.

U.S.

1 Founded on October 13, 1775, the U.S. Naval Corp is the largest navy on Earth. Including reserves, it boasts 450,000 personnel and nearly 4,000 aircraft.

The largest aircraft carriers can hold up to **90** planes

ORIGINS OF THE AIRCRAFT CARRIER

During the 1910s, the US Navy and British Royal Navy began developing ways to enable aircraft to take off from and land on a floating vessel. In 1918 the British navy's HMS *Argus* became the first official aircraft carrier.

TOP 10

MOST AIRCRAFT CARRIERS

Of all the countries that use these floating fortresses, these nations have the most...

	COUNTRY	NUMBER IN SERVICE	TOTAL NUMBER EVER BUILT
1	U.S.	10	68
2	UK	0	40
3	JAPAN	0	20
4	FRANCE	1	8
5	RUSSIA	1	7
6	INDIA	2	3
7	SPAIN	1	3
8	AUSTRALIA	0	3
=	CANADA	0	3
10	ITALY	2	2

AIRCRAFT NATIONS

These 5 countries have constructed the most...

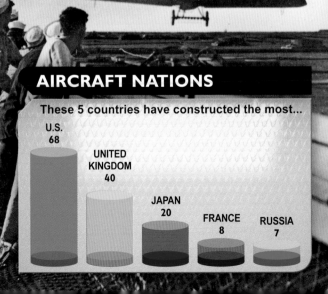

U.S. 68 — UNITED KINGDOM 40 — JAPAN 20 — FRANCE 8 — RUSSIA 7

The board game *Battleship* echoes the board game *Baslinda*, dating to

1890

GLOIRE

1 This French vessel had 4½-inch (11.4-cm) thick iron plating, which covered a bulky timber construction. It was armed with 36 guns.

MODERN BATTLESHIPS

Using battleships in war at sea is now a thing of the past. The British Royal Navy's battleship, HMS *Vanguard*, was one of the last in use. It was decommissioned in 1960.

TOP 10

FIRST CLASSES OF IRONCLAD BATTLESHIP

Once the all-wooden ships got superseded by metal, these were the original classes...

	CLASS	YEAR OF LAUNCH
1	GLOIRE	1859
2	WARRIOR	1860
3	MAGENTA	1861
=	TERRIBILE	1861
5	PROVENCE	1863
=	PRINCIPE DI CARIGNANO	1863
=	RE D'ITALIA	1863
=	REGINA MARIA PIA	1863
9	PERVENETS	1864
10	ROMA	1865

FORCES OF NATURE

ZONE 3

TOP 10

BIGGEST COUNTRIES
(LAND MASS)

Of the 196 countries on our planet, these are the 10 largest...

	COUNTRY	SIZE (MILES^2)	(KM^2)
1	RUSSIA	6,601,668	17,098,242
2	CANADA	3,855,100	9,984,670
3	CHINA	3,747,879	9,706,961
4	U.S.	3,705,407	9,629,091
5	BRAZIL	3,287,612	8,514,877
6	AUSTRALIA	2,969,907	7,692,024
7	INDIA	1,222,559	3,166,414
8	ARGENTINA	1,073,500	2,780,400
9	KAZAKHSTAN	1,052,100	2,724,900
10	ALGERIA	919,595	2,381,741

INDIA

7 The most popular sport in India is cricket. The nation's first team was established in 1792 and played its first Test cricket match in 1932.

Monaco, the second smallest country in the world, covers just

0.78 MILES^2

AUSTRALIA

6 This country's name comes from the Latin for "southern land," *Terra Australis*. Tourism contributes approximately $100 million a day to its economy.

NORWAY

7 A full 90 percent of Norway is mountainous, with a total of 291 peaks. Galdhøpiggen in Jotunheimen is the tallest at 8,100 feet (2,469 m).

RUSSIA

3 Nearly 30 million tourists visit Russia each year. St. Petersburg, founded in 1703 by Peter Alexeyevich (also known as Peter the Great), is the most popular place to visit.

TOP 10

LONGEST COASTLINES

These countries are connected to the oceans of the world more than any others...

COUNTRY	LENGTH OF COASTLINE (MILES)	(KM)
1 CANADA	164,988.34	265,523
2 U.S.	82,836.24	133,312
3 RUSSIA	68,543.46	110,310
4 INDONESIA	59,142.73	95,181
5 CHILE	48,816.78	78,563
6 AUSTRALIA	41,339.83	66,530
7 NORWAY	33,056.33	53,199
8 PHILIPPINES	21,064.48	33,900
9 BRAZIL	20,740.75	33,379
10 FINLAND	19,336.45	31,119

CANADA

1 Canada celebrates its original inhabitants, Canadian Aboriginals, and the history of the country every year on June 21, National Aboriginal Day. About 4 percent of Canada's population are Aboriginals.

USA's population is

325.9 MILLION

COASTLINE LENGTHS

This graph shows the 5 longest coastlines...

CANADA	U.S.	RUSSIA	INDONESIA	CHILE
164,988.34 MILES	82,836.24 MILES	68,543.46 MILES	59,142.73 MILES	48,816.78 MILES

1ST VS. 10TH

La Paz vs. Kabul: elevation above sea level…

- LA PAZ **11,942 FEET**
- KABUL **5,873 FEET**

QUITO

2 Founded in 1534, Quito is now home to nearly 3 million people. It has seven museums as well as seven professional soccer teams.

Nairobi covers **269** MI²

TOP 10

HIGHEST CAPITAL CITIES

Even the city at 10th place in this list is located more than a mile above sea level...

	NAME	COUNTRY	ELEVATION ABOVE SEA LEVEL (FT)	(M)
1	LA PAZ	BOLIVIA	11,942	3,640
2	QUITO	ECUADOR	9,350	2,850
3	THIMPHU	BHUTAN	8,688	2,648
4	BOGOTÁ	COLOMBIA	8,612	2,625
5	ADDIS ABABA	ETHIOPIA	7,726	2,355
6	ASMARA	ERITREA	7,628	2,325
7	SANA'A	YEMEN	7,382	2,250
8	MEXICO CITY	MEXICO	7,350	2,240
9	NAIROBI	KENYA	5,889	1,795
10	KABUL	AFGHANISTAN	5,873	1,790

ADDIS ABABA

5 This Ethiopian city is home to a childcare center called We Are the Future. The center is dedicated to improving the lives and well-being of children of Addis Ababa.

Lake Assal is **130** FEET deep

BADWATER BASIN

9 Natural salt at Badwater Basin in California is subject to repeated freezing, thawing, and evaporating. Tourists visit the site to see the unusual hexagonal salt shapes that form across the basin.

DEAD SEA

1 This sea is called "Dead" since the water is devoid of all life except bacteria and fungi. The Dead Sea is nine times saltier than the ocean, and 997 feet (304 m) deep.

TOP 10

COUNTRIES WITH THE **LOWEST** POINTS OF ELEVATION

In contrast with the list opposite, these locations are at extraordinary low points...

	PLACE	COUNTRY/COUNTRIES	LOWEST POINT BELOW SEA LEVEL (FT)	(M)
1	DEAD SEA	ISRAEL, JORDAN, PALESTINE	-1,402	-428
2	SEA OF GALILEE	ISRAEL	-702	-214
3	LAKE ASSAL	DJIBOUTI	-509	-155
4	AYDINGKOL	CHINA	-505	-154
5	QATTARA DEPRESSION	EGYPT	-436	-133
6	KARAGIYE DEPRESSION	KAZAKHSTAN	-433	-132
7	DANAKIL DEPRESSION	ETHIOPIA	-410	-125
8	LAGUNA DEL CARBÓN	ARGENTINA	-344	-105
9	BADWATER BASIN	U.S.	-279	-85
10	VPADINA AKCHANAYA	TURKMENISTAN	-266	-81

OCEANS VS. SEAS

The Top 10 compared...

- OCEAN **151,423,000** MILES^2
- SEAS **7,460,000** MILES^2

The Indian Ocean can reach

82 °F

LARGEST OCEANS & SEAS

Earth is often called the Blue Planet because 71 percent of its surface is covered in water...

	NAME	TYPE	AREA (MILES^2)	(KM^2)
1	PACIFIC	OCEAN	64,196,000	166,266,876
2	ATLANTIC	OCEAN	33,400,000	86,505,602
3	INDIAN	OCEAN	28,400,000	73,555,662
4	SOUTHERN	OCEAN	20,327,000	52,646,688
5	ARCTIC	OCEAN	5,100,000	13,208,939
6	PHILIPPINE	SEA	2,000,000	5,179,976
7	CORAL	SEA	1,850,000	4,791,478
8	ARABIAN	SEA	1,491,000	3,861,672
9	SOUTH CHINA	SEA	1,148,000	2,973,306
10	CARIBBEAN	SEA	971,000	2,514,878

ARCTIC WILDLIFE

A broad range of wildlife, including the walrus, narwal, beluga, snowy owl, polar bear, caribou, and lemming, thrive in the subzero temperatures of the Arctic region.

BERMUDA TRIANGLE MYSTERY

The area of the ocean between Bermuda, the state of Florida, and Puerto Rico is popularly known as the Devil's Triangle. Planes, ships, and their unlucky passengers have disappeared here without a trace.

CASPIAN SEA

1 The Beluga Sturgeon, the largest freshwater fish in the world, lives in this body of water. It can grow 24 feet (7.3 m) long, but is critically endangered due to overfishing.

TOP 10

LARGEST LAKES

There are an estimated 117 million lakes on our planet. Here are the 10 largest...

	NAME	LOCATION	AREA (MILES²)	(KM²)
1	**CASPIAN SEA**	IRAN, RUSSIA, TURKMENISTAN, KAZAKHSTAN, AZERBAIJAN	143,000	371,000
2	**SUPERIOR**	CANADA, U.S.	31,820	82,414
3	**VICTORIA**	UGANDA, KENYA, TANZANIA	26,828	69,485
4	**HURON**	CANADA, U.S.	23,000	59,600
5	**MICHIGAN**	U.S.	22,000	58,000
6	**TANGANYIKA**	TANZANIA, DEMOCRATIC REPUBLIC OF THE CONGO, BURUNDI, ZAMBIA	12,700	32,893
7	**BAIKAL**	RUSSIA	12,200	31,500
8	**GREAT BEAR**	CANADA	12,000	31,080
9	**MALAWI**	MOZAMBIQUE, TANZANIA, MALAWI	11,600	30,044
10	**GREAT SLAVE**	CANADA	11,170	28,930

GREAT LAKES CREATURE

2 Lake Superior, one of the five Great Lakes, reaches 1,333 feet (406.3 m) deep. Over the centuries, sightings of a huge, serpent-type creature called Pressie have been recorded here.

The Caspian Sea is home to **31** islands

YARLUNG TSANGPO GRAND CANYON

1 This is one of the rare places on Earth that hasn't been extensively explored and affected by humankind. It's so vast that it experiences both arctic and subtropical temperatures.

TOP 10

DEEPEST CANYONS

To put these measurements into context, the number 1 entry is almost four miles deep...

	NAME	LOCATION	DEEPEST POINT (FT)	(M)
1	YARLUNG TSANGPO GRAND CANYON	TIBET	19,714.6	6,009
2	THE KALI GANDAKI GORGE	NEPAL	18,277.6	5,571
3	INDUS GORGE	PAKISTAN	17,060.4	5,200
4	COLCA CANYON	PERU	13,648.3	4,160
5	TIGER LEAPING GORGE	CHINA	12,434.4	3,790
6	COTAHUASI CANYON	PERU	11,597.8	3,535
7	URIQUE CANYON (ONE OF THE 6 COPPER CANYONS)	MEXICO	6,164.7	1,879
8	THE GRAND CANYON	U.S.	5,997.4	1,828
9	BLYDE RIVER CANYON	SOUTH AFRICA	4,537.4	1,383
10	TARA RIVER CANYON	MONTENEGRO	4,265.1	1,300

Tibet's Yarlung Tsangpo Grand Canyon is

150

miles long

PERU CANYONS

This is how the featured Peruvian canyons compare...

COLCA CANYON
13,648.3 FT

COTAHUASI CANYON
11,597.8 FT

YANGTZE RIVER

3 This river has 700 tributaries. One of its dams, the Three Gorges Dam, is the largest power plant in the world. It took 14 years (from 1994 to 2008) to complete.

CONGO RIVER

9 There are 686 species of fish (that we know of) in the Congo River, including the air-breathing lungfish, and 80 percent of this river's species exist only there.

LONGEST RIVERS

These 10 rivers from all over the world total more than 35,000 miles in length...

	NAME	OUTFLOW	LENGTH (MILES)	(KM)
1	AMAZON—UCAYALI—APURÍMAC	ATLANTIC OCEAN	4,345	6,992
2	NILE—KAGERA	MEDITERRANEAN	4,258	6,853
3	YANGTZE	EAST CHINA SEA	3,917	6,300
4	MISSISSIPPI—MISSOURI—JEFFERSON	GULF OF MEXICO	3,902	6,275
5	YENISEI—ANGARA—SELENGE	KARA SEA	3,445	5,539
6	HUANG HE	BOHAI SEA	3,395	5,464
7	OB—IRTYSH	GULF OF OB	3,364	5,410
8	PARANÁ—RÍO DE LA PLATA	RÍO DE LA PLATA	3,030	4,880
9	CONGO—CHAMBESHI	ATLANTIC OCEAN	2,922	4,700
10	AMUR—ARGUN	SEA OF OKHOTSK	2,763	4,444

AMAZON RIVER

1 The Amazon River flows through four countries, for the most part Brazil and Peru. During the wet season, the river reaches 30 miles (48.2 km) wide.

The Amazon River sees **1,584** MILES^3 water flow through it each year

LAYA

10 The indigenous inhabitants of Laya are known as the Layap. They wear a distinctive, cone-shaped hat made of treated bamboo.

Bolivia's population is approximately **10** MILLION

COMPARING THE HIGHEST

Here is a graphic expression of this chart's top 5...

LA RINCONADA 16,728 FT	WENQUAN 15,980 FT	KORZOK 15,000 FT	PARINACOTA 14,435 FT	DOLPA 14,301 FT

TOP 10

HIGHEST RESIDENTIAL PLACES ABOVE SEA LEVEL

Although not actually the tallest points on Earth, these are the highest places that people live...

	PLACE	COUNTRY	ELEVATION ABOVE SEA LEVEL (FT)	(M)
1	LA RINCONADA	PERU	16,728	5,100
2	WENQUAN	CHINA	15,980	4,870
3	KORZOK	INDIA	15,000	4,570
4	PARINACOTA	CHILE	14,435	4,400
5	DOLPA	NEPAL	14,301	4,360
6	MINA PIRQUITAS	ARGENTINA	14,240	4,340
7	COLQUECHACA	BOLIVIA	13,680	4,170
8	QARABOLAQ	AFGHANISTAN	13,579	4,139
9	CHATYNDY	KYRGYZSTAN	13,166	4,013
10	LAYA	BHUTAN	12,533	3,820

LA RINCONADA

1 A colossal glacier called La Bella Durmiente (which translates as "The Sleeping Beauty") sits next to this Peruvian city, which has a population of 50,000.

DEEPEST REALMS

With depths ranging between five and six miles, these are the lowest known points on Earth...

	NAME	LOCATION	DEEPEST POINT BELOW SEA LEVEL	
			(FT)	(M)
1	**MARIANA TRENCH**	PACIFIC OCEAN	**36,197.5**	**11,033**
2	**TONGA TRENCH**	PACIFIC OCEAN	**35,702.1**	**10,882**
3	**JAPAN TRENCH**	PACIFIC OCEAN	**34,593.2**	**10,544**
4	**PHILIPPINE TRENCH**	PACIFIC OCEAN	**34,580**	**10,540**
5	**KURIL-KAMCHATKA TRENCH**	PACIFIC OCEAN	**34,448.8**	**10,500**
6	**KERMADEC TRENCH**	PACIFIC OCEAN	**32,962.6**	**10,047**
7	**IZU-OGASAWARA TRENCH**	PACIFIC OCEAN	**32,086.6**	**9,780**
8	**PUERTO RICO TRENCH**	ATLANTIC OCEAN	**28,372.7**	**8,648**
9	**SOUTH SANDWICH TRENCH**	ATLANTIC OCEAN	**27,650.9**	**8,428**
10	**ATACAMA TRENCH**	PACIFIC OCEAN	**26,460**	**8,065**

Just off the chart, the Atlantic Ocean's Romanche Trench is

25,459.3
FEET
deep

TONGA TRENCH

2 When the Apollo 13 space mission failed, its Lunar Module splashed down into the Tonga Trench. This is because it contained an RTG (Radioisotope Thermoelectric Generator) of radioactive plutonium and so needed to be as far away as possible from humans.

THE MARIANA TRENCH CHALLENGE

Filmmaker James Cameron made history when he piloted the *Deepsea Challenger* to the bottom of the Mariana Trench on March 26, 2012.

German explorer Paul Güssfeldt was the first European to attempt to climb Aconcagua in

1883

ANDES

3 Aconcagua forms the highest point along the Andes Mountain range. Its maximum elevation is 22,837 feet (6,960.8 m).

TOP 10

LONGEST MOUNTAIN RANGES

You may be familiar with the names of mountain ranges above water, but the biggest are beneath the waves...

	RANGE	MOUNTAIN TYPE	LOCATION	LENGTH (MILES)	(KM)
1	MID-OCEANIC RIDGE	OCEANIC	(GLOBAL)	40,389	65,000
2	MID-ATLANTIC RIDGE	OCEANIC	ATLANTIC OCEAN	6,214	10,000
3	ANDES	LAND	SOUTH AMERICA	4,350	7,000
4	ROCKY MOUNTAINS	LAND	NORTH AMERICA	2,983	4,800
5	TRANSANTARCTIC	LAND	ANTARCTICA	2,201	3,542
6	GREAT DIVIDING RANGE	LAND	AUSTRALIA	1,901	3,059
7	HIMALAYAS	LAND	ASIA	1,601	2,576
8	SOUTHEAST INDIAN RIDGE	OCEANIC	INDIAN OCEAN	1,429	2,300
9	SOUTHWEST INDIAN RIDGE	OCEANIC	RODRIGUEZ ISLAND TO PRINCE EDWARD ISLAND	1,200	1,931
10	PACIFIC-ANTARCTIC RIDGE	OCEANIC	SOUTH PACIFIC OCEAN	639	1,029

MID-OCEANIC RIDGE

1 The complete system of mid-oceanic ridges that exists in every ocean on the planet is known as the Ocean Ridge. It's almost 10 times the length of the Andes.

MID-ATLANTIC RIDGE

2 Some scientists believe the MAR (Mid-Atlantic Ridge) was formed when the original "super-continent" of Pangaea began to break apart 180 million years ago.

TUGELA FALLS

2 This system of five drops does not fall as one cascade of water. In cold periods, the higher falls freeze into icy columns. It's considered best to view the falls after rainfall.

ANGEL FALLS

1 Of its two drops, the longest is 2,648 feet (807 m). The falls drop into Venezuela's Canaima National Park, which is a UNESCO (United Nations Educational, Scientific, and Cultural Organization) World Heritage Site.

Vinnufossen is the tallest waterfall in Europe and has **4** drops

TOP 10

HIGHEST WATERFALLS

Have you ever visited any of the tallest, most famous waterfalls in the world?...

	NAME	LOCATION	HEIGHT (FT)	(M)
1	ANGEL FALLS	VENEZUELA	3,212	979
2	TUGELA FALLS	SOUTH AFRICA	3,110	948
3	CATARATAS LAS TRES HERMANAS	PERU	3,000	914
4	OLO'UPENA FALLS	HAWAII	2,953	900
5	CATARATA YUMBILLA	PERU	2,940	896
6	VINNUFOSSEN	NORWAY	2,822	860
7	BALÁIFOSSEN	NORWAY	2,788	850
8	PU'UKA'OKU FALLS	HAWAII	2,756	840
=	JAMES BRUCE FALLS	CANADA	2,756	840
10	BROWNE FALLS	NEW ZEALAND	2,743	836

Kuwait International Airport serves over

9 MILLION passengers each year

KEBILI

2 As well as being one of the hottest places on this planet, Kebili has evidence that points to human habitation near the town dating back 200,000 years.

DEATH VALLEY

1 The Native American Timbisha people have been living in Death Valley for more than 1,000 years.

TOP 10

HOTTEST PLACES

Cells in the human body start to die at around 113°F (45°C), so these highest-recorded air temperatures are dangerous...

	LOCATION	DATE	TEMPERATURE (°F)	(°C)
1	DEATH VALLEY, CALIFORNIA	JULY 10, 1913	134	56.7
2	KEBILI, TUNISIA	JULY 7, 1931	131	55
3	TIRAT ZVI, ISRAEL	JUNE 21, 1942	129	54
4	SULAIBYA, KUWAIT	JULY 31, 2012	128.5	53.6
5	KUWAIT INTERNATIONAL AIRPORT	AUGUST 3, 2011	128.3	53.5
=	MOHENJO-DARO, SINDH, PAKISTAN	MAY 26, 2010	128.3	53.5
7	NASIRIYAH, ALI AIR BASE, IRAQ	AUGUST 3, 2011	127.4	53
8	BASRA, IRAQ	JUNE 14, 2010	125.6	52
=	SAN LUIS RÍO COLORADO, MEXICO	JULY 6, 1966	125.6	52
=	JEDDAH, SAUDI ARABIA	JUNE 22, 2010	125.6	52

COLDEST PLACES

Pure water freezes at 32°F (0°C), which highlights
just how cold these realms are...

	LOCATION	DATE	TEMPERATURE (°F)	(°C)
1	VOSTOK STATION, ANTARCTICA	JULY 21, 1983	−128.6	−89.2
2	AMUNDSEN-SCOTT SOUTH POLE STATION, SOUTH POLE	JUNE 23, 1982	−117	−82.8
3	DOME A, EAST ANTARCTICA	JULY 5, 2007	−116.5	−82.5
4	VERKHOYANSK & OYMYAKON SAKHA REPUBLIC, RUSSIA	FEB. 6, 1933	−90	−68
5	NORTH ICE, GREENLAND	JAN. 9, 1954	−87	−66.1
6	SNAG, YUKON, CANADA	FEB. 3, 1947	−81	−63
7	PROSPECT CREEK, ALASKA	JAN. 23, 1971	−80	−62
8	UST-SHCHUGER, RUSSIA	DEC. 31, 1978	−72.6	−58.1
9	MALGOVIK, VÄSTERBOTTEN, SWEDEN	DEC. 13, 1941	−63.4	−53
10	MOHE COUNTY, CHINA	FEB. 13, 1969	−62.1	−52.3

VERKHOYANSK & OYMYAKON SAKHA REPUBLIC

4 It may be one of the coldest places on Earth, but in March 2014 it saw a deep-dive investigation into its Labynkyr Lake. Reported sightings of an unknown creature in the lake date back centuries.

AMUNDSEN-SCOTT SOUTH POLE STATION

2 The original version of this station was built in 1956. Nowadays, ongoing research of the galaxy is conducted there with the 32.8-foot (10-m) diameter South Pole Telescope.

Antarctica has

0

permanent residents

FAR BELOW FREEZING

Here is how the top 5 coldest places compare...

ANTARCTICA −128.6°F

SOUTH POLE −117°F

EAST ANTARCTICA −116.5°F

RUSSIA −90°F

GREENLAND −87°F

MOUNT ONTAKE

3 With a height of 10,062 feet (3,067 m), this is the second-tallest volcano in Japan. The biggest is Mount Fuji, towering at 12,388 feet (3,776 m).

MOUNT MERAPI

1 Appropriately for a volcano, Mount Merapi translates to mean "Fire Mountain." Scientific analysis dates Merapi at around 400,000 years old.

TOP 10

MOST RECENT & DEADLIEST VOLCANIC ERUPTIONS

They may be ancient, but many volcanoes remain active with the potential to devastate their surroundings...

WHAT IS "VEI"

The Volcanic Explosivity Index provides a way to measure the impact of a volcanic eruption. The 1 to 8 scale measures the volume of volcanic material that is discharged.

	NAME	LOCATION	YEAR	VEI	KNOWN FATALITIES
1	MOUNT MERAPI	INDONESIA	2010	4	353
2	NYIRAGONGO	DR CONGO	2002	1	147
3	MOUNT ONTAKE	JAPAN	2014	3	61
4	NABRO	ERITREA	2011	4	38
5	MOUNT SINABUNG	INDONESIA	2014	2	15
6	KELUD	INDONESIA	2014	4	2
7	CHAITÉN	CHILE	2008	4	1
8	CALBUCO	CHILE	2015	4	0
9	PUYEHUE-CORDÓN CAULLE	CHILE	2011	5	0
10	GRÍMSVÖTN	ICELAND	2011	4	0

Chile was the location of the cave-in that trapped

33

miners in 2010

TOP 10

BIGGEST EARTHQUAKES

Minor earthquakes occur unnoticed all over the world every day, but others are extremely deadly...

	LOCATION	DATE	MAGNITUDE (RICHTER SCALE)
1	VALDIVIA (CHILE)	MAY 22, 1960	9.5
2	ALASKA	MARCH 27, 1964	9.2
3	SUMATRA (INDONESIA)	DEC. 26, 2004	9.1–9.3
4	TŌHOKU REGION (JAPAN)	MARCH 11, 2011	9.0
=	KAMCHATKA (RUSSIA)	NOV. 4, 1952	9.0
6	SUMATRA (INDONESIA)	NOV. 25, 1833	8.8–9.2
7	ECUADOR/COLOMBIA	JAN. 31, 1906	8.8
=	MAULE (CHILE)	FEB. 27, 2010	8.8
=	ARICA (CHILE)	SEP. 16, 1615	8.8
10	KRAKATOA (INDONESIA)	AUGUST 26, 1883	8.75

TŌHOKU REGION

4

In addition to the 2011 quake, there was also one in 2006 that killed approximately 5,000 people. Nearly 250,000 people were also rendered homeless through fear of a full-blown volcanic eruption.

Indonesia has

150

active volcanoes

SUMATRA

3

Sumatra's landscape features several volcanoes. North Sumatra's most populated city is Medan, with 2.1 million residents.

Haiti covers
10,714
MILES²

SPIRIT LAKE

2 When Mount St. Helens erupted, Spirit Lake was struck with the full force. Now, this strange "raft" of more than a million trees felled from the blast can still be seen.

TOP 10

TALLEST TSUNAMIS

Any significant natural or man-made disturbance of a large area of water can cause a seismic sea wave...

	LOCATION	YEAR	HEIGHT OF TSUNAMI (FEET)	(M)
1	LITUYA BAY, ALASKA	1958	1,719	524
2	SPIRIT LAKE, WASHINGTON	1980	853	260
3	VAJONT DAM, ITALY	1963	820	250
4	MOUNT UNZEN, KYUSHU, JAPAN	1792	328	100
5	ISHIGAKI & MIYAKOJIMA ISLANDS, JAPAN	1771	262	79.9
6	INDIAN OCEAN, SOUTH ASIA	2004	98.4	30
7	LISBON, PORTUGAL	1755	66	20.1
8	MESSINA, ITALY	1908	40	12.2
9	HOEI, JAPAN	1707	32	9.8
10	MEIJI-SANRIKU, JAPAN	1896	30	9.1

VAJONT DAM

3 A reminder of how engineering and research can go wrong: on October 9, 1963, a landslide triggered an immense wave over the top of this dam, killing thousands.

ERAS COMPARED

Here's how the number of tsunamis in the chart compare by century...

21ST	20TH	19TH	18TH
1	4	1	4

DEADLIEST **FLOODS**

As much as water is needed for all life on this planet, it can fast become a cruel, unpredictable enemy...

	FLOOD (COUNTRY)	YEAR	FATALITIES
1	YANGTZE AND HUANG HE RIVERS (CHINA)	1931	2.5–3.7 MILLION
2	HUANG HE (CHINA)	1887	900,000–2 MILLION
3	HUANG HE (CHINA)	1938	500,000–700,000
▶ 4	INDIAN OCEAN TSUNAMI (SEVERAL)	2004	230,000–310,000
5	BANQIAO DAM FAILURE/TYPHOON NINA (CHINA)	1975	231,000
6	YANGTZE (CHINA)	1935	145,000
7	MESSINA EARTHQUAKE & TSUNAMI (ITALY)	1908	123,000
▶ 8	ST. FELIX'S FLOOD (NETHERLANDS)	1530	100,000+
9	HANOI & RED RIVER DELTA FLOODS (N. VIETNAM)	1971	100,000
=	LISBON EARTHQUAKE & TSUNAMI (PORTUGAL)	1755	100,000

ST. FELIX'S FLOOD

8 The day of this flood became known as Evil Saturday. Without its series of dikes, much of the Netherlands would be underwater. The country was made into a plain by sediment formed over millennia of floods.

Huang He is **3,395** MILES long

INDIAN OCEAN TSUNAMI

4 A 9.1 earthquake led to the catastrophic tsunami of 2004. The earthquake was so powerful, it caused earthquakes in Alaska. There were 25,120 earthquakes (of all magnitudes) in 2004.

TSUNAMI EVACUATION ROUTE

NEPAL 2015

8 Another 61 people were injured during this avalanche that was triggered by a deadly 7.8 earthquake. As a consequence, no one climbed Mount Everest in the spring of 2015.

Everest is the highest mountain on Earth at
29,029
FEET

AFGHANISTAN 2015

1 Extreme snowstorms led to this natural disaster in the Panjshir Province. In addition to the fatalities, a further 129 people were injured.

TOP 10

MOST FATAL AVALANCHES OF THE 21ST CENTURY

Examining the past 16 years, these have been the avalanches that have caused the highest loss of human life...

	LOCATION	EVENT	YEAR	FATALITIES
1	AFGHANISTAN	PANJSHIR PROVINCE AVALANCHES	2015	310
2	AFGHANISTAN	BADAKHSHAN PROVINCE AVALANCHES	2012	201*
3	AFGHANISTAN	SALANG AVALANCHES	2010	172
4	PAKISTAN	GAYARI SECTOR AVALANCHES	2012	138
5	RUSSIA	KOLKA-KARMADON ICE/ROCK SLIDE	2002	125
6	PAKISTAN	KOHISTAN AVALANCHE	2010	102
7	NEPAL	SEVERE SNOWSTORM	2014	43
8	NEPAL	MOUNT EVEREST AVALANCHES	2015	18
9	NEPAL	MOUNT EVEREST AVALANCHE	2014	16
10	CANADA	FLATHEAD VALLEY AVALANCHES	2008	11

*(INCL. 145 PRESUMED DEAD)

SÃO TOMÉ AND PRÍNCIPE

1 About 191,000 people live on this island nation, which is made up of the two main islands of its name and a series of archipelagos (clusters of small islands).

MOST RAINFALL

Hawaii is the wettest state in the U.S., with more than 63 inches (160 cm) of rain every year, but it doesn't even compare to these countries...

	LOCATION	AVERAGE ANNUAL RAINFALL	
		(INCHES)	(MM)
1	SÃO TOMÉ AND PRÍNCIPE	126	3,200
2	PAPUA NEW GUINEA	123.7	3,142
3	SOLOMON ISLANDS	119.2	3,028
4	COSTA RICA	115.2	2,926
5	MALAYSIA	113.2	2,875
6	BRUNEI	107.2	2,722
7	INDONESIA	106.4	2,702
8	PANAMA	105.9	2,692
9	BANGLADESH	105	2,666
10	COLOMBIA	102.8	2,612

A "wet season" for a tropical climate is defined by more than

2.4
INCHES
of rain

WETTEST PLACE ON EARTH

PAPUA NEW GUINEA

2 This, the 54th-largest country by area in the world, is 178,703 miles^2 (462,838.6 km^2). Across its 7.1 million residents, 848 languages are spoken.

MAWSYNRAM, MEGHALAYA, INDIA

This small village is the wettest place on Earth. It receives an average of 467 inches (1186.18 cm) of rain each year—that's more than an inch per day.

CHAMONIX

8 One of Chamonix's cable cars reaches a peak of 12,604.9 feet (3,842 m). This southeastern region of France has a population of just under 9,000.

PARADISE, MOUNT RAINIER

1 Not just famous for its record snowfall levels, Paradise also attracts visitors because of its paradise-like rolling wildflower meadows and views.

TOP 10

MOST SNOWFALL

The amount of annual snowfall in these regions means whole towns of people could build snowmen...

	LOCATION	AVERAGE ANNUAL SNOWFALL (INCHES)	(MM)
1	PARADISE, MOUNT RAINIER, WASHINGTON	642	16,307
2	NISEKO (JAPAN)	594	15,088
3	MOUNT FIDELITY, GLACIER NATIONAL PARK, BC (CANADA)	576	14,630
4	ALYESKA, ALASKA	516	13,106
5	ALTA, UTAH	510	12,954
6	KIRKWOOD MOUNTAIN, CALIFORNIA	472	11,988
7	NAGANO (JAPAN)	432	10,973
8	CHAMONIX (FRANCE)	376	9,550
9	AOMORI CITY, TŌHOKU (JAPAN)	312	7,925
10	MOUNT WASHINGTON, NEW HAMPSHIRE	261	6,629

Mount Rainier National Park was established **MARCH 2, 1899**

SNOWY COUNTRIES

This graph compares snowfall according to the countries listed...

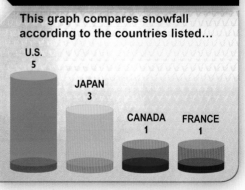

U.S. 5

JAPAN 3

CANADA 1

FRANCE 1

MYTHOLOGY OF LIGHTNING

The Marvel comic character Thor is based on the mythological Norse god of the same name. Associated with lightning and thunder, the Thor of Norse mythology also has a hammer and is devoted to protecting humankind.

TOP 10

DEADLIEST DISASTERS OF ALL TIME

Comparing the most fatalities caused by each kind of natural disaster, these 10 were the worst...

	TYPE	LOCATION	YEAR	ESTIMATED FATALITIES
1	VOLCANIC ERUPTION	ICELAND	1783	**6 MILLION**
2	FLOOD	CHINA	1931	**2.5–3.7 MILLION**
3	EARTHQUAKE	SHAANXI, CHINA	1556	**820,000–830,000**
4	CYCLONE	EAST PAKISTAN (NOW BANGLADESH)	1970	**500,000**
5	TSUNAMI	OCEANIA	2004	**230,000–310,000**
▶ 6	HEATWAVE	EUROPE	2003	**70,000**
7	AVALANCHE	PERU	1970	**20,000**
8	STORM	VENEZUELA	1999	**15,100**
9	BLIZZARD	IRAN	1972	**4,000**
=	LIGHTNING	GREECE	1856	**4,000**

HEATWAVE

6 In 2003, Europe saw its hottest summer since 1540. Scotland, UK, experienced an all-time record. The village of Greycrook reached 91.2°F (32.9°C).

Venezuela covers
353,841
MILES^2

DR CONGO

7 The deeply forested Democratic Republic of Congo is home to 81.7 million people. Although French is the official language, Swahili, Tshiluba, Kituba, and Lingala are also spoken.

BRAZIL

2 Less than one percent of Brazil's total area features water. The country has been the biggest exporter of coffee since the 1840s.

Russia is **13%** water (lakes, rivers, etc.)

RUSSIA

1 An eclectic mixture of 36 different languages are spoken in Russia. The country spans nine time zones and has 12.2 million people in its capital city, Moscow.

TOP 10

COUNTRIES WITH THE BIGGEST FOREST AREAS

The charts across these two pages show some places are a lot greener than others...

	COUNTRY	FORESTED AREA (MILES²)	(KM²)
1	RUSSIA	2,997,157	7,762,600
2	BRAZIL	1,844,402	4,776,980
3	CANADA	1,197,433	3,101,338
4	U.S.	1,170,233	3,030,890
5	CHINA	703,093.6	1,821,000
6	AUSTRALIA	567,891.4	1,470,832
7	DR CONGO	470,784.8	1,219,327
8	ARGENTINA	364,996.3	945,336
9	INDONESIA	341,681.5	884,950
10	INDIA	300,552	778,426

QATAR

1 This country is mostly surrounded by the Persian Gulf. Temperatures here can reach a sweltering 129°F (54°C). Qatar hosts the FIFA World Cup in 2022.

TOP 10

COUNTRIES WITH THE SMALLEST FOREST AREAS

Some places have a lack of forestry due to climate, and some because they're just too small to begin with....

	COUNTRY	FORESTED AREA (MILES²)	(KM²)
1	QATAR	0	0
2	SAN MARINO	0.4	1
3	MALTA	1.2	3
4	BAHRAIN	1.9	5
5	MALDIVES	3.9	10
6	BARBADOS	7.7	20
=	KIRIBATI	7.7	20
=	SINGAPORE	7.7	20
9	TUVALU	8.9	23
10	GRENADA	15.4	40

The population of the Maldives is approximately

341,500

MALTA

3 Malta is home to Hypogeum of Ħal-Saflieni, a 5,000-year-old underground temple. Birkirkara is Malta's largest town, with more than 22,000 residents, but it only covers one square mile.

Coast Redwoods have been recorded as living to

2,200

years of age

SOUTHERN BLUE GUM

7 Thanks to its rapid growth, this evergreen tree is cultivated all over the world and used for construction, oil, honey, and herbal tea.

TOP 10

TALLEST TREES

Although it is impossible to measure all of the trees in the world, these 10 are known to be the biggest...

	SPECIES	LOCATION	MAXIMUM KNOWN HEIGHT (FT)	(M)
1	COAST REDWOOD	CALIFORNIA	379.3	115.61
2	MOUNTAIN ASH	TASMANIA, AUSTRALIA	327.3	99.8
3	COAST DOUGLAS-FIR	OREGON	327	99.76
4	SITKA SPRUCE	CALIFORNIA	317	96.7
5	GIANT SEQUOIA	CALIFORNIA	314	95.8
6	MANNA GUM	TASMANIA, AUSTRALIA	299	91
7	SOUTHERN BLUE GUM	TASMANIA, AUSTRALIA	298	90.7
8	NOBLE FIR	WASHINGTON	295	89.9
9	KLINKI PINE	MONTANE RAIN FOREST, PAPUA NEW GUINEA	292	89
10	ALPINE ASH	TASMANIA, AUSTRALIA	291	88.71

COAST REDWOOD

1 This is the tallest species of tree on the planet. Its bark can grow to a foot in thickness, with its width often exceeding 30 feet (9 m).

COMPARE THE LOCATIONS

Number of trees from each country...

- U.S. **5**
- AUSTRALIA **4**
- PAPUA NEW GUINEA **1**

COBRA LILY

2 Once lured inside, the Cobra Lily's insect victims become trapped and are slowly dissolved by digestive enzymes.

VENUS FLYTRAP

7 Insects and arachnids that accidentally move a hair twice inside the flytrap's "jaws" trigger the plant to close tight. The prey is then digested over 10 days.

TOP 10

MOST CARNIVOROUS PLANTS

Far from being science fiction, meat-eating plants are very much science fact. These are ranked by size of their prey...

	NAME	LOCATION	TRAP TYPE	TRAPS & EATS
1	GIANT MALAYSIAN PITCHER PLANTS	MALAYSIA	PITFALL/CUP TRAP	RATS, MICE, LIZARDS, FROGS, INSECTS
2	COBRA LILY	CALIFORNIA	COBRA-LIKE PITCHER TRAP	FLIES, ANTS, BEETLES, CRAWLING INSECTS
3	COMMON BLADDERWORT	ACROSS U.S.	AQUATIC HAIR-TRIGGER BLADDER TRAPS	FISH FRY, TADPOLES, ROUND WORMS
4	WATERWHEEL PLANT	AFRICA, ASIA, AUSTRALIA, EUROPE	AQUATIC HAIR-TRIGGER BRISTLE TRAP	WATER FLEAS, TADPOLES
5	WEST AUSTRALIAN PITCHER PLANT	AUSTRALIA	PITFALL/CUP TRAP	ANTS, SMALL INSECTS
6	GREEN PITCHER PLANT	NORTH CAROLINA, GEORGIA	PITFALL/CUP TRAP	WASPS AND OTHER SMALL INSECTS
7	VENUS FLYTRAP	EAST COAST WETLANDS OF U.S.	HAIR-TRIGGER JAWS/TRAP	SMALL INSECTS AND ARACHNIDS
8	CAPE SUNDEW	CAPE OF GOOD HOPE (S. AFRICA)	STICKY TENTACLES	SMALL INSECTS AND ARACHNIDS
9	RAINBOW PLANT	AUSTRALIA, PAPUA NEW GUINEA, INDONESIA	STICKY BARBS	SMALL INSECTS
10	YELLOW BUTTERWORT	SOUTHEAST COAST OF U.S.	STICKY LEAVES	FLIES AND SMALL INSECTS

INVASION OF THE BODY SNATCHERS

There have been four movies made based on American author Jack Finney's 1955 novel *The Body Snatchers*, a tale of plant-like alien spores that replicate humans. The first version, in 1958, starred Kevin McCarthy.

The first version of killer-plant movie *The Little Shop of Horrors* was made in

1960

VIDEO GAMES

ZONE 4

TOP 10

BIGGEST-SELLING GAMING CONSOLES

Examining sales from every gaming system, these are the kings of sales figures...

	PLATFORM	MADE BY	RELEASED	UNIT SALES (MILLIONS)
1	PLAYSTATION 2	SONY	2000	157.68
2	NINTENDO DS	NINTENDO	2004	154.88
3	GAME BOY/GAME BOY COLOR	NINTENDO	1989/1998	118.69
4	PLAYSTATION	SONY	1994	104.25
5	WII	NINTENDO	2006	101.18
6	PLAYSTATION 3	SONY	2006	86.08
7	XBOX 360	MICROSOFT	2005	85.06
8	GAME BOY ADVANCE	NINTENDO	2001	81.51
9	PLAYSTATION PORTABLE	SONY	2004	80.82
10	NINTENDO ENTERTAINMENT SYSTEM	NINTENDO	1983	61.91

GAME BOY

3

Before the color version came along in 1998, the original Game Boy had reigned over the handheld gaming world since 1989. Manufacturing of both platforms ceased in 2003.

PS2 has sold the most units of games of any console:

1,661.95 MILLION

PS4 & XBOX ONE SALES

Both released in November 2013, Sony's PS4 has sold 36.1 million units, whereas Microsoft's game system has shifted only 19.5 million. The PS4 has seen game sales of 206.8 million units, with Xbox One trailing behind with 112.8 million.

GAMING BY ERA

Here is how the platforms' successes compare by the decades...

- 80s **2**
- 90s **1**
- 00s **7**

WII

10 The Nintendo Wii was so popular in 2007 that manufacturing could not keep up with public demand for the console. More than 958 million Wii games have been sold.

NINTENDO ENTERTAINMENT SYSTEM

1 The NES was first released in Japan on July 15, 1983. Its U.S. debut came on October 18, 1985. The basic set (just the console, no games) cost $89.99. A deluxe set with the ROB (Robotic Operating Buddy) peripheral retailed for $199.99.

Microsoft's original Xbox was in production for

7.3 years

TOP 10

LONGEST-RUNNING PLATFORMS

From the date they were first released, to when manufacturing stopped, these are the gaming systems that have stuck around the longest...

	PLATFORM	MADE BY	YEARS IN PRODUCTION	TOTAL YEARS
1	NINTENDO ENTERTAINMENT SYSTEM	NINTENDO	1983–2003	20
2	GAME BOY/GAME BOY COLOR	NINTENDO	1989–2003	14
3	PLAYSTATION	SONY	1994–2006	12
=	PLAYSTATION 2	SONY	2000–12	12
=	NINTENDO DS/3DS/3DSI XL	NINTENDO	2004–PRESENT	12
6	XBOX 360	MICROSOFT	2005–PRESENT	11
7	PLAYSTATION 3	SONY	2006–PRESENT	10
=	PLAYSTATION PORTABLE	SONY	2004–14	10
=	SUPER NINTENDO ENTERTAINMENT SYSTEM	NINTENDO	1993–2003	10
10	WII	NINTENDO	2006–13	7

TOP 10

BIGGEST-SELLING
HANDHELD CONSOLES

Gaming has been a popular portable pastime for decades, and these are the biggest successes...

	PLATFORM	MADE BY	RELEASED	UNIT SALES (MILLIONS)
1	NINTENDO DS	NINTENDO	2004	154.88
2	GAME BOY/GAME BOY COLOR	NINTENDO	1989/1998	118.69
3	GAME BOY ADVANCE	NINTENDO	2001	81.51
4	PLAYSTATION PORTABLE	SONY	2004	80.82
5	NINTENDO 3DS	NINTENDO	2011	55.27
6	PLAYSTATION VITA	SONY	2011	12.86
7	GAME GEAR	SEGA	1990	10.62
8	LEAPSTER	LEAPFROG ENTERPRISES	2008	4
9	NEO GEO POCKET/POCKET COLOR	SNK	1998/1999	2
10	TURBOEXPRESS	NEC	1990	1.5

PLAYSTATION VITA

6 About 52.8 million units of games have been sold for this Sony handheld console. In comparison, Nintendo's Game Boy saw 501.1 million games sold.

Sega's color handheld, the Game Gear, was released on **OCT. 6, 1990**

NINTENDO 3DS

5 Nintendo's 3DS XL (with a 90 percent bigger screen) was launched in July 2012. More than 229 million copies of games for the 3DS have been sold worldwide.

The *Animal Crossing* franchise has shifted
29.88 MILLION units

POKÉMON X/Y

1 Released on October 12, 2013, *Pokémon X/Y* had 70 new species of Pokémon for players to train. The game also saw the ability to evolve characters into new forms.

SUPER SMASH BROS.

7 *Super Smash Bros. for Wii U and 3DS* is the fifth title in the franchise, which debuted in 1999 on the N64. The brand has shifted more than 37 million units worldwide.

TOP 10

BIGGEST-SELLING 3DS GAMES

Nintendo's handheld continues to sell in the millions, and these are its most popular games...

	NAME	GENRE	RELEASED	UNIT SALES (MILLIONS)
1	POKÉMON X/Y	RPG	2013	13.17
2	MARIO KART 7	RACING	2011	11.13
3	SUPER MARIO 3D LAND	PLATFORM	2011	10.37
4	POKÉMON OMEGA RUBY/ ALPHA SAPPHIRE	RPG	2014	9.07
5	NEW SUPER MARIO BROS. 2	PLATFORM	2012	9.01
6	ANIMAL CROSSING: NEW LEAF	ACTION	2012	8.25
7	SUPER SMASH BROS. FOR WII U AND 3DS	FIGHTING	2014	6.6
8	TOMODACHI LIFE	SIMULATION	2013	4.45
9	LUIGI'S MANSION: DARK MOON	ADVENTURE	2013	4.33
10	THE LEGEND OF ZELDA: OCARINA OF TIME	ACTION	2011	3.82

The Legend of Zelda: The Wind Waker is the **10**TH Zelda game

SUPER MARIO 3D WORLD

5 Rosalina watches over the cosmos and is a playable character once World 2 of *Super Mario 3D World* has been completed.

SPLATOON

6 A brand new game title, *Splatoon* features humanoid creatures that can take on the form of a squid. Players' challenges include rescuing the Great Zapfish.

TOP 10

BIGGEST WII U GAMES

Since the Wii U was first released on November 18, 2012, these games have been the big sellers...

	NAME	GENRE	RELEASED	UNIT SALES (MILLIONS)
1	MARIO KART 8	RACING	2014	5.43
2	NEW SUPER MARIO BROS. U	ACTION	2012	4.89
3	NINTENDO LAND	ACTION	2012	4.21
4	SUPER SMASH BROS. FOR WII U AND 3DS	FIGHTING	2014	3.81
▷ 5	SUPER MARIO 3D WORLD	PLATFORM	2013	3.66
▷ 6	SPLATOON	SHOOTER	2015	2.25
7	NEW SUPER LUIGI U	PLATFORM	2013	2.14
8	WII PARTY U	PARTY	2013	1.65
9	THE LEGEND OF ZELDA: THE WIND WAKER	ACTION	2013	1.46
10	SUPER MARIO MAKER	PLATFORM	2015	1.39

TOP 10

BIGGEST WII GAMES

Even though new Nintendo Wiis haven't been produced since 2013, gaming on them is still very popular...

Wii Fit was first released in Japan on **DECEMBER 1, 2007**

	NAME	GENRE	RELEASED	UNIT SALES (MILLIONS)
1	WII SPORTS	SPORTS	2006	82.57
2	MARIO KART WII	RACING	2008	35.4
3	WII SPORTS RESORT	SPORTS	2009	32.78
4	WII PLAY	PARTY	2006	28.94
5	NEW SUPER MARIO BROS. WII	PLATFORM	2009	28.2
6	WII FIT	SPORTS	2007	22.69
7	WII FIT PLUS	SPORTS	2009	21.84
8	SUPER SMASH BROS. BRAWL	FIGHTING	2008	12.75
9	SUPER MARIO GALAXY	PLATFORM	2007	11.34
10	JUST DANCE 3	PARTY	2011	10.13

GENRE FACE-OFF

Ranking the Wii's biggest hits by their style...

- SPORTS **4**
- PARTY **2**
- PLATFORM **2**
- RACING **1**
- FIGHTING **1**

JUST DANCE 3

10 The third game in this series was released on October 7, 2011. The *Just Dance* game franchise has shifted 57.3 million copies since the first game debuted in 2009.

WII FIT

6 The Wii Fit Balance Board can be used to play the slalom skiing and snowboard elements of the game. The activities can help strengthen core muscles.

7.3

TOP 10

BIGGEST-SELLING PS4 GAMES

This next-generation console is a clear hit for those who love action and shooting games...

	NAME	GENRE	RELEASED	UNIT SALES (MILLIONS)
1	GRAND THEFT AUTO V	ACTION	2014	8.21
2	CALL OF DUTY: ADVANCED WARFARE	SHOOTER	2014	7.08
3	FIFA 15	SPORTS	2014	6.47
4	CALL OF DUTY: BLACK OPS 3	SHOOTER	2015	5.55
5	DESTINY	ACTION	2014	5.24
6	FIFA 16	SPORTS	2015	5
7	WATCH DOGS	ACTION	2014	3.9
8	ASSASSIN'S CREED: UNITY	ACTION	2014	3.56
9	FAR CRY 4	SHOOTER	2014	3.55
10	THE LAST OF US	ADVENTURE	2014	3.54

CALL OF DUTY: ADVANCED WARFARE

2 Incorporating a sci-fi element, this *Call of Duty* title is set in the 2050s. Actor Kevin Spacey provides the voice for key character Jonathan Irons.

The first *Far Cry* game was released in

2004

THE LAST OF US

10 It was first released on the PS3 on June 14, 2013, and the remastered PS4 edition emerged the following year on July 29, 2014.

GRAND THEFT AUTO V

1 At the 2014 Game Developers Choice Awards, *Grand Theft Auto V* won Best Technology.

The *Call of Duty* franchise has sold
230.84
MILLION
units

TOP 10

BIGGEST-SELLING PS3, PS2, & PLAYSTATION GAMES
Combining all three of Sony's previous home consoles, these were their best-selling titles...

	NAME	PLATFORM	GENRE	RELEASED	UNIT SALES (MILLIONS)
1	GRAND THEFT AUTO V	PS3	ACTION	2013	21.04
2	GRAND THEFT AUTO: SAN ANDREAS	PS2	ACTION	2004	20.81
3	GRAND THEFT AUTO: VICE CITY	PS2	ACTION	2002	16.15
4	GRAN TURISMO 3: A-SPEC	PS2	RACING	2001	14.98
5	CALL OF DUTY: BLACK OPS II	PS3	SHOOTER	2012	13.75
6	CALL OF DUTY: MODERN WARFARE 3	PS3	SHOOTER	2011	13.32
7	GRAND THEFT AUTO III	PS2	ACTION	2001	13.1
8	CALL OF DUTY: BLACK OPS	PS3	SHOOTER	2010	12.58
9	GRAN TURISMO 4	PS2	RACING	2004	11.66
10	GRAN TURISMO	PS	RACING	1997	10.95

GRAN TURISMO 4

9 This racing franchise has sold more than 71 million copies worldwide. *Gran Turismo 4* was first released in Japan on December 28, 2004.

BEST-SELLING PS VITA GAMES

Fans of gaming on the go are still enjoying this six-year-old handheld system...

Number of main *Persona* games in the *Shin Megami Tensei* franchise:

6

	NAME	GENRE	RELEASED	UNIT SALES (MILLIONS)
1	UNCHARTED: GOLDEN ABYSS	ACTION	2011	**1.53**
2	CALL OF DUTY: BLACK OPS: DECLASSIFIED	ACTION	2012	**1.34**
3	ASSASSIN'S CREED III: LIBERATION	ACTION	2012	**1.32**
▷ 4	LITTLEBIGPLANET PS VITA	PLATFORM	2012	**1.2**
=	MINECRAFT	ADVENTURE	2014	**1.2**
6	PERSONA 4: THE GOLDEN	RPG	2012	**1.07**
▷ 7	NEED FOR SPEED: MOST WANTED	RACING	2012	**0.97**
8	KILLZONE: MERCENARY	SHOOTER	2013	**0.81**
=	FINAL FANTASY X/X-2 HD REMASTER	RPG	2013	**0.81**
10	TEARAWAY	ACTION	2013	**0.63**

LITTLEBIGPLANET PS VITA

4 Since the 2008 LittleBigPlanet arrived on the PS3, this franchise has sold more than 16 million copies. The PS Vita's touchscreen allows for more ways to create levels.

SONY

PS VITA

DIFFERENT TYPES OF GAMES

Here's how the PS Vita's biggest games compare by genre....

ACTION
4

RPG
2

PLATFORM
1

ADVENTURE
1

RACING
1

SHOOTER
1

NEED FOR SPEED: MOST WANTED

7 The 19th game in the *Need for Speed* franchise gave players the ability to compete in races of their choosing in an open world environment.

Number of *God of War* releases:

12

CRISIS CORE: FINAL FANTASY VII

10 Japanese composer Takeharu Ishimoto has written the music for several major games, including *Crisis Core: Final Fantasy VII* and *Dissidia Final Fantasy*, released November 26, 2015.

DAXTER

5 This game was spun out of the *Jak and Daxter* series, which began in 2001 with *Jak and Daxter: The Precursor Legacy* for the PS2. Daxter (the sixth release) is set between that debut game and 2003's *Jak II*.

TOP 10

BEST-SELLING PSP

It lasted 10 years as a handheld console, and these were the games that counted the most...

	NAME	GENRE	RELEASED	UNIT SALES (MILLIONS)
1	GRAND THEFT AUTO: LIBERTY CITY STORIES	ACTION	2005	**7.68**
2	MONSTER HUNTER FREEDOM UNITE	RPG	2008	**5.48**
3	GRAND THEFT AUTO: VICE CITY STORIES	ACTION	2006	**5.04**
4	MONSTER HUNTER FREEDOM 3	RPG	2010	**4.87**
5	DAXTER	PLATFORM	2006	**4.17**
6	RATCHET & CLANK: SIZE MATTERS	PLATFORM	2007	**3.74**
7	MIDNIGHT CLUB 3: DUB EDITION	RACING	2005	**3.64**
8	GRAN TURISMO	RACING	2009	**3.24**
9	GOD OF WAR: CHAINS OF OLYMPUS	ACTION	2008	**3.17**
10	CRISIS CORE: FINAL FANTASY VII	RPG	2007	**3.16**

DESTINY

Titanfall's total international award wins:

28

5 This first-person shooter was developed by Bungie, the team behind the *Halo* franchise. Its original soundtrack included new music by Paul McCartney.

FORZA MOTORSPORT 5

10 Exclusive to the Xbox One console, this racing game has 200 cars to choose from, with more available as downloadable content. Players can race on more than 20 circuits.

TOP 10

BIGGEST-SELLING XBOX ONE GAMES

Like its 360 predecessor, Microsoft's latest home console is beloved by fans of shooting games...

	NAME	GENRE	RELEASED	UNIT SALES (MILLIONS)
1	CALL OF DUTY: ADVANCED WARFARE	SHOOTER	2014	4.73
2	GRAND THEFT AUTO V	ACTION	2014	3.37
3	CALL OF DUTY: BLACK OPS 3	SHOOTER	2015	3.31
4	ASSASSIN'S CREED: UNITY	ACTION	2014	3.06
5	DESTINY	ACTION	2014	3.01
6	TITANFALL	SHOOTER	2014	2.71
7	HALO: THE MASTER CHIEF COLLECTION	SHOOTER	2014	2.67
8	CALL OF DUTY: GHOSTS	SHOOTER	2013	2.62
9	ASSASSIN'S CREED IV: BLACK FLAG	ACTION	2013	2.11
10	FORZA MOTORSPORT 5	RACING	2013	2.05

TOP 10

BIGGEST-SELLING XBOX 360 GAMES

The *Call of Duty* franchise has sold millions on this system, but the number 1 belongs to a party game...

	NAME	GENRE	RELEASED	UNIT SALES (MILLIONS)
1	KINECT ADVENTURES!	PARTY	2010	21.63
2	GRAND THEFT AUTO V	ACTION	2013	15.6
3	CALL OF DUTY: MODERN WARFARE 3	SHOOTER	2011	14.59
4	CALL OF DUTY: BLACK OPS	SHOOTER	2010	14.41
5	CALL OF DUTY: BLACK OPS II	SHOOTER	2012	13.49
6	CALL OF DUTY: MODERN WARFARE 2	SHOOTER	2009	13.44
7	HALO 3	SHOOTER	2007	12.06
8	GRAND THEFT AUTO IV	ACTION	2008	10.94
9	CALL OF DUTY: GHOSTS	SHOOTER	2013	9.87
10	HALO: REACH	SHOOTER	2010	9.77

HALO 2

Released on the Xbox console, *Halo 2* (2004) almost made this Top 10 with worldwide unit sales of 8.49 million.

The first *Grand Theft Auto* game was released in

1997

KINECT ADVENTURES!

1 Released on November 4, 2010, this was a launch title for the Xbox 360's Kinect motion-camera system. Its five challenge areas require full-body movement and interaction with puzzles on the screen.

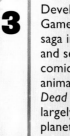

DEVIL MAY CRY 4 (ACTION)

1 Capcom's *Devil May Cry* action series has sold 15.1 million units. *Devil May Cry 4: Special Edition* was released on PS4 and Xbox One on June 18, 2015.

Total sales of the adventure genre:

237.81
MILLION

DEAD SPACE 3 (SHOOTER)

3 Developer Visceral Games' *Dead Space* saga includes six games and several tie-in comics, novels, and animated movies. *Dead Space 3* was largely set on ice-planet Tau Volantis.

TOP 10

MOST SUCCESSFUL GENRES

Combining games of all types, across all platforms, here are the genres that sell the most units...

	GENRE	ALL PLATFORMS' UNIT SALES (MILLIONS)
1	ACTION	1,648.08
2	SPORTS	1,279.45
3	SHOOTER	958.86
4	RPG	881.35
5	PLATFORM	815.05
6	PARTY	782.19
7	RACING	716.08
8	FIGHTING	435.94
9	SIMULATION	382.3
10	PUZZLE	242.63

GENRE WINNERS

Here's how the top 5 compare visually...

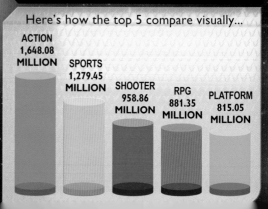

ACTION
1,648.08
MILLION

SPORTS
1,279.45
MILLION

SHOOTER
958.86
MILLION

RPG
881.35
MILLION

PLATFORM
815.05
MILLION

GENRE BEST-SELLERS

Taking a look at each genre, here are the biggest sellers from each of those gaming worlds...

	GENRE	GAME	RELEASED	PLATFORM	UNIT SALES (MILLIONS)
1	SPORTS	WII SPORTS	2006	WII	82.57
2	PLATFORM	SUPER MARIO BROS.	1985	NES	40.24
3	RACING	MARIO KART WII	2008	WII	35.4
4	RPG	POKÉMON RED/BLUE/GREEN	1996	GAME BOY	31.37
5	PUZZLE	TETRIS	1989	GAME BOY	30.26
6	PARTY	WII PLAY	2006	WII	28.94
7	SHOOTER	DUCK HUNT	1985	NES	28.31
8	SIMULATION	NINTENDOGS	2005	DS	24.69
9	ACTION	GRAND THEFT AUTO: SAN ANDREAS	2004	PS2	20.81
10	FIGHTING	SUPER SMASH BROS. BRAWL	2008	WII	12.75

Tetris has appeared in

71

games

GRAND THEFT AUTO: SAN ANDREAS

9 Released across multiple platforms between 2004 and 2015, the *San Andreas* sub-brand of *Grand Theft Auto* has sold nearly 24 million units.

SUPER MARIO BROS.

2 Japanese composer Koji Kondo wrote the iconic music for not only *Super Mario Bros.* and *Super Mario Bros. 2* (pictured), but also numerous other Nintendo

The *Dr. Mario* games have sold

11.5
MILLION
units

NEW SUPER MARIO BROS. WII

3 This *Super Mario Bros.* title features the traditional sideways-scrolling platform gameplay associated with the original game. Its worldwide debut was in Australia on November 11, 2009. Its U.S. release was November 15, 2009.

TIME: 00:19.66
BEST TIME: 01:30.00

SUPER MARIO GALAXY

8 Similar to *Super Mario 64* (1996) and *Super Mario Sunshine* (2002), this 2007 platformer utilized 3D environments, instead of the traditional side-scrolling Mario style.

TOP 10

BIGGEST PLATFORM GAMES

In 1981 japanese game designer Shigeru Miyamoto created Mario (formerly Jumpman), the king of games involving platform-jumping...

	NAME	PLATFORM	RELEASED	UNIT SALES (MILLIONS)
1	SUPER MARIO BROS.	NES	1985	40.24
2	NEW SUPER MARIO BROS.	DS	2006	29.79
3	NEW SUPER MARIO BROS. WII	WII	2009	28.20
4	SUPER MARIO WORLD	SNES	1990	20.61
5	SUPER MARIO LAND	GAME BOY	1989	18.14
6	SUPER MARIO BROS. 3	NES	1988	17.28
7	SUPER MARIO 64	N64	1996	11.89
8	SUPER MARIO GALAXY	WII	2007	11.34
9	SUPER MARIO LAND 2: 6 GOLDEN COINS	GAME BOY	1992	11.18
10	SUPER MARIO ALL-STARS	SNES	1993	10.55

ASSASSIN'S CREED III

6

The 2012 entry in the *Assassin's Creed* series had new downloadable extras. These included *The Tyranny of King Washington*, a game set in the alternate reality of the United Kingdom of America.

Number of versions of *The Legend of Zelda: Ocarina of Time*:

5

RED DEAD REDEMPTION

7

This open-world western adventure had a downloadable zombie-filled extra that became its own fully-released game, *Red Dead Redemption: Undead Nightmare*.

TOP 10

BIGGEST ADVENTURE GAMES

This genre often features sprawling landscapes, complex journeys, puzzles, and explosive action...

	NAME	PLATFORM	RELEASED	UNIT SALES (MILLIONS)
1	**MINECRAFT**	XBOX 360	2013	**8.09**
2	**THE LEGEND OF ZELDA: OCARINA OF TIME**	N64	1998	**7.6**
3	**THE LEGEND OF ZELDA: TWILIGHT PRINCESS**	WII	2006	**7.18**
4	**THE LEGEND OF ZELDA**	NES	1986	**6.51**
5	**RED DEAD REDEMPTION**	PS3	2010	**6.45**
6	**ASSASSIN'S CREED III**	PS3	2012	**6.44**
7	**RED DEAD REDEMPTION**	XBOX 360	2010	**6.23**
8	**METAL GEAR SOLID 2: SONS OF LIBERTY**	PS2	2001	**6.05**
9	**METAL GEAR SOLID**	PS	1998	**6.03**
10	**METAL GEAR SOLID 4: GUNS OF THE PATRIOTS**	PS3	2008	**6**

113

KINECT SPORTS

10 Launched as a key title for Xbox's Kinect system, this game included soccer, beach volleyball, boxing, table tennis, and track and field events.

MARIO & SONIC AT THE OLYMPIC GAMES

5 Total sales of this franchise have surpassed 13.7 million units. The latest, *Mario & Sonic at the Rio 2016 Olympic Games*, was released on February 18, 2016, for Nintendo 3DS and Wii U.

TOP 10

BIGGEST SPORTS GAMES

From fitness games that feature martial arts to Olympic Games hits, these are the 10 medal winners...

Total *FIFA* soccer games:

23

	NAME	PLATFORM	RELEASED	UNIT SALES (MILLIONS)
1	WII SPORTS	WII	2006	82.57
2	WII SPORTS RESORT	WII	2009	32.78
3	WII FIT	WII	2007	22.69
4	WII FIT PLUS	WII	2009	21.84
5	MARIO & SONIC AT THE OLYMPIC GAMES	WII	2007	8
6	FIFA SOCCER 14	PS3	2013	6.91
7	ZUMBA FITNESS	WII	2010	6.72
8	FIFA SOCCER 12	PS3	2011	6.66
9	FIFA 15	PS4	2014	6.47
10	KINECT SPORTS	XBOX 360	2010	6.12

TOP 10

BIGGEST PARTY GAMES

The evolution of peripherals like guitar controllers and microphones amped up this gaming genre...

	NAME	PLATFORM	RELEASED	UNIT SALES (MILLIONS)
1	WII PLAY	WII	2006	28.94
2	KINECT ADVENTURES!	XBOX 360	2010	21.63
3	JUST DANCE 3	WII	2011	10.13
4	JUST DANCE 2	WII	2010	9.45
5	MARIO PARTY DS	DS	2007	8.93
6	WII PARTY	WII	2010	8.4
7	MARIO PARTY 8	WII	2007	8.27
8	JUST DANCE	WII	2009	7.2
9	JUST DANCE 4	WII	2012	6.78
10	GUITAR HERO II	PS2	2006	5.12

GUITAR HERO II

10 Nine years after the release of *Guitar Hero II*, *Guitar Hero Live* was released in October 2015. It swapped stylized graphics for full-motion video.

MARIO PARTY 8

7 This was the first time a *Mario Party* title appeared on the Wii. On March 12, 2015, *Mario Party 10* was released for the Wii U.

WII: PARTY MACHINE

Proof that one platform rules party gaming...

■ WII **7**

The *Just Dance* franchise has sold

53.69

POKÉMON BLACK/WHITE VERSION

5 This edition was the most popular in Japan, where it sold 5.65 million units. The second most successful market was the U.S., where it sold 5.55 million copies.

Including all platforms' editions, total *Pokémon* releases:

83

POKÉMON DIAMOND/ PEARL VERSION

3 The box art showcases the Pokémon called Palkia. The character also appeared in *Super Smash Bros.* for Nintendo 3DS and Wii U.

TOP 10

BIGGEST RPG GAMES

Just as Mario dominates platform games, Role Playing Games changed forever when Pokémon debuted in 1996...

	NAME	PLATFORM	RELEASED	UNIT SALES (MILLIONS)
1	POKÉMON RED/BLUE/GREEN VERSION	GAME BOY	1996	**31.37**
2	POKÉMON GOLD/SILVER VERSION	GAME BOY	1999	**23.1**
3	POKÉMON DIAMOND/PEARL VERSION	GAME BOY	2006	**18.26**
4	POKÉMON RUBY/SAPPHIRE VERSION	GAME BOY	2002	**15.85**
5	POKÉMON BLACK/WHITE VERSION	GAME BOY	2010	**15.17**
6	POKÉMON YELLOW: SPECIAL PIKACHU EDITION	GAME BOY	1998	**14.64**
7	POKÉMON X/Y	3DS	2013	**13.17**
8	POKÉMON HEART GOLD/SOUL SILVER VERSION	DS	2009	**11.79**
9	POKÉMON FIRERED/LEAFGREEN VERSION	GBA	2004	**10.49**
10	FINAL FANTASY VII	PS	1997	**9.72**

BIGGEST STRATEGY GAMES

This genre involves a lot of tactical planning and strategic maneuvering to triumph over numerous challenges...

	NAME	PLATFORM	RELEASED	UNIT SALES (MILLIONS)
1	POKÉMON STADIUM	N64	1999	5.45
2	WARZONE 2100	PS	1999	5.01
3	POKÉMON TRADING CARD GAME	GAME BOY	1998	3.7
4	POKÉMON STADIUM 2	N64	2000	2.73
5	HALO WARS	XBOX 360	2009	2.55
6	YU-GI-OH! THE ETERNAL DUELIST SOUL	GAME BOY	2001	2.07
7	PIKMIN	GAMECUBE	2001	1.63
8	YU-GI-OH! DUEL MASTERS	GAME BOY	1998	1.61
9	LEGO BATTLES: NINJAGO	DS	2011	1.46
10	POCKET MONSTERS STADIUM	N64	1998	1.37

HALO WARS

5

Halo Wars, the fourth *Halo* game, got a sequel seven years later in 2016. *Halo Wars 2* is the 13th release in the franchise.

LEGO BATTLES: NINJAGO

9

Based on the hit *LEGO* franchise of *Ninjago*, this game is part of the expanded universe that also includes the TV series *LEGO Ninjago: Masters of Spinjitzu*.

The first ever *LEGO* game was released in

1997

TOP 10

BIGGEST PUZZLE GAMES

Simplicity is the key to a successful puzzle, and as this chart proves, Tetris with its turning shapes is still king...

	NAME	PLATFORM	RELEASED	UNIT SALES (MILLIONS)
1	TETRIS	GAME BOY	1989	30.26
2	BRAIN AGE 2: MORE TRAINING IN MINUTES A DAY	DS	2005	15.29
3	PAC-MAN	ATARI 2600	1982	7.81
4	TETRIS	NES	1988	5.58
5	DR. MARIO	GAME BOY	1989	5.34
6	PROFESSOR LAYTON AND THE CURIOUS VILLAGE	DS	2007	5.21
7	DR. MARIO	NES	1990	4.85
8	PROFESSOR LAYTON AND THE DIABOLICAL BOX	DS	2007	3.96
9	PROFESSOR LAYTON AND THE UNWOUND FUTURE	DS	2008	3.27
10	PAC-MAN COLLECTION	GBA	2001	2.94

PROFESSOR LAYTON AND THE UNWOUND FUTURE

9 The first three titles of the *Professor Layton* trilogy feature in this Top 10. The franchise's total sales across seven titles exceed 18 million units.

TETRIS

1 Prior to Tetris's huge success on the Nintendo Game Boy, Russian creator Alexey Pajitnov's game appeared in arcades and on home computers.

PUZZLING FRANCHISES

Here's this Top 10 ranked by brand...

- PROFESSOR LAYTON **3**
- MARIO **2**
- PAC-MAN **2**
- TETRIS **2**
- BRAIN AGE **1**

Pac-Man franchise total unit sales:

27.26 MILLION

GRAND THEFT AUTO V

4

Demand for this sequel was so high that sales surpassed $1 billion during its first week of release in September 2013.

The *Grand Theft Auto* games have sold more than

159 MILLION units

HISTORY OF GRAND THEFT AUTO

The *Grand Theft Auto* series spans 20 years. The latest, a remastered edition for PS4 and Xbox One, was released on November 18, 2014.

BIGGEST ACTION GAMES

The open-world, exploratory nature of the *Grand Theft Auto* franchise has undoubtedly helped its popularity...

	NAME	PLATFORM	RELEASED	UNIT SALES (MILLIONS)
1	GRAND THEFT AUTO: SAN ANDREAS	PS2	2004	20.81
2	GRAND THEFT AUTO V	PS3	2013	20.56
3	GRAND THEFT AUTO: VICE CITY	PS2	2002	16.15
4	GRAND THEFT AUTO V	XBOX 360	2013	15.6
5	GRAND THEFT AUTO III	PS2	2001	13.1
6	GRAND THEFT AUTO IV	XBOX 360	2008	10.94
7	GRAND THEFT AUTO IV	PS3	2008	10.44
8	GRAND THEFT AUTO V	PS4	2014	8.21
9	GRAND THEFT AUTO: LIBERTY CITY STORIES	PSP	2005	7.68
10	THE LEGEND OF ZELDA: OCARINA OF TIME	N64	1998	7.6

CALL OF DUTY: MODERN WARFARE 3

2 Brian Tyler, the composer behind movies including *Iron Man 3* (2013) and *Avengers: Age Of Ultron* (2015), wrote the music for this game.

HALO 3

9 This game brought an end to the storyline that ran through *Halo: Combat Evolved* (2001) and *Halo 2* (2004). It hit stores on September 25, 2007.

TOP 10

BIGGEST SHOOTING GAMES

For all of its many iterations, the *Call of Duty* franchise still cannot topple a Nintendo classic...

	NAME	PLATFORM	RELEASED	UNIT SALES (MILLIONS)
1	DUCK HUNT	NES	1985	28.31
2	CALL OF DUTY: MODERN WARFARE 3	XBOX 360	2011	14.59
3	CALL OF DUTY: BLACK OPS	XBOX 360	2010	14.41
4	CALL OF DUTY: BLACK OPS II	PS3	2012	13.75
5	CALL OF DUTY: BLACK OPS II	XBOX 360	2012	13.49
6	CALL OF DUTY: MODERN WARFARE 2	XBOX 360	2009	13.44
7	CALL OF DUTY: MODERN WARFARE 3	PS3	2011	13.32
8	CALL OF DUTY: BLACK OPS	PS3	2010	12.58
9	HALO 3	XBOX 360	2007	12.06
10	CALL OF DUTY: MODERN WARFARE 2	PS3	2009	10.6

The *Call of Duty* franchise has released **24** titles

BIGGEST FIGHTING GAMES

A popular genre in arcades and home systems, combat-based games are dominated by these three best-selling franchises...

	NAME	PLATFORM	RELEASED	UNIT SALES (MILLIONS)
1	SUPER SMASH BROS. BRAWL	WII	2008	12.75
2	TEKKEN 3	PS	1998	7.16
3	SUPER SMASH BROS. MELEE	GAMECUBE	2001	7.07
4	SUPER SMASH BROS. FOR WII U AND 3DS	3DS	2014	6.6
5	STREET FIGHTER II: THE WORLD WARRIOR	SNES	1992	6.3
6	TEKKEN 2	PS	1996	5.74
7	SUPER SMASH BROS.	N64	1999	5.55
8	STREET FIGHTER IV	PS3	2009	4.13
9	STREET FIGHTER II TURBO	SNES	1992	4.1
10	TEKKEN TAG TOURNAMENT	PS2	2000	4.05

STREET FIGHTER IV

8 After its initial release as an arcade game in 2008, this arrived on PS3 and Xbox 360 in February 2009. The first *Street Fighter* game appeared in arcades in 1987.

SUPER SMASH BROS. BRAWL

1 The third game in the *Super Smash Bros.* franchise features 39 playable characters from other game worlds, including Solid Snake from *Metal Gear Solid* and Pikachu from *Pokémon*.

Total number of *Tekken* games:

10

BIGGEST CONSOLE GAMES OF ALL TIME

No matter which platform the title was released on, these 10 games are the most popular of them all...

	NAME	GENRE	RELEASED	PLATFORM	UNIT SALES (MILLIONS)
1	WII SPORTS	SPORTS	2006	WII	82.57
2	SUPER MARIO BROS.	PLATFORM	1985	NES	40.24
3	MARIO KART WII	RACING	2008	WII	35.4
4	WII SPORTS RESORT	SPORTS	2009	WII	32.78
5	POKÉMON RED/BLUE/GREEN	RPG	1996	GAME BOY	31.37
6	TETRIS	PUZZLE	1989	GAME BOY	30.26
7	NEW SUPER MARIO BROS.	PLATFORM	2006	DS	29.79
8	WII PLAY	PARTY	2006	WII	28.94
9	DUCK HUNT	SHOOTER	1985	NES	28.31
10	NEW SUPER MARIO BROS. WII	PLATFORM	2009	WII	28.2

TOP 5 SMASH HITS

Here's how the top 5 compare visually...

WII SPORTS
82.57
MILLION

SUPER MARIO BROS.
40.24
MILLION

MARIO KART WII
35.4
MILLION

WII SPORTS RESORT
32.78
MILLION

POKÉMON RED/BLUE/GREEN
31.37
MILLION

Duck Hunt was first released on the NES on **APRIL 21, 1984**

GAME BOY

Nintendo

Pokémon
Gotta catch 'em all!

EVERYONE
E
ESRB

RED VERSION

USE RED BLUE VERSION TO CATCH ALL 150 MONSTERS!

Nintendo

MARIO KART WII

3 A spin-off of the main *Mario* franchise, the *Mario Kart* series has shifted more than 108 million units alone. *Mario Kart Wii*'s worldwide debut was in Japan on April 10, 2008. Its U.S. release was April 27 of the same year.

POKÉMON RED/BLUE/GREEN

5 This was the first *Pokémon* game ever. The second installment, Gold/Silver, ranks as the second best-selling *Pokémon* release with 23.1 million units sold.

Final Fantasy games have sold more than **110 MILLION** units

LEGO

7 Across all gaming platforms, there have been 230 official *LEGO* video games made since 1997. *LEGO Marvel's Avengers* was released on January 26, 2016.

SONIC THE HEDGEHOG

8 The super-fast blue hero debuted on the Sega Genesis in 1991 in *Sonic the Hedgehog.* The latest title, *Sonic Boom: Fire & Ice*, was released in 2016 for Nintendo 3DS.

TOP 10

BIGGEST GAME BRANDS

Come up with a popular character or series, and you could sell hundreds of millions...

	FRANCHISE	UNIT SALES (MILLIONS)
1	SUPER MARIO BROS.	580.83
2	POKÉMON	244.98
3	CALL OF DUTY	230.66
4	WII FIT/SPORTS/PARTY	199.8
5	GRAND THEFT AUTO	159.54
6	FIFA	158.02
7	LEGO	126.25
8	SONIC THE HEDGEHOG	114.24
9	FINAL FANTASY	110.03
10	NEED FOR SPEED	98.33

BATMAN: ARKHAM CITY

1 There have been four games in the *Batman: Arkham* series released between 2009 and 2015. Across all platforms, the second game of the franchise, *Batman: Arkham City*, has sold 11.03 million units.

Across all platforms, *LEGO Batman: The Videogame* has sold

13.3
MILLION
units

SPIDER-MAN: THE MOVIE

3 Based on the 2002 film directed by Sam Raimi, this Spider-Man game includes narration by Bruce Campbell. The *Ash vs. Evil Dead* star made a cameo appearance as the ring announcer in the movie.

TOP 10

BIGGEST SUPERHERO GAMES

Those caped crusaders don't just sell millions of movie theater tickets, they triumph in the gaming market too...

	NAME	PLATFORM	RELEASED	UNIT SALES (MILLIONS)
1	BATMAN: ARKHAM CITY	PS3	2011	5.37
2	BATMAN: ARKHAM CITY	XBOX 360	2011	4.67
3	SPIDER-MAN: THE MOVIE	PS2	2002	4.48
4	BATMAN: ARKHAM ASYLUM	PS3	2009	4.19
5	BATMAN: ARKHAM ASYLUM	XBOX 360	2009	3.44
6	SPIDER-MAN 2	PS2	2004	3.41
7	BATMAN: ARKHAM KNIGHT	PS4	2015	3.37
8	LEGO BATMAN: THE VIDEOGAME	XBOX 360	2008	3.33
9	SPIDER-MAN	PS	2000	3.13
10	LEGO BATMAN: THE VIDEOGAME	WII	2008	3.06

BIGGEST TOLKIEN TIE-IN GAMES

The expansive world of Middle Earth has inspired dozens of very different video games...

	NAME	PLATFORM	RELEASED	UNIT SALES (MILLIONS)
1	THE LORD OF THE RINGS: THE TWO TOWERS	PS2	2002	**4.67**
2	THE LORD OF THE RINGS: THE RETURN OF THE KING	PS2	2003	**3.28**
3	MIDDLE-EARTH: SHADOW OF MORDOR	PS4	2014	**2.52**
4	LEGO THE LORD OF THE RINGS	XBOX 360	2012	**1.21**
5	THE LORD OF THE RINGS: THE FELLOWSHIP OF THE RING	PS2	2002	**1.2**
6	THE LORD OF THE RINGS: THE RETURN OF THE KING	XBOX	2003	**1.14**
7	MIDDLE-EARTH: SHADOW OF MORDOR	XBOX ONE	2014	**1.1**
8	LEGO THE LORD OF THE RINGS	PS3	2012	**1.06**
9	LEGO THE LORD OF THE RINGS	WII	2012	**0.91**
10	THE LORD OF THE RINGS: WAR IN THE NORTH	PS3	2011	**0.84**

THE LORD OF THE RINGS: THE RETURN OF THE KING

6 This tie-in game saw Elijah Wood reprise his role as Frodo Baggins. His voice performance won a 2004 DICE (Design, Innovate, Communicate, Entertain) award.

MIDDLE-EARTH: SHADOW OF MORDOR

3 Set during the 60-year time period between the storylines of *The Hobbit* and *The Lord of the Rings*, this was developed by Monolith Productions.

J. R. R. Tolkien wrote *The Lord of the Rings* over a period of

12 years

BIGGEST ZELDA GAMES

Ever since Link appeared in the 1986 debut title, the Zelda franchise has enchanted millions of fans worldwide...

	NAME	PLATFORM	RELEASED	UNIT SALES (MILLIONS)
1	THE LEGEND OF ZELDA: OCARINA OF TIME	N64	1998	7.6
2	THE LEGEND OF ZELDA: TWILIGHT PRINCESS	WII	2006	7.18
3	THE LEGEND OF ZELDA	NES	1986	6.51
4	THE LEGEND OF ZELDA: THE PHANTOM HOURGLASS	DS	2007	5.1
5	THE LEGEND OF ZELDA: A LINK TO THE PAST	SNES	1991	4.61
6	THE LEGEND OF ZELDA: THE WIND WAKER	GAMECUBE	2002	4.6
7	ZELDA II: THE ADVENTURE OF LINK	NES	1987	4.38
8	THE LEGEND OF ZELDA: SKYWARD SWORD	WII	2011	3.98
9	THE LEGEND OF ZELDA: LINK'S AWAKENING	GAME BOY	1992	3.83
10	THE LEGEND OF ZELDA: OCARINA OF TIME	3DS	2011	3.82

THE LEGEND OF ZELDA: SKYWARD SWORD

8 Although it is the 16th title in the series, this prequel is set before any other *Zelda* game. It was released on November 18, 2011, exclusively for the Nintendo Wii.

THE LEGEND OF ZELDA: TWILIGHT PRINCESS

2 The 13th *Zelda* game was originally planned for release on the GameCube, Nintendo's predecessor to the Wii. In 2016 an HD version was released for the Wii U.

The *Legend Of Zelda: Tri-Force Heroes* was released on **OCT. 22, 2015**

STAR WARS: BATTLEFRONT

9 On November 17, 2015, eleven years after the hit PS2 version, a brand new take on this *Star Wars* game franchise was released for the PS4 and Xbox One.

THE SIMPSONS: ROAD RAGE

9 This is the 19th official video game based on *The Simpsons*. Since 1991, there have been 25 games based on this TV show, created by Matt Groening.

Across all platforms, the *LEGO Indiana Jones* games have sold

16.98 MILLION units

TOP 10

BIGGEST MOVIE/TV TIE-IN GAMES

There have been hundreds of official video games made of TV/movie franchises, including these 10 best-sellers...

	NAME	GENRE	PLATFORM	RELEASED	UNIT SALES (MILLIONS)
1	GOLDENEYE 007	SHOOTER	N64	1997	8.09
2	LEGO STAR WARS: THE COMPLETE SAGA	ACTION	WII	2007	5.61
3	LEGO STAR WARS: THE COMPLETE SAGA	ACTION	DS	2007	4.76
4	THE SIMPSONS: HIT & RUN	RACING	PS2	2003	4.7
5	THE LORD OF THE RINGS: THE TWO TOWERS	ACTION	PS2	2002	4.67
6	SPIDER-MAN: THE MOVIE	ACTION	PS2	2002	4.48
7	LEGO INDIANA JONES: THE ORIGINAL ADVENTURES	ADVENTURE	XBOX 360	2008	3.74
8	HARRY POTTER & THE SORCERER'S STONE	ACTION	PS	2001	3.73
9	STAR WARS: BATTLEFRONT	SHOOTER	PS2	2004	3.61
=	THE SIMPSONS: ROAD RAGE	RACING	PS2	2001	3.61

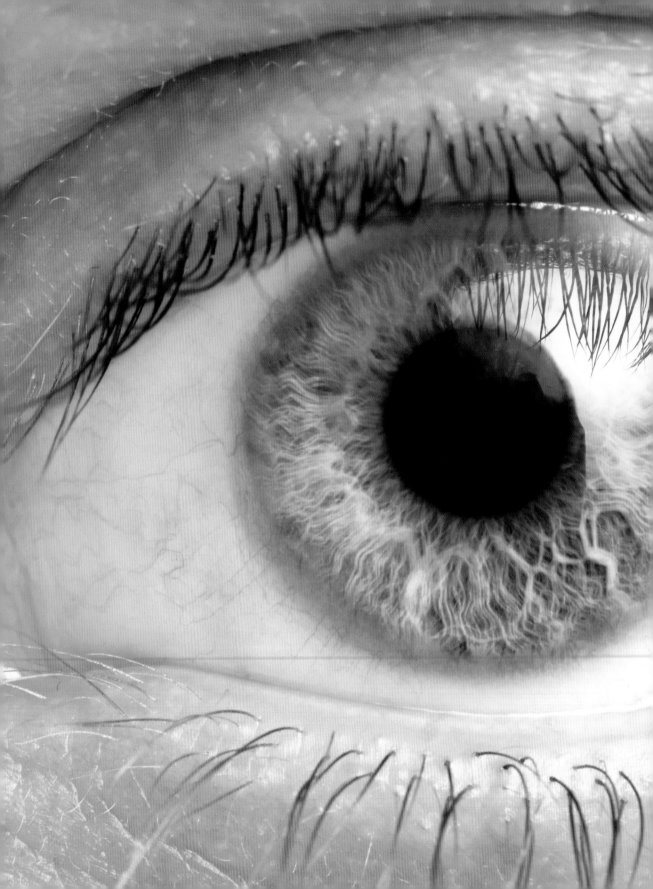

HUMANKIND

ZONE **5**

MOST POPULATED COUNTRIES

Of all the 196 recognized countries on Earth, these are inhabited by the most humans...

	COUNTRY	POPULATION
1	CHINA	1,373,180,000
2	INDIA	1,280,040,000
3	U.S.	322,230,000
4	INDONESIA	255,461,700
5	BRAZIL	205,190,000
6	PAKISTAN	188,925,000
7	NIGERIA	182,202,000
8	BANGLADESH	159,365,000
9	RUSSIA	146,435,680
10	JAPAN	126,890,000

CHINA

1 This country's official full name is the People's Republic of China. The population of its capital city, Beijing (measured by its core districts), is 11.72 million.

W 58 ST

U.S.

3 The state of Pennsylvania (home to the city of Philadelphia, where the Declaration of Independence was approved and issued) has a population of 12.8 million.

Population of California, the biggest state:

38.8 MILLION

Liechtenstein's size:

61
SQUARE MILES

VATICAN CITY

1 Located behind a series of walls in Rome, Italy, Vatican City has been recognized as a country since February 11, 1929.

NAURU

3 An island in the central region of the Pacific Ocean, Nauru covers just over 8 square miles (20.9 km²). Its capital, Yaren, is home to an underground lake, the Moqua Well.

TOP 10

LEAST POPULATED COUNTRIES

This Top 10 contains countries that have a smaller population than most large towns in the U.S....

	COUNTRY	POPULATION
1	VATICAN CITY	839
2	NIUE	1,490
3	NAURU	10,084
4	TUVALU	10,640
5	COOK ISLANDS	14,974
6	PALAU	20,901
7	SAN MARINO	32,831
8	LIECHTENSTEIN	37,370
9	MONACO	37,800
10	SOUTH OSSETIA	51,547

SMALLEST POPULATIONS

Here's how the top 5 compare graphically...

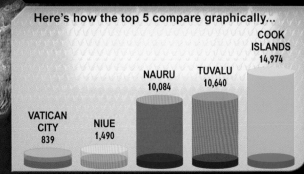

VATICAN CITY 839

NIUE 1,490

NAURU 10,084

TUVALU 10,640

COOK ISLANDS 14,974

LAGOS

3

Paul McCartney recorded his third Wings album, *Band on The Run* (his fifth post-Beatles record), mostly in a studio in Lagos between August and September 1973.

MUMBAI

9

Up until 1995, this city was known as Bombay. Mumbai is the home of the Indian movie industry. Known throughout the world as "Bollywood," it produces more than 1,000 films a year.

TOP 10

MOST POPULATED CITIES

Do you know the population of the city you live in/near? Compare it to this Top 10...

	CITY	COUNTRY	POPULATION
1	SHANGHAI	CHINA	24,150,000
2	KARACHI	PAKISTAN	23,500,000
3	LAGOS	NIGERIA	21,324,000
4	DELHI	INDIA	16,787,941
5	ISTANBUL	TURKEY	14,377,019
6	TOKYO	JAPAN	13,297,629
7	TIANJIN	CHINA	12,938,224
8	GUANGZHOU	CHINA	12,700,800
9	MUMBAI	INDIA	12,478,447
10	MOSCOW	RUSSIA	12,197,596

Shanghai's summer temperatures can reach

103.8°F

MADRID

10 The Manzanares River flows through the Spanish capital. It's popular with fishing enthusiasts, because carp, pike, common trout, and rainbow trout are all found in the river.

Wenzhou's first ever railroad opened **JUNE 11, 1998**

NAIROBI

7 Kenya's largest city (and also its capital) is home to the country's oldest hospital. Established in 1901, the Kenyatta National Hospital employs more than 6,000 staff.

TOP 10

LEAST POPULATED CITIES

Of all the places officially classified as a city, these have the lowest population figures...

	CITY	COUNTRY	POPULATION
1	**WENZHOU**	CHINA	3,039,439
2	**BUENOS AIRES**	ARGENTINA	3,054,300
3	**JAIPUR**	INDIA	3,073,350
4	**ADDIS ABABA**	ETHIOPIA	3,103,673
5	**PUNE**	INDIA	3,115,431
6	**ZHONGSHAN**	CHINA	3,121,275
7	**NAIROBI**	KENYA	3,138,369
8	**EKURHULENI**	SOUTH AFRICA	3,178,470
9	**PESHAWAR**	PAKISTAN	3,201,000
10	**MADRID**	SPAIN	3,207,247

SELMA LAGERLÖF

10 Born on November 20, 1858, Lagerlöf was the first woman to earn the Nobel Prize in Literature. Her other honors include becoming the first woman to be featured on Swedish currency—her face adorns the 20 kronor bill.

ШВЕДСКАЯ ПИСАТЕЛЬНИЦА

СЕЛЬМА ЛАГЕРЛЁФ

ПОЧТА СССР

1858

40 коп.

Bjørnstjerne Bjørnson's total published works:

32

RUDYARD KIPLING

8 Known for such works as *The Jungle Book* (1894) and *Captains Courageous* (1897), the author was born in 1865 in the then British-ruled part of India, Bombay (now called Mumbai).

WINNING NATIONS

Ranked by country, this Top 10 is almost an even split...

FRANCE | POLAND
GERMANY | ITALY
NORWAY | UK
SPAIN | SWEDEN

FIRST **NOBEL PRIZE IN LITERATURE** WINNERS

This coveted prize celebrates outstanding contributions to literature...

TOP 10

	NAME	COUNTRY	YEAR
1	SULLY PRUDHOMME	FRANCE	1901
2	THEODOR MOMMSEN	GERMANY	1902
3	BJØRNSTJERNE BJØRNSON	NORWAY	1903
4	FRÉDÉRIC MISTRAL	FRANCE	1904
=	JOSÉ ECHEGARAY	SPAIN	1904
6	HENRYK SIENKIEWICZ	POLAND	1905
7	GIOSUÈ CARDUCCI	ITALY	1906
8	RUDYARD KIPLING	UK	1907
9	RUDOLF CHRISTOPH EUCKEN	GERMANY	1908
10	SELMA LAGERLÖF	SWEDEN	1909

ARTHUR B. MCDONALD

1

Aged 73, McDonald is a board member of the Perimeter Institute for Theoretical Physics, based in his home province of Ontario, Canada.

SAUL PERLMUTTER

This American astrophysicist also won the 2015 Fundamental Physics Prize for his part in discovering that the expansion of the universe is accelerating, not slowing down.

TOP 10

MOST RECENT NOBEL PRIZE IN PHYSICS WINNERS

Winners are awarded for their highly significant scientific work in the physics spectrum...

	NAME	COUNTRY	YEAR
1	ARTHUR B. MCDONALD	CANADA	2015
=	TAKAAKI KAJITA	JAPAN	2015
3	SHUJI NAKAMURA	JAPAN	2014
=	HIROSHI AMANO	JAPAN	2014
=	ISAMU AKASAKI	JAPAN	2014
6	PETER HIGGS	UNITED KINGDOM	2013
=	FRANÇOIS ENGLERT	BELGIUM	2013
8	DAVID J. WINELAND	U.S.	2012
=	SERGE HAROCHE	FRANCE	2012
10	SAUL PERLMUTTER, ADAM G. RIESS & BRIAN P. SCHMIDT	U.S. & AUSTRALIA	2011

David J. Wineland's total awards in the field of physics:

10

135

WHAT IS THE GLOBAL INNOVATION INDEX?

Analyzing 143 different international economies, and using 79 indicators (such as technological and creative outputs), the GII attributes rankings based on how well an economy has innovated change to help its output.

Ireland's coastline length:

1,738
MILES

TOP 10

MOST INNOVATIVE COUNTRIES

These nations were ranked the most innovative of 2015...

	COUNTRY	GLOBAL INNOVATION INDEX
1	SWITZERLAND	68.30
2	UNITED KINGDOM	62.42
3	SWEDEN	62.40
4	NETHERLANDS	61.58
5	U.S.	60.10
6	FINLAND	59.97
7	SINGAPORE	59.36
8	IRELAND	59.13
9	LUXEMBOURG	59.02
10	DENMARK	57.70

IRELAND

8 Ireland was ranked as the 21st most innovative country in 2007. By 2015, it had climbed 13 places and into the top 10.

SWITZERLAND

1 Since 2010, Switzerland has topped the Global Innovation Index. It receives particular commendation for its world-class universities and creative business innovations, including the number of patent applications.

GRAMEEN BANK

5 Established in 1983 in Dhaka, Bangladesh, this independent bank provides collateral-free small loans. These allow borrowers to grow a business and then repay the money from their profit.

MÉDECINS SANS FRONTIÈRES

8 Also known as Doctors Without Borders, this NGO (nongovernmental organization) dedicated to humanitarian aid was founded on December 20, 1971.

TOP 10

MOST RECENT NOBEL PEACE PRIZE WINNERS (ORGANIZATIONS)

It's not just individuals who are awarded this special prize for promoting peace between nations...

IPCC (Intergovernmental Panel on Climate Change) was established in

1988

	ORGANIZATION	LOCATION	YEAR
1	TUNISIAN NATIONAL DIALOGUE QUARTET	TUNISIA	2015
2	ORGANIZATION FOR THE PROHIBITION OF CHEMICAL WEAPONS	(WORLDWIDE)	2013
3	EUROPEAN UNION	EUROPE	2012
4	INTERGOVERNMENTAL PANEL ON CLIMATE CHANGE (IPCC)	UNITED NATIONS	2007
5	GRAMEEN BANK	BANGLADESH	2006
6	INTERNATIONAL ATOMIC ENERGY AGENCY	UNITED NATIONS	2005
7	UNITED NATIONS	UNITED NATIONS	2001
8	MÉDECINS SANS FRONTIÈRES	SWITZERLAND	1999
9	INTERNATIONAL CAMPAIGN TO BAN LANDMINES	SWITZERLAND	1997
10	PUGWASH CONFERENCES ON SCIENCE AND WORLD AFFAIRS	CANADA	1995

YURI GAGARIN

1 Russian Gagarin (March 9, 1934–March 27, 1968) was the solo crew member of the Vostok 1 mission, which was the only time he went into space. After reentry, he ejected at 23,000 feet (7,000 m) and parachuted to the ground.

Alan Shepard's total time spent in space:
9 DAYS
57 MINS

MIROSŁAW HERMASZEWSKI

4 This Polish astronaut holds the record of being the only person born in Poland to go on a space mission. His total time spent in space is 7 days, 22 hours, and 2 minutes.

FIRSTS BY DECADE

Here are the first astronauts categorized by era...

- 1960s **2**
- 1970s **4**
- 1980s **4**

TOP 10

NATIONS' FIRST ASTRONAUTS

These are the first people sent into space by their respective homelands...

	NATION	FIRST ASTRONAUT	LAUNCH DATE
1	**RUSSIA (SOVIET UNION ERA)**	YURI GAGARIN	**APRIL 12, 1961**
2	**U.S.**	ALAN SHEPARD	**MAY 5, 1961**
3	**CZECHOSLOVAKIA**	VLADIMÍR REMEK	**MARCH 2, 1978**
4	**POLAND**	MIROSŁAW HERMASZEWSKI	**JUNE 27, 1978**
5	**EAST GERMANY (NOW GERMANY)**	SIGMUND JÄHN	**AUGUST 26, 1978**
6	**BULGARIA**	GEORGI IVANOV	**APRIL 10, 1979**
7	**HUNGARY**	BERTALAN FARKAS	**MAY 26, 1980**
8	**VIETNAM**	PHẠM TUÂN	**JULY 23, 1980**
9	**CUBA**	ARNALDO TAMAYO MÉNDEZ	**SEPT. 18, 1980**
10	**MONGOLIA**	JÜGDERDEMIDIIN GÜRRAGCHAA	**MAR. 22, 1981**

FIRST SPACE STATIONS

The history of constructing and manning space stations looks like this...

	NAME	NATION	TOTAL CREW	LAUNCH DATE	BROKEN UP REENTERING ORBIT
1	SALYUT 1	RUSSIA (SOVIET UNION ERA)	3	APRIL 19, 1971	OCT. 11, 1971
2	SKYLAB	U.S.	3	MAY 14, 1973	JULY 11, 1979
3	SALYUT 3	RUSSIA (SOVIET UNION ERA)	2	JUNE 25, 1974	JAN. 24, 1975
4	SALYUT 4	RUSSIA (SOVIET UNION ERA)	2	DEC. 26, 1974	FEB. 3, 1977
5	SALYUT 5	RUSSIA (SOVIET UNION ERA)	2	JUNE 22, 1976	AUGUST 8, 1977
6	SALYUT 6	RUSSIA (SOVIET UNION ERA)	2	SEPT. 29, 1977	JULY 29, 1982
7	SALYUT 7	RUSSIA (SOVIET UNION ERA)	3	APRIL 19, 1982	FEB. 7, 1991
8	MIR	RUSSIA (SOVIET UNION ERA)	3	FEB. 19, 1986	MARCH 23, 2001
9	ISS	U.S., RUSSIA, EUROPE, CANADA, JAPAN	6	NOV. 20, 1998	–
10	TIANGONG 1	CHINA	3	SEPT. 29, 2011	–

Total days Mir had crew:

4,592

TIANGONG 1

10 This is China's first space station. With a length of 34.1 feet (10.4 m), it can hold a crew of three. The structure is part of China's testing and preparation for its larger space station, planned for 2020.

ISS

9 Traveling at 17,100 mph (27,519.8 kph), the ISS (International Space Station) completes 15.54 orbits of the Earth each day.

139

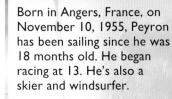

BRUNO PEYRON

3 Born in Angers, France, on November 10, 1955, Peyron has been sailing since he was 18 months old. He began racing at 13. He's also a skier and windsurfer.

TOP 10

FASTEST AROUND THE WORLD BY SAILBOAT

Navigating the world's oceans is a challenge taken up by numerous sailors, but only a few have successfully made their way entirely around the Earth...

	SKIPPER/NO. OF CREW	COUNTRY	SHIP	DATE	TIME
1	LOÏCK PEYRON/14	FRANCE	BANQUE POPULAIRE V	JAN. 2012	**45D, 13H, 42M, 53S**
2	FRANCK CAMMAS/10	FRANCE	GROUPAMA 3	MAR. 2010	**48D, 7H, 44M, 52S**
3	BRUNO PEYRON/14	FRANCE	ORANGE II	MAR. 2005	**50D, 16H, 20M, 4S**
4	FRANCIS JOYON/1*	FRANCE	IDEC 2	JAN. 2008	**57D, 13H, 34M, 6S**
5	STEVE FOSSETT/13	U.S.	CHEYENNE	APRIL 2004	**58D, 9H, 32M, 45S**
6	BRUNO PEYRON/13	FRANCE	ORANGE	MAY 2002	**64D, 8H, 37M, 24S**
7	OLIVIER DE KERSAUSON/7	FRANCE	SPORT-ELEC	MAR. 1997	**71D, 14H, 18M, 8S**
8	ELLEN MACARTHUR/1*	UK	CASTORAMA	FEB. 2005	**71D, 14H, 18M, 33S**
9	FRANCIS JOYON/1*	FRANCE	IDEC	FEB. 2004	**72D, 22H, 54M, 22S**
10	PETER BLAKE & ROBIN KNOX-JOHNSTON/6	NZ/UK	ENZA	JAN. 1994	**74D, 22H, 17M, 22S**

*Single-handed/solo

FRANCK CAMMAS

2 This French yachtsman has won numerous other coveted titles during his career. These include the 2013 Formula 18 St. Barth Cata-Cup and 2013 Tour de France à la Voile.

Steve Fossett's total aviation and sailing world records achieved:

114

Will Goodman's dive set the record for the longest scuba dive:
48 HOURS
8 MINUTES

TRIMIX SCUBA DIVERS

To achieve depths much greater than amateur scuba divers who enjoy diving as a hobby, experts will often use a "trimix" breathing gas. This is a combination of oxygen, helium, and nitrogen.

AHMED GABR

1 Gabr began training for his record attempts in 2010. He holds two world records for Deepest Scuba Dive in Sea Water, and also the Deepest Scuba Dive achieved by a male.

TOP 10

DEEPEST SCUBA DIVES

This Top 10 doesn't include depths achieved by deep-sea diving equipment. Only those using traditional SCUBA breathing apparatus and gear qualify...

	NAME	COUNTRY	LOCATION OF DIVE	YEAR	DEPTH (FEET)	(M)
1	AHMED GABR	EGYPT	RED SEA	2014	1,090.4	332.35
2	NUNO GOMES	SOUTH AFRICA	RED SEA	2005	1,043	318
3	MARK ELLYATT	UNITED KINGDOM	ANDAMAN SEA	2003	1,027	313
4	JOHN BENNETT	UNITED KINGDOM	PHILIPPINES	2001	1,010	308
5	WILL GOODMAN	UNITED KINGDOM	INDONESIA	2014	950	290
6	NUNO GOMES	SOUTH AFRICA	SOUTH AFRICA	1996	928	283
=	KRZYSZTOF STARNAWSKI	POLAND	RED SEA	2011	928	283
8	JIM BOWDEN	U.S.	MEXICO	1994	925	282
9	AARON BUTLER	AUSTRALIA	AUSTRALIA	2015	915	279
10	GILBERTO M DE OLIVEIRA	BRAZIL	BRAZIL	2002	899	274

Total children Susannah Mushatt Jones's parents had:

11

EMMA MORANO-MARTINUZZI

2 During an interview, she credited her long life to the consumption of three raw eggs every day since her teenage years.

TOP 10

OLDEST PEOPLE ALIVE TODAY

These people continue to break records for the length of their lives, all well exceeding a century...

EUDOXIE BABOUL

8 Living in the South American region of French Guiana, Baboul once worked as a dressmaker and also a farm worker. She now lives with her grandson, Joubert, a schoolteacher.

	NAME	COUNTRY	DATE OF BIRTH	AGE (YEARS)
1	SUSANNAH MUSHATT JONES	U.S.	JULY 6, 1899	116+
2	EMMA MORANO-MARTINUZZI	ITALY	NOV. 29, 1899	115+
3	VIOLET BROWN	JAMAICA	MARCH 10, 1900	115+
4	NABI TAJIMA	JAPAN	AUGUST 4, 1900	115+
5	KIYOKO ISHIGURO	JAPAN	MARCH 4, 1901	114+
6	CHIYO MIYAKO	JAPAN	MAY 2, 1901	114+
7	TOSHIE YORIMITSU	JAPAN	SEPT. 30, 1901	114+
8	EUDOXIE BABOUL	FRANCE	OCT. 1, 1901	114+
9	MATSUYO KAGEYAMA	JAPAN	OCT. 10, 1901	114+
10	ANA VELA RUBIO	SPAIN	OCT. 29, 1901	114+

TOP 10

OLDEST PEOPLE OF ALL TIME

Half of the entries in this chart experienced what life was like in three centuries...

	NAME	COUNTRY	DATE OF BIRTH	DATE OF DEATH	AGE
1	JEANNE CALMENT	FRANCE	FEB. 21, 1875	AUG. 4, 1997	**122 YEARS, 164 DAYS**
2	SARAH KNAUSS	U.S.	SEPT. 24, 1880	DEC. 30, 1999	**119 YEARS, 97 DAYS**
3	LUCY HANNAH	U.S.	JULY 16, 1875	MAR. 21, 1993	**117 YEARS, 248 DAYS**
4	MARIE-LOUISE MEILLEUR	CANADA	AUG. 29,1880	APRIL 16, 1998	**117 YEARS, 230 DAYS**
5	MISAO OKAWA	JAPAN	MAR. 5, 1898	APRIL 1, 2015	**117 YEARS, 27 DAYS**
6	MARÍA CAPOVILLA	ECUADOR	SEPT. 14, 1889	AUG. 27, 2006	**116 YEARS, 347 DAYS**
7	GERTRUDE WEAVER	U.S.	JULY 4, 1898	APRIL 6, 2015	**116 YEARS 276 DAYS**
8	SUSANNAH MUSHATT JONES	U.S.	JULY 6, 1899	–	**116 YEARS, 211 DAYS+**
9	TANE IKAI	JAPAN	JAN. 18, 1879	JULY 12, 1995	**116 YEARS, 175 DAYS**
10	ELIZABETH BOLDEN	U.S.	AUG. 15, 1890	DEC. 11, 2006	**116 YEARS, 118 DAYS**

AGE BY THE NATIONS

There must be something special in American water...

- U.S. **5**
- JAPAN **2**
- FRANCE **1**
- CANADA **1**
- ECUADOR **1**

MISAO OKAWA

5 Her 117-year-long life was assisted by plenty of sushi and rest, Okawa once said. She had four grandchildren and six great-grandchildren.

Jeanne Calment met artist Vincent Van Gogh in

1888

KHAGENDRA THAPA MAGAR

9 The Nepalese actor and dancer was born in his home country's Baglung District.

Madge Bester's mother Winnie's height was:

27.6 INCHES

PAULINE MUSTERS

3 The shortest woman ever was a highly accomplished dancer and acrobat under the stage name of Princess Pauline.

TOP 10

SHORTEST HUMANS OF ALL TIME

These records for short heights come from people all over the world, from Nepal to Mexico...

	NAME	COUNTRY	LIFESPAN	HEIGHT (INCH)	(CM)
1	CHANDRA BAHADUR DANGI	NEPAL	1939–2015	21.5	54.6
2	GUL MOHAMMED	INDIA	1957–1997	22.4	57
3	PAULINE MUSTERS*	NETHERLANDS	1876–1895	22.8	58
4	JYOTI AMGE*	INDIA	1993–PRESENT	23	58.4
5	JUNREY BALAWING	PHILIPPINES	1993–PRESENT	23.6	60
6	LUCIA ZARATE	MEXICO	1864–1890	24	61
7	MADGE BESTER*	SOUTH AFRICA	1963–PRESENT	25.6	65
=	ISTVÁN TÓTH	HUNGARY	1963–2011	25.6	65
9	KHAGENDRA THAPA MAGAR	NEPAL	1992–PRESENT	26.4	67
10	LIN YÜ-CHIH	TAIWAN	1972–PRESENT	26.6	67.5

Female; the rest are male.

Édouard Beaupré weighed **375 POUNDS**

ROBERT WADLOW

1 By the time he was eight years old, Wadlow was taller than his father, Harold, who was 5′ 11″ (1.82 m). As an adult, Wadlow wore a size 25 shoe.

LEONID STADNYK

4 The Ukranian height record-holder died of a brain hemorrhage on August 24, 2014, at the age of 44.

TOP 10

TALLEST HUMANS OF ALL TIME

The top 3 in this chart, all Americans, were almost a towering 9 feet (2.7 m) in height...

	NAME	COUNTRY	LIFESPAN	HEIGHT (FEET)	(M)
1	ROBERT WADLOW	U.S.	1918–1940	8.92	2.72
2	JOHN ROGAN	U.S.	1868–1905	8.79	2.68
3	JOHN F. CARROLL	U.S.	1932–1969	8.63	2.63
4	LEONID STADNYK	UKRAINE	1970–2014	8.43	2.57
5	VÄINÖ MYLLYRINNE	FINLAND	1909–1963	8.23	2.51
=	ÉDOUARD BEAUPRÉ	CANADA	1881–1904	8.23	2.51
=	SULTAN KÖSEN	TURKEY	1982–PRESENT	8.23	2.51
8	BERNARD COYNE	U.S.	1897–1821	8.17	2.49
=	DON KOEHLER	U.S.	1925–1881	8.17	2.49
10	PATRICK COTTER O'BRIEN	IRELAND	1760–1806	8.07	2.46

TOP 10

OLDEST LIVING STATE LEADERS

For these people, the idea of retiring from work in their sixties was something that they ignored for many decades...

	NAME	POSITION	PERIOD OF RULE	AGE
1	TELMO VARGAS	HEAD OF STATE OF ECUADOR	1966	**103 YEARS, 36 DAYS**
2	PIET DE JONG	PRIME MINISTER OF THE NETHERLANDS	1967–71	**100 YEARS, 225 DAYS**
▶ **3**	ĐỖ MƯỜI	PRIME MINISTER OF VIETNAM GENERAL SECRETARY OF THE COMMUNIST PARTY OF VIETNAM	1988–91 1991–97	**98 YEARS, 285 DAYS**
4	ÉMILE DERLIN ZINSOU	PRESIDENT OF DAHOMEY	1968–69	**97 YEARS, 236 DAYS**
▶ **5**	YASUHIRO NAKASONE	PRIME MINISTER OF JAPAN	1982–87	**97 YEARS, 171 DAYS**
6	KONSTANTINOS MITSOTAKIS	PRIME MINISTER OF GREECE	1990–93	**97 YEARS, 27 DAYS**
7	PATRICIO AYLWIN	PRESIDENT OF CHILE	1990–94	**96 YEARS, 353 DAYS**
8	HYUN SOONG-JONG	PRIME MINISTER OF SOUTH KOREA	1992–93	**96 YEARS, 292 DAYS**
9	MOHAMMED KARIM LAMRANI	PRIME MINISTER OF MOROCCO	1971–72, 1983–86, 1992–94	**96 YEARS, 197 DAYS**
10	WALTER SCHEEL	PRESIDENT OF WEST GERMANY	1974–79	**96 YEARS, 129 DAYS**

Piet de Jong achieved several military ranks, including Captain at Sea in

1958

YASUHIRO NAKASONE

5 The former Japanese Prime Minister also served in the Imperial Japanese Navy from 1941–45. He's currently a Senior Advisor to the Japan Karate Association.

ĐỖ MƯỜI

3 Born in Vietnam's Thanh Trì District, part of the Hanoi province, on February 2, 1917, Mười has been called the Godfather of Vietnamese politics.

U.S.

1 The 44th President of the United States of America, Barack Obama assumed office on January 20, 2009. Serving two terms, Obama will hand over power to the next president on January 20, 2017.

CANADA

9 Justin Trudeau became the 23rd Prime Minister of Canada on November 4, 2015. The leader of the Liberal Party was born on December 25, 1971.

Total politicians and advisers in UK: approximately

30,000

BIGGEST GOVERNMENTS

TOP 10

Too bad governments tend to spend as much as, if not more than, they actually make...

	COUNTRY	REVENUE ($ MILLIONS)
1	U.S.	3,029,721
2	CHINA	2,285,000
3	GERMANY	1,680,000
4	JAPAN	1,512,000
5	FRANCE	1,507,500
6	ITALY	990,000
7	UNITED KINGDOM	936,200
8	BRAZIL	861,300
9	CANADA	675,800
10	SPAIN	545,200

TOP 5 EARNERS

These governments generate the most revenue...

U.S. $3,029,721 MILLION

CHINA $2,285,000 MILLION

GERMANY $1,680,000 MILLION

JAPAN $1,512,000 MILLION

FRANCE $1,507,500 MILLION

Hassanal Bolkiah is the

29TH

Sultan and Yang di-Pertuan of Brunei

GOODWILL ZWELITHINI KABHEKUZULU

6 The current reigning king of the Zulu nation took over after the death of his father, King Cyprian Bhekuzulu kaSolomon, on September 17, 1968.

ELIZABETH II

2 Elizabeth Alexandra Mary's coronation took place on June 2, 1953. She married her husband, Prince Philip, Duke of Edinburgh, on November 20, 1947, in London's Westminster Abbey. She is the longest-reigning monarch in UK history.

LONGEST REIGNING MONARCHS ALIVE

TOP 10

Being in their senior years is not a time to slow down, or step down, for these world leaders...

	NAME	COUNTRY	YEARS CURRENTLY REIGNED
1	BHUMIBOL ADULYADEJ	THAILAND	70
2	ELIZABETH II	UNITED KINGDOM	64
3	ABDUL HALIM	MALAYSIA	58
4	SIKIRU KAYODE ADETONA	NIGERIA	56
5	HASSANAL BOLKIAH	BRUNEI	49
6	GOODWILL ZWELITHINI KABHEKUZULU	SOUTH AFRICA	48
7	QABOOS BIN SAID AL SAID	OMAN	46
8	MARGRETHE II	DENMARK	44
9	SULTAN BIN MOHAMED AL-QASSIMI III	UNITED ARAB EMIRATES	44
10	CARL XVI GUSTAF	SWEDEN	43

LONGEST REIGNING MONARCHS OF ALL TIME

All of these entries in this Top 10 remained on their respective thrones for more than seven decades...

	NAME	LOCATION	REIGN BEGAN	REIGN ENDED	TOTAL TIME
1	SOBHUZA II	SWAZILAND	DEC. 10, 1899	AUG. 21, 1982	**82 YEARS, 254 DAYS**
2	BERNHARD VII	LIPPE (HOLY ROMAN EMPIRE)	AUG. 12, 1429	APRIL 2, 1511	**81 YEARS, 234 DAYS**
3	WILLIAM IV	HENNEBERG-SCHLEUSINGEN (HOLY ROMAN EMPIRE)	MAY 26, 1480	JAN. 24, 1559	**78 YEARS, 243 DAYS**
4	HEINRICH XI	REUSS-OBERGREIZ (HOLY ROMAN EMPIRE)	MAR. 17, 1723	JUNE 28, 1800	**77 YEARS, 103 DAYS**
5	IDRIS IBNI MUHAMMAD AL-QADRI	TAMPIN (MALAYSIA)	MAY 1, 1929	DEC. 26, 2005	**76 YEARS, 239 DAYS**
6	CHRISTIAN AUGUST	PALATINATE-SULZBACH (HOLY ROMAN EMPIRE)	AUG. 14, 1632	APRIL 23, 1708	**75 YEARS, 253 DAYS**
7	MUDHOJI IV RAO NAIK NIMBALKAR	PHALTAN STATE (INDIA)	DEC. 7, 1841	OCT. 17, 1916	**74 YEARS, 315 DAYS**
8	BHAGVATSINGH SAHIB	GONDAL STATE (INDIA)	DEC. 14, 1869	MAR. 10, 1944	**74 YEARS, 87 DAYS**
9	GEORG WILHELM	SCHAUMBURG-LIPPE (HOLY ROMAN EMPIRE)	FEB. 13, 1787	NOV. 21, 1860	**73 YEARS, 282 DAYS**
10	KARL FRIEDRICH	BADEN (HOLY ROMAN EMPIRE)	MAY 12, 1738	JUNE 10, 1811	**73 YEARS, 29 DAYS**

Sobhuza II was born on
JULY 22, 1899

LIPPE FAMILY

The House of Lippe (coat of arms shown) presided over the German principality of Lippe from 1123 to 1918.

BHAGVATSINGH SAHIB

8 Born October 24, 1865, in Dhoraji, Gujarat, India, Sahib received numerous political and academic honors throughout his life. These included a Bachelor of Medicine.

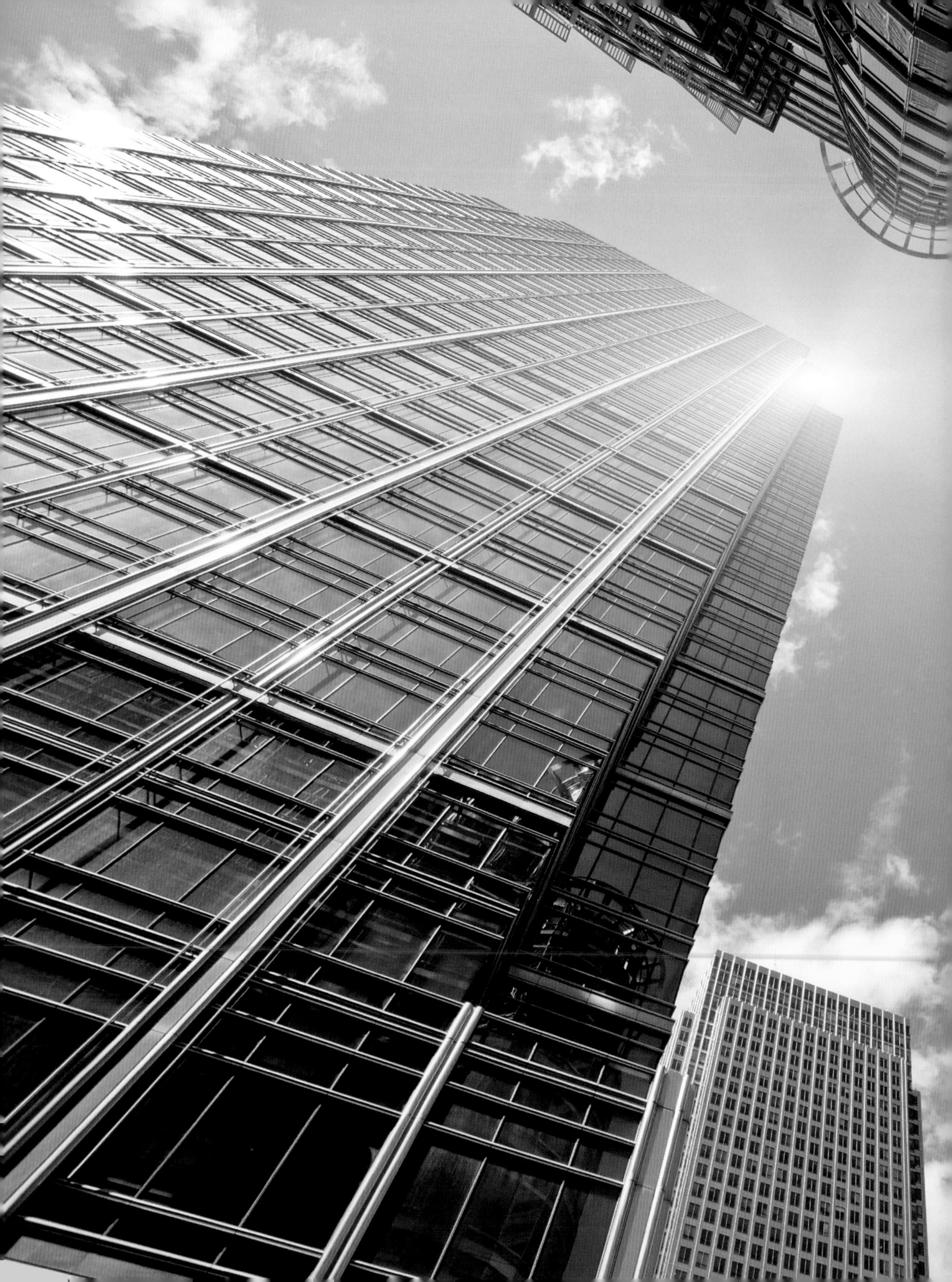

EPIC
STRUCTURES

ZONE 6

TOP 10

LARGEST ALL-RESIDENTIAL BUILDINGS

Some skyscrapers combine offices and homes, but these are just for residents...

	BUILDING	CITY	COUNTRY	YEAR COMPLETED	FLOORS	HEIGHT (FT)	(M)
1	PRINCESS TOWER	DUBAI	UNITED ARAB EMIRATES	2012	101	1,356	413.4
2	23 MARINA	DUBAI	UNITED ARAB EMIRATES	2012	88	1,287	392.4
3	BURJ MOHAMMED BIN RASHID TOWER	ABU DHABI	UNITED ARAB EMIRATES	2014	88	1,251	381.2
4	ELITE RESIDENCE	DUBAI	UNITED ARAB EMIRATES	2012	87	1,248	380.5
5	THE TORCH	DUBAI	UNITED ARAB EMIRATES	2011	86	1,155	352
6	Q1 TOWER	GOLD COAST	AUSTRALIA	2005	78	1,058	322.5
7	HHHR TOWER	DUBAI	UNITED ARAB EMIRATES	2010	72	1,042	317.6
8	OCEAN HEIGHTS	DUBAI	UNITED ARAB EMIRATES	2010	83	1,017	310
9	CAYAN TOWER	DUBAI	UNITED ARAB EMIRATES	2013	73	1,005	306.4
10	EAST PACIFIC CENTRE TOWER A	SHENZHEN	CHINA	2013	85	1,004	306

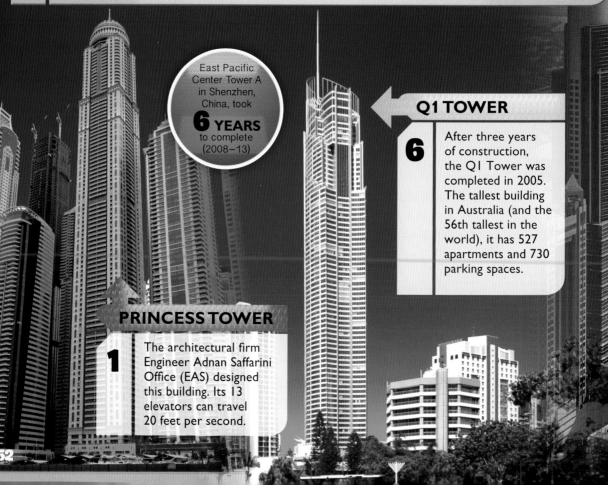

East Pacific Center Tower A in Shenzhen, China, took **6** YEARS to complete (2008–13)

Q1 TOWER

6
After three years of construction, the Q1 Tower was completed in 2005. The tallest building in Australia (and the 56th tallest in the world), it has 527 apartments and 730 parking spaces.

PRINCESS TOWER

1
The architectural firm Engineer Adnan Saffarini Office (EAS) designed this building. Its 13 elevators can travel 20 feet per second.

Skyscrapers are buildings taller than 492 feet (150 m). Total in Shanghai:

126

SCRAPING THE SKY

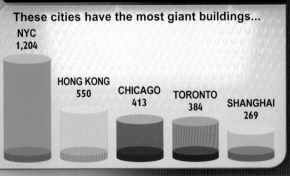

These cities have the most giant buildings...

NYC 1,204
HONG KONG 550
CHICAGO 413
TORONTO 384
SHANGHAI 269

TOP 10

CITIES WITH THE MOST SKYSCRAPERS

If you walk the streets of these places, you'll spend most of your time staring upward...

	CITY	COUNTRY	TOTAL SKYSCRAPERS
1	NEW YORK CITY	USA	1,204
2	HONG KONG	CHINA	550
3	CHICAGO	USA	413
4	TORONTO	CANADA	384
5	SHANGHAI	CHINA	269
6	DUBAI	UNITED ARAB EMIRATES	253
7	SYDNEY	AUSTRALIA	194
8	TOKYO	JAPAN	189
9	HOUSTON	USA	175
10	MELBOURNE	AUSTRALIA	163

DUBAI

6 With an average building age of seven years, Dubai is a very modern-looking city with a population of more than 2.2 million. The 2,333-ft (711-m) tall Dubai One will be completed by 2020 and will be the tallest building on Earth.

CHICAGO

3 More than 60 percent of Chicago's buildings are made primarily of concrete. Nearly half of the city's buildings are used for offices.

China's Shanghai World Financial Center has

91

elevators

RUSSIA

4

Along with its four completed buildings taller than 1,000 feet, Russia's capital city Moscow has another two under development, including the 1,226-foot (373.7-m) high Federation Towers.

USA

3

Started in 2014 and planned for a 2019 opening, New York City's Central Park Tower will be 1,775 feet (541 m) high and will have residential, retail, and hotel facilities.

TOP 10

COUNTRIES WITH THE MOST 1,000 FOOT+ BUILDINGS

These are the nations that have constructed the giant towers that dwarf all others...

	COUNTRY	NUMBER OF 1,000 FOOT + BUILDINGS
1	CHINA	36
2	UNITED ARAB EMIRATES	22
3	USA	16
4	RUSSIA	4
5	MALAYSIA	3
=	SAUDI ARABIA	3
7	SOUTH KOREA	2
=	TAIWAN	2
=	KUWAIT	2
10	AUSTRALIA/CHILE/JAPAN/QATAR/THAILAND/UK/VIETNAM	1

Bibliothque Nationale de France was first opened to the public in
1692

NATIONAL LIBRARY OF CHINA

9 Established in 1909, this was originally called the Imperial Library of Peking. Among its vast collection are over 1.6 million ancient handmade Chinese texts.

TOP 10

BIGGEST LIBRARIES

Does your local library have your favorite books? Next time you visit, find out if its inventory rivals these...

	NAME	CITY	COUNTRY	NUMBER OF BOOKS (MILLIONS)
1	THE BRITISH LIBRARY	LONDON	UK	170
2	LIBRARY OF CONGRESS	WASHINGTON, D.C.	USA	160
3	LIBRARY AND ARCHIVES	OTTAWA	CANADA	54
4	NEW YORK PUBLIC LIBRARY	NEW YORK CITY	USA	53.1
5	RUSSIAN STATE LIBRARY	MOSCOW	RUSSIA	44.4
6	BIBLIOTHÈQUE NATIONALE DE FRANCE	PARIS	FRANCE	40
7	NATIONAL LIBRARY OF RUSSIA	ST. PETERSBURG	RUSSIA	36.5
8	NATIONAL DIET LIBRARY	TOKYO/KYOTO	JAPAN	35.6
9	NATIONAL LIBRARY OF CHINA	BEIJING	CHINA	31.2
10	ROYAL DANISH LIBRARY	COPENHAGEN	DENMARK	30.2

LIBRARY OF CONGRESS

2 Thomas Jefferson's own collection of 6,487 books was bought by Congress for this library in 1815. There are also books featuring 460 different languages.

SHANGHAI WORLD FINANCIAL CENTER

Jin Mao Tower's total parking spaces:

993

3

Eleven years in the making, the second-tallest building in China opened in 2008. The two arcs and square prism echo the Chinese symbols for heaven and earth.

TOP 10

BIGGEST HOTELS

If you enjoy a room with a view, these are the 10 hotels you need to put on your vacation wishlist...

	BUILDING	COUNTRY	YEAR COMPLETED	FLOORS	ROOMS	HEIGHT (FT)	(M)
1	BURJ KHALIFA	UNITED ARAB EMIRATES	2010	163	304	2,717	828
2	MAKKAH ROYAL CLOCK TOWER HOTEL	SAUDI ARABIA	2012	120	858	1,972	601
3	SHANGHAI WORLD FINANCIAL CENTER	CHINA	2008	101	174	1,614	492
4	INTERNATIONAL COMMERCE CENTER	CHINA	2010	108	312	1,588	484
5	ZIFENG TOWER	CHINA	2010	66	450	1,476	450
6	KK100	CHINA	2011	100	249	1,449	441.8
7	GUANGZHOU INTERNATIONAL FINANCE CENTER	CHINA	2010	103	374	1,439	438.6
8	TRUMP INTERNATIONAL HOTEL & TOWER	USA	2009	98	339	1,389	423.2
9	JIN MAO TOWER	CHINA	1999	88	555	1,380	420.5
10	JW MARRIOTT MARQUIS HOTEL DUBAI TOWERS	UNITED ARAB EMIRATES	2013	82	1,608	1,166	355.4

BURJ KHALIFA

1

This tower has more than 2,000,000 square feet (185,800m²) of luxurious interiors and the highest outdoor observatory in the world.

MOST FLOORS OF ALL

Ranked by floors, these are the top 5...

BURJ KHALIFA
163

MAKKAH ROYAL CLOCK TOWER HOTEL
120

INTERNATIONAL COMMERCE CENTER
108

GUANGZHOU INTERNATIONAL FINANCE CENTER
103

SHANGHAI WORLD FINANCIAL CENTER
101

Tokyo Haneda Airport's early incarnation as Haneda Airfield opened in

1931

LONDON HEATHROW AIRPORT

3 Since its airfield beginnings in 1929, Heathrow now serves nearly 100 airlines that take passengers to 170 countries. Its fifth terminal, built to cope with increased usage, opened March 27, 2008.

BEIJING CAPITAL INTERNATIONAL AIRPORT

2 The first incarnation of this airport opened on March 2, 1958. In 2009 it was awarded the World's Best Airport by a renowned travel magazine.

TOP 10

AIRPORTS WITH THE MOST PASSENGERS

When it comes to air travel, these 10 complexes move the most people...

	AIRPORT	LOCATION	TOTAL PASSENGERS PER YEAR (MILLIONS)
1	HARTSFIELD–JACKSON ATLANTA INTERNATIONAL AIRPORT	GEORGIA	96.18
2	BEIJING CAPITAL INTERNATIONAL AIRPORT	BEIJING (CHINA)	86.13
3	LONDON HEATHROW AIRPORT	LONDON (UK)	73.41
4	TOKYO HANEDA AIRPORT	TOKYO (JAPAN)	72.83
5	LOS ANGELES INTERNATIONAL AIRPORT	CALIFORNIA	70.67
6	DUBAI INTERNATIONAL AIRPORT	DUBAI (UNITED ARAB EMIRATES)	70.48
7	O'HARE INTERNATIONAL AIRPORT	CHICAGO	70.02
8	PARIS-CHARLES DE GAULLE AIRPORT	ÎLE-DE-FRANCE (FRANCE)	63.81
9	DALLAS-FORT WORTH INTERNATIONAL AIRPORT	TEXAS	63.52
10	HONG KONG INTERNATIONAL AIRPORT	HONG KONG (CHINA)	63.15

TALLEST CONSTRUCTIONS

PETRONAS TWIN TOWERS

7 Ground broke on these office towers in Kuala Lumpur in 1992. A sky bridge between the 41st and 42nd floors unites the buildings. Facilities around these floors, such as a prayer room, can be shared.

The Willis Tower, originally the Sears Tower, took **4** years to construct

TAIPEI 101

4 Being in a typhoon-prone region of the world, this building contains a 728-ton pendulum device that counters any movement caused by intense winds.

TALLEST BUILDINGS

TOP 10

In the battle of the highest constructions in the world, these are the 10 victors...

	BUILDING	COUNTRY	YEAR COMPLETED	FLOORS	HEIGHT (FT)	(M)
1	BURJ KHALIFA	UNITED ARAB EMIRATES	2010	163	2,717	828
2	MAKKAH ROYAL CLOCK TOWER HOTEL	SAUDI ARABIA	2012	120	1,972	601
3	ONE WORLD TRADE CENTER	USA	2014	104	1,776	541
4	TAIPEI 101	TAIWAN	2004	101	1,667	508
5	SHANGHAI WORLD FINANCIAL CENTER	CHINA	2008	101	1,614	492
6	INTERNATIONAL COMMERCE CENTER	CHINA	2010	108	1,588	484
7	PETRONAS TWIN TOWERS	MALAYSIA	1998	88	1,483	451.9
8	ZIFENG TOWER	CHINA	2010	66	1,476	450
9	WILLIS TOWER	USA	1974	108	1,451	442.1
10	KK100	CHINA	2011	100	1,449	441.8

TOP 10

BUILDINGS WITH THE MOST FLOORS

Spires and other attributes aside, this chart is all about the number of floors above ground level...

	BUILDING	CITY	COUNTRY	YEAR COMPLETED	FLOORS
1	**BURJ KHALIFA**	DUBAI	UNITED ARAB EMIRATES	2010	**163**
2	**MAKKAH ROYAL CLOCK TOWER HOTEL**	MECCA	SAUDI ARABIA	2012	**120**
3	**INTERNATIONAL COMMERCE CENTRE**	HONG KONG	CHINA	2010	**108**
=	**WILLIS TOWER**	CHICAGO	USA	1974	**108**
5	**GUANGZHOU INTERNATIONAL FINANCE CENTER**	GUANGZHOU	CHINA	2010	**103**
6	**EMPIRE STATE BUILDING**	NEW YORK CITY	USA	1931	**102**
7	**TAIPEI 101**	TAIPEI	TAIWAN	2004	**101**
=	**SHANGHAI WORLD FINANCIAL CENTER**	SHANGHAI	CHINA	2008	**101**
=	**PRINCESS TOWER**	DUBAI	UNITED ARAB EMIRATES	2012	**101**
10	**JOHN HANCOCK CENTER**	CHICAGO	USA	1969	**100**

INTERNATIONAL COMMERCE CENTRE

3 There are 83 elevators and 1,700 parking spaces serving this complex, which features 312 hotel rooms.

EMPIRE STATE BUILDING

6 Located at 350 Fifth Avenue, this building was completed in just one year, from 1930–31. It is the star of countless movies including the 1933 and 2005 versions of *King Kong*.

John Hancock Center's global ranking for tallest building:

37TH

Transamerica Pyramid is the tallest building in San Francisco at:

853 FEET

LOS ANGELES

2 In the City of Angels, 95 percent of buildings are made primarily from steel. Three towers of the Oceanwide Plaza are set to be completed by 2018.

SEOUL

1 More than 60 percent of the buildings in South Korea's capital are residential. Along with the 70 buildings in Seoul that exceed 492 feet (150 m) in height, there are another ten under construction.

TOP 10

CITIES WITH THE MOST HELIPADS

A helicopter provides amazing views of any city, but these cities have the most places to land one...

	CITY	COUNTRY	NUMBER OF 650-FOOT+ BUILDINGS WITH HELIPADS
1	SEOUL	SOUTH KOREA	12
2	BUSAN	SOUTH KOREA	10
=	LOS ANGELES	USA	10
4	GOYANG	SOUTH KOREA	8
=	TOKYO	JAPAN	8
6	INCHEON	SOUTH KOREA	5
7	HWASEONG	SOUTH KOREA	4
=	OSAKA	JAPAN	4
9	DALIAN	CHINA	3
=	GUANGZHOU	CHINA	3

TOP 10

BUILDINGS WITH THE HIGHEST HELIPADS

If you've got enough of a head for heights for a helicopter flight, these helipads will suit you fine...

	BUILDING	CITY	COUNTRY	YEAR COMPLETED	HELIPAD HEIGHT (FT)	(M)
1	GUANGZHOU INTERNATIONAL FINANCE CENTER	GUANGZHOU	CHINA	2010	1,437	438
2	CHINA WORLD TOWER	BEIJING	CHINA	2010	1,082.7	330
3	U.S. BANK TOWER	LOS ANGELES	USA	1990	1,017.1	310
4	NORTHEAST ASIA TRADE TOWER	INCHEON	SOUTH KOREA	2011	984.3	300
=	ABENO HARUKAS	OSAKA	JAPAN	2014	984.3	300
6	DOOSAN HAEUNDAE WE'VE THE ZENITH TOWER A	BUSAN	SOUTH KOREA	2011	981	299
7	LANDMARK TOWER	YOKOHAMA	JAPAN	1993	971.1	296
8	SEG PLAZA	SHENZHEN	CHINA	2000	958	292
9	UNITED INTERNATIONAL MANSION	CHONGQING	CHINA	2013	941.6	287
10	THREE INTERNATIONAL FINANCE CENTER	SEOUL	SOUTH KOREA	2012	931.7	284

The highest helipad in the world is on the Siachen glacier in the Himalayas:

20,997 FEET

above sea level

CHINA WORLD TOWER

2 The 48th-tallest building in the world is the third phase of Beijing's China World Trade Center.

GUANGZHOU INTERNATIONAL FINANCE CENTER

1 This is the ninth-tallest building in Asia. It houses offices with a hotel added in 2010.

HELIPAD CENTRAL

These countries have the highest ones...

- CHINA **4**
- SOUTH KOREA **3**
- JAPAN **2**
- USA **1**

TALLEST CONSTRUCTIONS

TALLEST CELL PHONE AND OBSERVATION TOWERS

Constructions like these need height to serve their purpose, and these are the highest in the world...

	BUILDING	COUNTRY	YEAR COMPLETED	HEIGHT (FT)	(M)
1	TOKYO SKY TREE	JAPAN	2012	2,080	634
2	CANTON TOWER	CHINA	2010	1,969	600
3	CN TOWER	CANADA	1976	1,815	553.3
4	OSTANKINO TOWER	RUSSIA	1967	1,772	540
5	ORIENTAL PEARL TELEVISION TOWER	CHINA	1995	1,535	468
6	MILAD TOWER	IRAN	2008	1,427	435
7	MENARA KUALA LUMPUR	MALAYSIA	1996	1,379	420.4
8	TIANJIN RADIO & TV TOWER	CHINA	1991	1,362	415.1
9	CENTRAL RADIO & TV TOWER	CHINA	1992	1,347	410.5
10	HENAN PROVINCE RADIO & TV TOWER	CHINA	2011	1,273	388

TOKYO SKY TREE

1 Although initially proposed in 2006, the construction of the Tokyo Sky Tree didn't begin until 2008. The tower has 13 elevators, which can travel at 33 feet per second.

CANTON TOWER

2 It may not be the tallest building in the world, but the Canton Tower is home to the world's highest post office, perched 1,404.2 feet (428 m) up.

Menara Kuala Lumpur's top elevator speed:

19 FEET PER SECOND

UK's British Telecom Tower height:

581
FEET

← **USA**

3 The tallest tower in the United States is the Stratosphere Tower in Las Vegas. It extends up 1,149 feet (350.2 m) and has towered over the skyline since 1996.

TOP 10

COUNTRIES WITH THE MOST CELL PHONE TOWERS

The tallest towers are on the opposite page, and these are the nations that boast the most...

	COUNTRY	NUMBER OF TELECOM TOWERS
1	THE NETHERLANDS	49
2	CHINA	25
3	USA	18
4	GERMANY	13
5	UK	7
6	CANADA	6
=	JAPAN	6
8	RUSSIA	4
9	ITALY	3
10	BELGIUM/GEORGIA/INDIA/SOUTH AFRICA/SOUTH KOREA/SPAIN	2

GERMANY

4 The Fernsehturm (also known as the Berlin TV Tower) attracts 1.2 million visitors each year. Its antenna contributes to its height of 1,207.45 feet (368.03 m).

HANGZHOU BAY BRIDGE

9 Constructed over four years (2003–07), this gigantic bay-spanning bridge is 22 miles long and took more than a decade to carefully design and plan.

Tianjin Grand Bridge is more than **70** MILES long

SPANNING TENS OF MILES

The number 1 actually exceeds 100 miles...

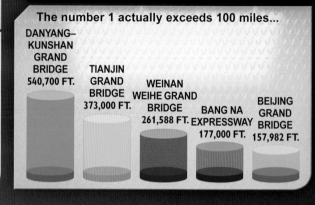

DANYANG–KUNSHAN GRAND BRIDGE 540,700 FT.

TIANJIN GRAND BRIDGE 373,000 FT.

WEINAN WEIHE GRAND BRIDGE 261,588 FT.

BANG NA EXPRESSWAY 177,000 FT.

BEIJING GRAND BRIDGE 157,982 FT.

TOP 10

LONGEST BRIDGES

Humans have been constructing bridges to connect places for centuries, but these are record breakers...

	BRIDGE	COUNTRY	LENGTH (FT)	(M)
1	DANYANG–KUNSHAN GRAND BRIDGE	CHINA	540,700	164,800
2	TIANJIN GRAND BRIDGE	CHINA	373,000	113,700
3	WEINAN WEIHE GRAND BRIDGE	CHINA	261,588	79,732
4	BANG NA EXPRESSWAY	THAILAND	177,000	54,000
5	BEIJING GRAND BRIDGE	CHINA	157,982	48,153
6	LAKE PONTCHARTRAIN CAUSEWAY	USA	126,122	38,442
7	MANCHAC SWAMP BRIDGE	USA	120,440	36,710
8	YANGCUN BRIDGE	CHINA	117,493	35,812
9	HANGZHOU BAY BRIDGE	CHINA	117,037	35,673
10	RUNYANG BRIDGE	CHINA	116,990	35,660

BANG NA EXPRESSWAY

4 This colossal bridge is 137.8 feet (42 m) wide. It is a toll bridge, and required nearly 63,566,400 cubic feet (1.8 million cubic m) of concrete to complete.

TOP 10

LONGEST ROLLER COASTERS

Theme park rides often feature twists and turns, but these roller coasters take you the greatest distances...

The Voyage ride lasts
2 MINUTES
45 SECONDS

	ROLLER COASTER	LOCATION	LENGTH (FT)	(M)
1	STEEL DRAGON 2000	NAGASHIMA SPA LAND (JAPAN)	8,133	2,479
2	THE ULTIMATE	LIGHTWATER VALLEY (UK)	7,442	2,268
3	THE BEAST	KINGS ISLAND (USA)	7,359	2,243
4	FUJIYAMA	FUJI-Q HIGHLAND (JAPAN)	6,709	2,045
5	FURY 325	CAROWINDS (USA)	6,602	2,012
6	MILLENNIUM FORCE	CEDAR POINT (USA)	6,595	2,010
7	FORMULA ROSSA	FERRARI WORLD (UNITED ARAB EMIRATES)	6,562	2,000
8	THE VOYAGE	HOLIDAY WORLD & SPLASHIN' SAFARI (USA)	6,442	1,964
9	CALIFORNIA SCREAMIN'	DISNEY CALIFORNIA ADVENTURE (USA)	6,072	1,851
10	DESPERADO	BUFFALO BILL'S (USA)	5,843	1,781

STEEL DRAGON 2000

1 Located in Mie Prefecture, Japan, this roller coaster gets its name from the fact that it was opened in the "Year of the Dragon."

THE ULTIMATE

2 Situated in the English village of North Stainley, this coaster ride is among 44 acres of woodland in the Lightwater Valley park.

The Melbourne Star reopened with its new wheel:

DEC. 23, 2013

HIGH ROLLER

1 This appropriately named ferris wheel, set in the heart of the gambling city of Las Vegas, was opened on March 31, 2014.

LONDON EYE

4 Open since March 2000, this iconic landmark on London's South Bank is the tallest ferris wheel in Europe. It features 32 passenger pods, which can hold 25 people each.

TOP 10

BIGGEST FERRIS WHEELS

Providing spectacular views at great heights, these have become popular landmarks in many cities...

	FERRIS WHEEL	LOCATION	YEAR COMPLETED	HEIGHT (FT)	(M)
1	HIGH ROLLER	LAS VEGAS	2014	550	167.6
2	SINGAPORE FLYER	MARINA CENTER, SINGAPORE	2008	541	165
3	STAR OF NANCHANG	NANCHANG, CHINA	2006	525	160
4	LONDON EYE	SOUTH BANK, LONDON	2000	443	135
5	ORLANDO EYE	ORLANDO, FLORIDA	2015	400	122
6	SUZHOU FERRIS WHEEL	SUZHOU, CHINA	2009	394	120
=	MELBOURNE STAR	DOCKLANDS, AUSTRALIA	2008	394	120
=	TIANJIN EYE	TIANJIN, CHINA	2008	394	120
=	CHANGSHA FERRIS WHEEL	CHANGSHA, CHINA	2004	394	120
=	ZHENGZHOU FERRIS WHEEL	HENAN, CHINA	2003	394	120

TOP 10

MOST POPULAR WATER PARKS

Have you visited any of these water parks? They attract more than a million people each year...

	WATER PARK	LOCATION	AVERAGE ANNUAL ATTENDANCE
1	CHIMELONG WATER PARK	GUANGZHOU, CHINA	2.26 MILLION
2	TYPHOON LAGOON (WALT DISNEY WORLD)	FLORIDA	2.19 MILLION
3	BLIZZARD BEACH (WALT DISNEY WORLD)	FLORIDA	2.01 MILLION
4	THERMAS DOS LARANJAIS	OLÍMPIA, BRAZIL	1.94 MILLION
5	OCEAN WORLD	GANGWON-DO, SOUTH KOREA	1.60 MILLION
6	AQUATICA	FLORIDA	1.57 MILLION
7	CARIBBEAN BAY (EVERLAND RESORT)	GYEONGGI-DO, SOUTH KOREA	1.49 MILLION
8	AQUAVENTURE	DUBAI, UNITED ARAB EMIRATES	1.4 MILLION
9	HOT PARK RIO QUENTE	CALDAS NOVAS, BRAZIL	1.29 MILLION
10	WET 'N' WILD ORLANDO	FLORIDA	1.28 MILLION

AQUATICA

6

This water park includes two wave pools and 14 different slides, rides, and areas. There's also an 80,000-square foot (7,432-m²) artificial beach.

Wet 'n' Wild Orlando's total water slides:

17

CHIMELONG WATER PARK

1

This water park has been operational for more than ten years. Its neighboring Chimelong Safari Park became home to giant panda cubs in 2014. Nearby, the main Chimelong Paradise Park offers five roller coasters.

LEVIATHAN

10 A ride lasting 3 minutes 28 seconds, Leviathan has a drop height of 306 feet (93 m). Although it was the sixth Canadian roller coaster to be constructed, it's the country's fastest and tallest.

Superman: Escape From Krypton roller coaster height:

415 FEET

KINGDA KA

2 This roller coaster can carry 1,400 riders every hour, at speeds of 128 mph (206 kph). It opened May 21, 2005.

TOP 10

FASTEST ROLLER COASTERS

For those of you who go on rides for the acceleration, these are the 10 you should seek out...

	ROLLER COASTER	LOCATION	TOP SPEED (MPH)	(KPH)
1	FORMULA ROSSA	FERRARI WORLD (UNITED ARAB EMIRATES)	149.1	240
2	KINGDA KA	SIX FLAGS GREAT ADVENTURE (USA)	128	206
3	TOP THRILL DRAGSTER	CEDAR POINT (USA)	120	193.1
4	DODONPA	FUJI-Q HIGHLAND (JAPAN)	106.9	172
5	SUPERMAN: ESCAPE FROM KRYPTON	SIX FLAGS MAGIC MOUNTAIN (USA)	100.8	162.2
6	TOWER OF TERROR II	DREAMWORLD (AUSTRALIA)	100	160.9
7	STEEL DRAGON 2000	NAGASHIMA SPA LAND (JAPAN)	95	152.9
=	FURY 325	CAROWINDS (USA)	95	152.9
9	MILLENNIUM FORCE	CEDAR POINT (USA)	93	149.7
10	LEVIATHAN	CANADA'S WONDERLAND (CANADA)	92	148.1

TOP 10

BIGGEST **MOVIE SCREENS** EVER

From temporary screens used for film events to permanent IMAX theaters, this top 10 has the places film fans wish they could go...

	CINEMA SCREEN	LOCATION	TOTAL AREA (FT²)	(M²)
1	LOVELL RADIO TELESCOPE*	CHESHIRE, UK	49,087	4,560.37
2	NOKIA N8*	MALMÖ, SWEDEN	15,371	1,428
3	PINEWOOD STUDIOS*	MIDDLESEX, UK	14,399	1,337.73
4	IMAX DARLING HARBOUR	SYDNEY, AUSTRALIA	11,369	1,056.24
5	IMAX MELBOURNE	MELBOURNE, AUSTRALIA	7,922.2	736
6	OSLO SPEKTRUM*	OSLO, NORWAY	7,276.4	676
7	TOKYO DOME	TOKYO, JAPAN	6,964.2	647
8	MEYDAN IMAX	DUBAI, UNITED ARAB EMIRATES	6,867.4	638
=	PRASADS IMAX	HYDERABAD, INDIA	6,867.4	638
10	KRUNGSRI IMAX	BANGKOK, THAILAND	6,329.2	588

Temporary screen erected for one-night event

TOP 5 BIGGEST IMAX SCREENS

Proving that IMAXs come in very different sizes...

IMAX DARLING HARBOUR 11,369 FT.

IMAX MELBOURNE 7,922.2 FT.

MEYDAN IMAX 6,867.4 FT.

PRASADS IMAX 6,867.4 FT.

KRUNGSRI IMAX 6,329.2 FT.

Total IMAX movie screens in the world: **1,000**

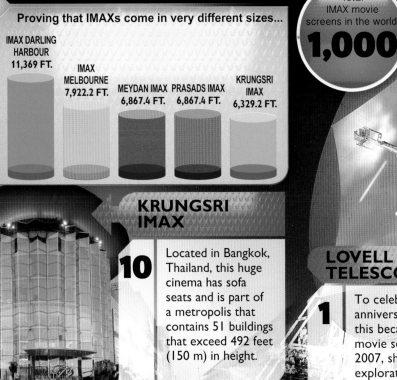

KRUNGSRI IMAX

10 Located in Bangkok, Thailand, this huge cinema has sofa seats and is part of a metropolis that contains 51 buildings that exceed 492 feet (150 m) in height.

LOVELL RADIO TELESCOPE

1 To celebrate the 50th anniversary of the telescope, this became a temporary movie screen on October 5, 2007, showing astronomy and exploration films.

Preparation to construct Baku Crystal Hall began

AUGUST 2, 2011

SMART ARANETA COLISEUM

6 This huge arena is appropriately known as "The Big Dome." Although mainly home to basketball events, the 56-year-old venue also hosts music and religious events.

TOP 10

LARGEST INDOOR ARENAS

From rock and pop events to world-class sports championships, these arenas have hosted them all...

	NAME	LOCATION	CAPACITY CROWD
1	PHILIPPINE ARENA	BOCAUE, PHILIPPINES	55,000
2	SAITAMA SUPER ARENA	SAITAMA, JAPAN	37,000
3	OLIMPIYSKIY	MOSCOW, RUSSIA	35,000
4	GWANGMYEONG VELODROME	GWANGMYEONG, SOUTH KOREA	30,000
5	TELENOR ARENA	BÆRUM, NORWAY	26,000
6	KOMBANK ARENA	BELGRADE, SERBIA	25,000
=	MINEIRINHO	BELO HORIZONTE, BRAZIL	25,000
=	SMART ARANETA COLISEUM	QUEZON CITY, PHILIPPINES	25,000
=	BAKU CRYSTAL HALL	BAKU, AZERBAIJAN	25,000
=	SCC PETERBURGSKIY	ST. PETERSBURG, RUSSIA	25,000

SAITAMA SUPER ARENA

2 This Japanese arena was also the home to the official John Lennon Museum (2000–10). It featured a vast collection of personal items owned by Lennon's widow, artist Yoko Ono.

BIGGEST STADIUMS

TOP 10

When the demand for an event can fill the biggest
arena a few times over, it's time to relocate a stadium...

	NAME	LOCATION	CAPACITY CROWD
1	RUNGRADO 1ST OF MAY STADIUM	PYONGYANG (NORTH KOREA)	150,000
2	MICHIGAN STADIUM	MICHIGAN	107,601
3	BEAVER STADIUM	PENNSYLVANIA	107,572
4	OHIO STADIUM	OHIO	104,944
5	KYLE FIELD	TEXAS	102,512
6	NEYLAND STADIUM	TENNESSEE	102,455
7	TIGER STADIUM	LOUISIANA	102,321
8	BRYANT-DENNY STADIUM	ALABAMA	101,821
9	DARRELL K. ROYAL-TEXAS MEMORIAL STADIUM	TEXAS	100,119
10	MELBOURNE CRICKET GROUND	MELBOURNE, AUSTRALIA	100,024

BEAVER STADIU

3 This stadium isn't nam
after a team, but after
Pennsylvania governo
James A. Beaver
(1837–1914).

MELBOURNE CRICKET GROUND

10 This has been the home
of the world-famous
MCC (Melbourne
Cricket Club) since the
first match was played
on September 30, 1854.

Louisiana's
Tiger Stadium
first opened in

1924

Taiwan's National Palace Museum total exhibits:

696,344

LOUVRE

1 The Louvre is home to more than 35,000 antiquities and works of art, including those of Greek, Egyptian, Islamic, and Roman origins. It first opened on August 10, 1793. It has housed the *Mona Lisa* since 1797.

TOP 10

MOST POPULAR ART GALLERIES

Cities all over the world have galleries that are home to some of the most important works of art ever created...

NAME	LOCATION	ANNUAL VISITORS (AVERAGE)
1 LOUVRE	PARIS, FRANCE	9.3 MILLION
2 BRITISH MUSEUM	LONDON, UK	6.7 MILLION
3 NATIONAL GALLERY	LONDON, UK	6.4 MILLION
4 METROPOLITAN MUSEUM OF ART	NEW YORK CITY, USA	6.2 MILLION
5 VATICAN MUSEUMS	VATICAN CITY, VATICAN CITY	5.9 MILLION
6 TATE MODERN	LONDON, UK	5.8 MILLION
7 NATIONAL PALACE MUSEUM	TAIPEI, TAIWAN	5.4 MILLION
8 NATIONAL GALLERY OF ART	WASHINGTON, D.C., USA	4.1 MILLION
9 MUSÉE NATIONAL D'ART MODERNE	PARIS, FRANCE	3.7 MILLION
10 MUSÉE D'ORSAY	PARIS, FRANCE	3.5 MILLION

BRITISH MUSEUM

2 With more than eight million pieces, including the Rosetta Stone, London's British Museum has been open to the public for more than 250 years.

DISPLAYING THE DIFFERENCE

Attendance is similar between the top 5...

LOUVRE
9.3 MILLION

BRITISH MUSEUM
6.7 MILLION

NATIONAL GALLERY
6.4 MILLION

METROPOLITAN MUSEUM OF ART
6.2 MILLION

VATICAN MUSEUMS
5.9 MILLION

VATICAN MUSEUMS

2 Located in Vatican City (officially the smallest country in the world), there are 54 galleries inside the complex.

CAPITOLINE MUSEUMS

1 In the Capitoline's square, you will find a replica of the museum's statue of Marcus Aurelius, the Roman Emperor.

By request, visitors could view the Uffizi Gallery's contents as early as **1591**

TOP 10

OLDEST OPERATIONAL MUSEUMS

These museums, still open to the public today, have been functioning for hundreds of years...

	NAME	LOCATION	YEAR OFFICIALLY OPENED TO THE PUBLIC
1	CAPITOLINE MUSEUMS	ROME, ITALY	1471
2	VATICAN MUSEUMS	VATICAN CITY	1506
3	ROYAL ARMOURIES, THE TOWER OF LONDON	LONDON, UK	1660
4	KUNSTMUSEUM BASEL (FORMERLY AMERBACH CABINET)	BASEL, SWITZERLAND	1671
5	MUSÉE DES BEAUX-ARTS ET D'ARCHÉOLOGIE DE BESANÇON	BESANÇON, FRANCE	1694
6	KUNSTKAMERA	ST. PETERSBURG, RUSSIA	1727
7	BRITISH MUSEUM	LONDON, UK	1759
8	UFFIZI GALLERY	FLORENCE, ITALY	1769
9	MUSEUM OF THE HISTORY OF RIGA AND NAVIGATION	RIGA, LATVIA	1773
=	TEYLERS MUSEUM	HAARLEM, NETHERLANDS	1784

NIKOLAI ANDRIANOV

3 During his long career, the Russian gymnast won a total of 21 gold, 19 silver, and 5 bronze medals from all of the international events he competed in.

TOP 10

MOST SUCCESSFUL OLYMPIANS

Tallying up the medal winners from the 1896 to 2015 Olympics, these are the 10 biggest winners...

	NAME	DISCIPLINE	COUNTRY	YEARS	GOLD	SILVER	BRONZE	TOTAL
1	MICHAEL PHELPS	SWIMMING	USA	2004–12	18	2	2	22
2	LARISA LATYNINA	GYMNASTICS	SOVIET UNION (NOW RUSSIA)	1956–64	9	5	4	18
3	NIKOLAI ANDRIANOV	GYMNASTICS	SOVIET UNION (NOW RUSSIA)	1972–80	7	5	3	15
4	OLE EINAR BJØRNDALEN	BIATHLON	NORWAY	1998–2014	8	4	1	13
5	BORIS SHAKHLIN	GYMNASTICS	SOVIET UNION (NOW RUSSIA)	1956–64	7	4	2	13
6	EDOARDO MANGIAROTTI	FENCING	ITALY	1936–60	6	5	2	13
7	TAKASHI ONO	GYMNASTICS	JAPAN	1952–64	5	4	4	13
8	PAAVO NURMI	ATHLETICS	FINLAND	1920–28	9	3	0	12
9	BJØRN DÆHLIE	CROSS-COUNTRY SKIING	NORWAY	1992–98	8	4	0	12
=	BIRGIT FISCHER	CANOEING	GERMANY	1980–2004	8	4	0	12

MICHAEL PHELPS

1 Born in Baltimore, Maryland, on June 30, 1985, swimmer Phelps competes in these events: butterfly, backstroke, freestyle, and individual medley.

Norwegian skiing legend Bjørn Dæhlie was born on

JUNE 19, 1967

OLE EINAR BJØRNDALEN

4 The "King of Biathlon" (combining cross-country skiing and rifle shooting) is the most successful athlete of this sport, with 135 career medals to date.

SALT LAKE 2002

HEINZ FREI

2 The 58-year-old athlete has been crowned Swiss Sportsperson of the Year ten times. He has also won 112 wheelchair marathons all over the world.

RAGNHILD MYKLEBUST

4 Her 27 Paralympic medals were won in ice sled speed racing, biathlon, and cross-country skiing (where she picked up 16 gold medals).

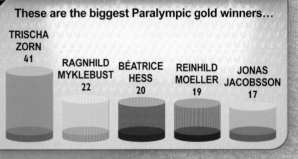

TOP 5 BY GOLD MEDALS

These are the biggest Paralympic gold winners…

| TRISCHA ZORN 41 | RAGNHILD MYKLEBUST 22 | BÉATRICE HESS 20 | REINHILD MOELLER 19 | JONAS JACOBSSON 17 |

Ragnhild Myklebust competed at **5** Winter Paralympics

MOST SUCCESSFUL PARALYMPIANS

Fifty-five years since the first Paralympic Games were held, these are the greatest champions…

	NAME	DISCIPLINE(S)	COUNTRY	YEARS	GOLD	SILVER	BRONZE	TOTAL
1	TRISCHA ZORN	SWIMMING	USA	1980–2004	41	9	5	55
2	HEINZ FREI	ATHLETICS, CYCLING, CROSS-COUNTRY SKIING	SWITZERLAND	1984–2000	14	6	11	31
3	JONAS JACOBSSON	SHOOTING	SWEDEN	1980–2012	17	4	9	30
4	RAGNHILD MYKLEBUST	BIATHLON, CROSS-COUNTRY SKIING, ICE SLED RACING	NORWAY	1988–2002	22	3	2	27
5	ROBERTO MARSON	ATHLETICS, FENCING	ITALY	1964–76	16	7	3	26
6	BÉATRICE HESS	SWIMMING	FRANCE	1984–2004	20	5	0	25
7	CLAUDIA HENGST	SWIMMING	GERMANY	1988–2004	13	4	8	25
8	FRANK HÖFLE	BIATHLON, CROSS-COUNTRY SKIING, CYCLING	GERMANY	1992–2002	14	5	5	24
9	REINHILD MOELLER	ALPINE SKIING, ATHLETICS	GERMANY	1980–2006	19	3	1	23
10	MATTHEW COWDREY	SWIMMING	AUSTRALIA	2004–12	13	7	3	23

FRANCE

5 The disciplines that have garnered France the most medals at Olympic Games are fencing (115), cycling (90), alpine skiing (45), and biathlon (21).

TOP 10

MOST SUCCESSFUL OLYMPIC NATIONS

Combining wins from the Olympic Games up to 2015, these countries scored the most medals...

	COUNTRY/TEAM	TOTAL SUMMER GAMES MEDALS	TOTAL WINTER GAMES MEDALS	TOTAL MEDALS
1	USA	2,399	281	2,680
2	RUSSIA (+ SOVIET UNION ERA)	1,407	318	1,725
3	GERMANY (+ EAST & WEST ERA)	1,186	358	1,544
4	UK	780	26	806
5	FRANCE	671	109	780
6	ITALY	549	114	663
7	SWEDEN	483	144	627
8	CHINA	473	53	526
9	HUNGARY	476	6	482
10	AUSTRALIA	468	12	480

SWEDEN

7 Swedish competitors excel the most at athletics, wrestling, and cross-country skiing, in which a total of 239 medals have been won since the 1896 games.

Hungary has competed at

47

Olympic Games

USA has won **96** gold medals from **11** Winter Paralympics

SPAIN

8 Spain has competed at every Paralympics except for the 1960 and 1965 Summer Games and the 1976 and 1980 Winter Games.

CANADA

4 Founded in 1981, nonprofit organization the CPC (Canadian Paralympic Committee) represents 43 sports organizations.

TOP 10

MOST SUCCESSFUL PARALYMPIC NATIONS

These are the countries that triumphed the most at the 1960–2015 Paralympic Games...

	COUNTRY/TEAM	TOTAL SUMMER GAMES MEDALS	TOTAL WINTER GAMES MEDALS	TOTAL MEDALS
1	USA	1,939	277	2,216
2	GERMANY (+ EAST & WEST ERA)	1,327	345	1,672
3	UK	1,557	21	1,578
4	CANADA	947	135	1,082
5	FRANCE	921	152	1,073
6	AUSTRALIA	1,013	30	1,043
7	CHINA	794	0	794
8	SPAIN	630	43	673
9	POLAND	626	44	670
10	SWEDEN	564	99	663

LONDON 1908

4 It was the longest Olympic Games in history, at 187 days. Of the 2,008 athletes involved, only 37 were women. Still, that was more than had appeared in any prior modern Olympics. Women had been banned from the 1896 Games.

FIRST 10 OLYMPICS

TOP 10

Counting from the first modern Olympic Games, these were the first 10 with the new motto "swifter, higher, stronger"...

	HOST CITY	COUNTRY	OFFICIAL NAME	HELD	YEAR
1	ATHENS	GREECE	GAMES OF THE I OLYMPIAD	APRIL 6–15	1896
2	PARIS	FRANCE	GAMES OF THE II OLYMPIAD	MAY 14–OCT. 28	1900
3	ST. LOUIS	USA	GAMES OF THE III OLYMPIAD	AUG. 29–SEPT. 3	1904
4	LONDON	UK	GAMES OF THE IV OLYMPIAD	APRIL 27–OCT. 31	1908
5	STOCKHOLM	SWEDEN	GAMES OF THE V OLYMPIAD	MAY 5–JULY 22	1912
6	ANTWERP	BELGIUM	GAMES OF THE VII OLYMPIAD	AUG. 14–SEPT. 12	1920
7	CHAMONIX	FRANCE	I OLYMPIC WINTER GAMES	JAN. 25–FEB. 5	1924
8	PARIS	FRANCE	GAMES OF THE VIII OLYMPIAD	MAY 4–JULY 27	1924
9	ST. MORITZ	SWITZERLAND	II OLYMPIC WINTER GAMES	FEB. 11–19	1928
10	AMSTERDAM	NETHERLANDS	GAMES OF THE IX OLYMPIAD	JULY 28–AUG 12	1928

ANTWERP 1920

6 USA triumphed at the 1920 Games, winning a total of 95 medals, including 41 gold. Sweden came second with 64, of which 19 were gold.

Due to the outbreak of World War I, the **1916** Olympics were cancelled

180

TOKYO 1964

2 These Paralympic Games included 375 athletes from 21 different nations. In 2020 Tokyo will become the first country to host the Summer Paralympics twice.

USA/UK 1984

10 The 1984 Summer Paralympics, held across the U.S. and the UK, involved 18 different sports, including snooker and fencing.

Total athletes at Geilo, Norway's 1980 event:

299

TOP 10

FIRST 10 PARALYMPICS

Since the Paralympics began in 1960, these were the first cities ever to host the Games...

	HOST CITY	COUNTRY	SEASON	HELD	YEAR
1	ROME	ITALY	SUMMER	SEPT. 18–25	**1960**
2	TOKYO	JAPAN	SUMMER	NOV. 3–12	**1964**
3	TEL AVIV	ISRAEL	SUMMER	NOV. 4–13	**1968**
4	HEIDELBERG	(W) GERMANY	SUMMER	AUGUST 2–11	**1972**
5	ÖRNSKÖLDSVIK	SWEDEN	WINTER	FEB. 21–28	**1976**
6	TORONTO	CANADA	SUMMER	AUGUST 3–11	**1976**
7	GEILO	NORWAY	WINTER	FEB. 1–7	**1980**
8	ARNHEM	NETHERLANDS	SUMMER	JUNE 21–30	**1980**
9	INNSBRUCK	AUSTRIA	WINTER	JAN. 14–20	**1984**
10	NEW YORK/STOKE MANDEVILLE	USA/UK	SUMMER	JUN. 17–30/JUL. 22–AUG. 1	**1984**

RIO DE JANEIRO

1 Held between August 5 and 21, 2016, these were the 31st Summer Olympics. Rio de Janeiro was officially announced as the host city on October 2, 2009.

The 2012 Olympics in London, England, had **10,768** athletes

TOP 10

10 MOST RECENT OLYMPICS

Including Summer and Winter Games, these Olympics from the past two decades saw numerous records broken...

	HOST CITY	COUNTRY	OFFICIAL NAME	HELD	YEAR
1	RIO DE JANEIRO	BRAZIL	GAMES OF THE XXXI OLYMPIAD	AUGUST 5–21	**2016**
2	SOCHI	RUSSIA	XXII OLYMPIC WINTER GAMES	FEBRUARY 7–23	**2014**
3	LONDON	UK	GAMES OF THE XXX OLYMPIAD	JULY 27–AUG. 12	**2012**
4	VANCOUVER	CANADA	XXI OLYMPIC WINTER GAMES	FEBRUARY 12–28	**2010**
5	BEIJING	CHINA	GAMES OF THE XXIX OLYMPIAD	AUGUST 8–24	**2008**
6	TURIN	ITALY	XX OLYMPIC WINTER GAMES	FEBRUARY 10–26	**2006**
7	ATHENS	GREECE	GAMES OF THE XXVIII OLYMPIAD	AUGUST 13–29	**2004**
8	SALT LAKE CITY	USA	XIX OLYMPIC WINTER GAMES	FEBRUARY 8–24	**2002**
9	SYDNEY	AUSTRALIA	GAMES OF THE XXVII OLYMPIAD	SEPT. 15–OCT. 1	**2000**
10	NAGANO	JAPAN	XVIII OLYMPIC WINTER GAMES	FEBRUARY 7–22	**1998**

SOCHI

2 Nearly 3,000 athletes took part in these Winter Olympics across 98 different events. The city of Sochi has around 344,000 residents.

RIO DE JANEIRO

1 The swirling orange and yellow logo of the 2016 Summer Paralympics was revealed on November 26, 2011, nearly five years before the Games.

TOP 10

10 MOST RECENT PARALYMPICS

These were the past ten Paralympic Games, where dreams were achieved (and some were dashed)...

	HOST CITY	COUNTRY	OFFICIAL NAME	HELD	YEAR
1	RIO DE JANEIRO	BRAZIL	XV PARALYMPIC GAMES	SEPT. 7–18	2016
2	SOCHI	RUSSIA	XI PARALYMPIC WINTER GAMES	MARCH 7–16	2014
3	LONDON	UK	XIV PARALYMPIC GAMES	AUG. 29–SEPT. 9	2012
4	VANCOUVER	CANADA	X PARALYMPIC WINTER GAMES	MARCH 12–21	2010
5	BEIJING	CHINA	XIII PARALYMPIC GAMES	SEPT. 6–17	2008
6	TURIN	ITALY	IX PARALYMPIC WINTER GAMES	MARCH 10–19	2006
7	ATHENS	GREECE	XII PARALYMPIC GAMES	SEPT. 17–28	2004
8	SALT LAKE CITY	USA	VIII PARALYMPIC WINTER GAMES	MARCH 7–16	2002
9	SYDNEY	AUSTRALIA	XI PARALYMPIC GAMES	OCT. 18–29	2000
10	NAGANO	JAPAN	VII PARALYMPIC WINTER GAMES	MARCH 5–14	1998

VANCOUVER

4 In 2010 there were 506 athletes from 44 countries. The main stadium was B.C. Place in False Creek, which opened in 1983.

The 1998 Paralympic Winter Games in Nagano, Japan, featured

122

events

183

GRAPH OF OLYMPIC COSTS

Here's how the 5 most expensive compare visually...

SOCHI
$51 BILLION

BEIJING
$44 BILLION

LONDON
$14.6 BILLION

RIO
$9.82 BILLION

BARCELONA
$9.3 BILLION

SOCHI

1

These Winter Games in 2014 featured 98 events, compared to Moscow's 203 in its 1980 Summer Games.

The 2008 Olympics in Beijing, China, featured

28

different sporting disciplines

MOST EXPENSIVE OLYMPICS

TOP 10

Being a host nation is a prestigious event, but it also comes with a massive price tag...

	HOST CITY	COUNTRY	YEAR	EST. TOTAL BUDGET ($ BILLIONS)
1	SOCHI	RUSSIA	2014	51
2	BEIJING	CHINA	2008	44
3	LONDON	UNITED KINGDOM	2012	14.6
4	RIO DE JANEIRO	BRAZIL	2016	9.82
5	BARCELONA	SPAIN	1992	9.3
6	ATHENS	GREECE	2004	9
7	SYDNEY	AUSTRALIA	2000	6.6
8	VANCOUVER	CANADA	2010	6.4
9	MOSCOW	SOVIET UNION (NOW RUSSIA)	1980	1.35
10	SALT LAKE CITY	UNITED STATES	2002	1.2

BEIJING

2

At this 2008 Summer Olympics, 43 world records were achieved. China won the most gold medals at the games, 51 in total.

TOP 10

MOST HOSTED OLYMPIC & PARALYMPIC NATIONS

These countries have hosted Games more than any others...

COUNTRY	TOTAL TIMES OLYMPIC & PARALYMPIC GAMES
1	UNITED STATES	11
2	FRANCE	6
3	CANADA	5
=	ITALY	5
=	JAPAN	5
=	UNITED KINGDOM	5
7	AUSTRIA	4
=	GERMANY	4
=	GREECE	4
=	NORWAY	4

FRANCE

2 France hosted Games in 1900 (Summer Olympics), 1924 (Summer and Winter Olympics), 1968 (Winter Olympics), and 1992 (Winter Olympics and Winter Paralympics).

France's total medals from all the Paralympic Games (before Rio 2016):

1,148

BRAZIL 2016

Rio de Janeiro's Summer Olympics was the first held by a South American country. The Organizing Committee President (right) launched the Torch Relay in January 2016.

185

Florence Griffith Joyner's 100 m record has remained unbeaten for more than

28
years

CHRISTINE ARRON

5

Now retired, the French runner achieved the 4 x 100 m relay gold medal at the 2003 World Championships in Athletics held in Paris.

KERRON STEWART

7

Born in Kingston, the capital of Jamaica, Stewart has amassed 26 career medals. Her three world championship golds include the 4 x 100 m relay at Beijing in 2015.

TOP 10

FASTEST 100 m FEMALE SPRINTERS

This chart reveals the 10 fastest women of all time, plus their average speed...

	NAME	COUNTRY	YEAR	TIME (SECS)	AVERAGE SPEED (MPH)	(KPH)
1	FLORENCE GRIFFITH JOYNER	USA	1988	10.49	21.32	34.31
2	CARMELITA JETER	USA	2009	10.64	21.02	33.83
3	MARION JONES	USA	1998	10.65	21.00	33.80
4	SHELLY-ANN FRASER-PRYCE	JAMAICA	2012	10.70	20.91	33.65
5	CHRISTINE ARRON	FRANCE	1998	10.73	20.85	33.56
6	MERLENE OTTEY	JAMAICA	1996	10.74	20.83	33.52
7	KERRON STEWART	JAMAICA	2009	10.75	20.81	33.49
8	EVELYN ASHFORD	USA	1984	10.76	20.79	33.46
=	VERONICA CAMPBELL-BROWN	JAMAICA	2011	10.76	20.79	33.46
10	IRINA PRIVALOVA/IVET LALOVA-COLLIO	RUSSIA/BULGARIA	1994/2004	10.77	33.43	20.77

JUSTIN GATLIN

5 The 34-year-old Gatlin achieved his new personal best in the chart below at the Qatar Athletic Super Grand Prix on May 15, 2015.

Usain Bolt, the fastest man on Earth, is **6 FT. 5 IN.** tall

TOP 10

FASTEST 100 M MALE SPRINTERS

Think about how fast it feels to travel 30 mph (48 kph) in a car, and then have a look at how fast these men can move...

	NAME	COUNTRY	YEAR	TIME (SECS)	AVERAGE SPEED (MPH)	(KPH)
1	USAIN BOLT	JAMAICA	2009	9.58	23.35	37.58
2	TYSON GAY	USA	2009	9.69	23.08	37.14
=	YOHAN BLAKE	JAMAICA	2012	9.69	23.08	37.14
▶ 4	ASAFA POWELL	JAMAICA	2008	9.72	23.01	37.03
▶ 5	JUSTIN GATLIN	USA	2014	9.74	22.90	36.85
6	NESTA CARTER	JAMAICA	2010	9.78	22.87	36.81
7	MAURICE GREENE	USA	1999	9.79	22.85	36.77
8	STEVE MULLINGS	JAMAICA	2011	9.80	22.83	36.74
9	RICHARD THOMPSON	TRINIDAD AND TOBAGO	2014	9.82	22.78	36.66
10	DONOVAN BAILEY/BRUNY SURIN/TRAYVON BROMWELL	CANADA/CANADA/USA	1996/1999/2015	9.84	22.73	36.58

ASAFA POWELL

4 Although he is currently the fourth-fastest man on Earth, Powell held the world record for the 100 m for nearly three years between 2005 and 2008.

SPEED MASTERS

FLORENCE GRIFFITH JOYNER

1 Flo-Jo's career included four gold and three silver medals, won between 1984 and 1987. She sadly passed away in her sleep on September 21, 1998.

JARMILA KRATOCHVÍLOVÁ

4 The Czech athlete's world record for the 800 m has not been bested in 33 years. Between 1980 and 1983, Kratochvílová won five gold medals in 400 m and 800 m.

TOP 10

QUICKEST SPORTSWOMEN

Focusing on 10 sports that require explosive bursts of acceleration, these are their 10 fastest women...

	SPORT	DISTANCE	FASTEST PERSON	COUNTRY	YEAR	TIME	AVERAGE SPEED (MPH)	(KPH)
1	RUNNING	100 M	FLORENCE GRIFFITH JOYNER	USA	1988	0:10.49	21.32	34.32
2	RUNNING	200 M	FLORENCE GRIFFITH JOYNER	USA	1988	0:21.34	20.96	33.74
3	RUNNING	400 M	MARITA KOCH	GERMANY	1985	0:47.60	18.8	30.25
4	RUNNING	800 M	JARMILA KRATOCHVÍLOVÁ	CZECH REPUBLIC	1983	1:53.28	15.8	25.42
5	SWIMMING: FREESTYLE	50 M	RANOMI KROMOWIDJOJO	NETHERLANDS	2013	0:23.24	4.81	7.74
6	SWIMMING: BUTTERFLY	50 M	THERESE ALSHAMMAR	SWEDEN	2009	0:24.38	4.59	7.39
7	SWIMMING: FREESTYLE	100 M	LIBBY TRICKETT	AUSTRALIA	2009	0:51.01	4.39	7.07
8	SWIMMING: BACKSTROKE	50 M	ETIENE MEDEIROS	BRAZIL	2014	0:25.67	4.36	7.02
9	SWIMMING: BUTTERFLY	100 M	SARAH SJÖSTRÖM	SWEDEN	2014	0:54.61	4.1	6.59
10	SWIMMING: FREESTYLE	200 M	SARAH SJÖSTRÖM	SWEDEN	2014	1:50.78	4.04	6.5

5 to 10 performed in Short Course (25-m/82-ft.) pools

LIBBY TRICKETT

7 The world record-holder in 100 m freestyle picked up her first international individual medal, a bronze, at the 2003 World Championships.

Therese Alshammar was born

AUGUST 26, 1977

TATYANA MCFADDEN

3

Russian-born USA athlete Tatyana McFadden, 27, won three gold medals at the Summer Olympics in 2012.

QUICKEST FEMALE PARALYMPIANS

This is not a definitive Top 10 because comparing the different disability classes is unfair. This chart merely shows the fastest speeds in each sprint event...

	SPORT	DISTANCE	FASTEST PERSON	CLASS	COUNTRY	YEAR	TIME	AVERAGE SPEED (MPH)	(KPH)
1	**RUNNING**	100 M	OMARA DURAND	T12	CUBA	2015	**0:11.65**	**19.62**	**31.58**
2	**RUNNING**	200 M	OMARA DURAND	T13	CUBA	2015	**0:23.67**	**18.9**	**30.42**
3	**RUNNING**	800 M	TATYANA MCFADDEN	T54	USA	2015	**1:42.72**	**17.42**	**28.03**
4	**RUNNING**	400 M	TATYANA MCFADDEN	T54	USA	2015	**0:51.90**	**17.24**	**27.75**
5	**SWIMMING: FREESTYLE**	50 M	OXANA SAVCHENKO	S12	RUSSIA	2009	**0:26.54**	**4.21**	**6.78**
6	**SWIMMING: BUTTERFLY**	50 M	SOPHIE PASCOE	S10	NEW ZEALAND	2013	**0:29.08**	**3.85**	**6.19**
7	**SWIMMING: FREESTYLE**	100 M	OXANA SAVCHENKO	S12	RUSSIA	2009	**0:58.60**	**3.82**	**6.14**
8	**SWIMMING: BACKSTROKE**	50 M	SOPHIE PASCOE	S10	NEW ZEALAND	2013	**0:30.49**	**3.67**	**5.9**
9	**SWIMMING: FREESTYLE**	200 M	VALÉRIE GRAND'MAISON	S13	CANADA	2008	**2:08.53**	**3.48**	**5.6**
10	**SWIMMING: BUTTERFLY**	100 M	JOANNA MENDAK	S12	POLAND	2009	**1:05.10**	**3.44**	**5.53**

5 to 10 performed in Short Course (25-m/82-ft.) pools

Joanna Mendak's total Paralympics Games' medals:

6

QUICKEST COUNTRIES

Here's how the above chart looks ranked by nation...

- CUBA **2**
- USA **2**
- RUSSIA **2**
- NEW ZEALAND **2**
- CANADA **1**
- POLAND **1**

FLORENT MANAUDOU

5 The 6.5-ft. (1.96-m) tall French swimmer achieved his two world records at the 2014 FINA World Swimming Championships, held in Qatar from December 3 to 7.

MICHAEL JOHNSON

3 This sprinter achieved eight gold medals during international competitions between 1991 and 2000. These include four Olympic golds.

TOP 10

QUICKEST SPORTSMEN

These are the 10 fastest men from the sports that involve high speeds...

	SPORT	DISTANCE	FASTEST PERSON	COUNTRY	YEAR	TIME	AVERAGE SPEED (MPH)	(KPH)
1	RUNNING	100 M	USAIN BOLT	JAMAICA	2009	0:09.58	23.35	37.58
2	RUNNING	200 M	USAIN BOLT	JAMAICA	2009	0:19.19	23.31	37.52
3	RUNNING	400 M	MICHAEL JOHNSON	USA	1999	0:43.18	20.72	33.35
4	RUNNING	800 M	DAVID RUDISHA	KENYA	2012	1:40.91	17.73	28.54
5	SWIMMING: FREESTYLE	50 M	FLORENT MANAUDOU	FRANCE	2014	0:20.26	5.52	8.88
6	SWIMMING: BUTTERFLY	50 M	STEFFEN DEIBLER	GERMANY	2009	0:21.80	5.13	8.26
7	SWIMMING: BACKSTROKE	50 M	FLORENT MANAUDOU	UK	2014	0:22.22	5.03	8.1
8	SWIMMING: FREESTYLE	100 M	AMAURY LEVEAUX	FRANCE	2008	0:44.94	4.98	8.01
9	SWIMMING: BUTTERFLY	100 M	CHAD LE CLOS	SOUTH AFRICA	2014	0:48.44	4.62	7.44
10	SWIMMING: FREESTYLE	200 M	PAUL BIEDERMANN	GERMANY	2009	1:39.37	4.51	7.26

5 to 10 performed in Short Course (25-m/82-ft.) pools

Chad le Clos holds

2 world records for 100 m and 200 m butterfly

QUICKEST MALE PARALYMPIANS

Although not a definitive chart, because comparing classifications is unfair, this Top 10 reveals the fastest speeds achieved in the "sprint" sports...

	SPORT	DISTANCE	FASTEST PERSON	CLASS	COUNTRY	YEAR	TIME	AVERAGE SPEED (MPH)	(KPH)
1	RUNNING	200 M	ALAN FONTELES CARDOSO OLIVEIRA	T43	BRAZIL	2013	0:20.66	21.65	34.85
2	RUNNING	100 M	JASON SMYTH	T13	IRELAND	2012	0:10.46	21.39	34.42
3	RUNNING	400 M	LIXIN ZHANG	T54	CHINA	2008	0:45.07	19.85	31.95
4	RUNNING	800 M	MARCEL HUG	T54	SWITZERLAND	2010	1:31.12	19.64	31.61
5	SWIMMING: FREESTYLE	50 M	ANDRE BRASIL	S10	BRAZIL	2009	0:22.44	4.98	8.02
6	SWIMMING: FREESTYLE	100 M	ANDRE BRASIL	S10	BRAZIL	2009	0:48.70	4.59	7.39
7	SWIMMING: BUTTERFLY	50 M	TIMOTHY ANTALFY	S13	AUSTRALIA	2014	0:24.60	4.55	7.32
8	SWIMMING: BACKSTROKE	50 M	SEAN RUSSO	S13	AUSTRALIA	2013	0:27.30	4.1	6.59
9	SWIMMING: BUTTERFLY	100 M	ANDRE BRASIL	S10	BRAZIL	2009	0:54.76	4.08	6.57
10	SWIMMING: FREESTYLE	200 M	PHILIPPE GAGNON	S10	CANADA	2002	1:52.83	3.97	6.38

5 to 10 performed in Short Course (25-m/82-ft.) pools

LIXIN ZHANG

3 The Chinese athlete won four gold medals at the 2008 Summer Paralympics in Beijing. He won an additional gold medal at the London 2012 Paralympics.

Philippe Gagnon's total medals at the 2000 Paralympics:

4

(3 gold, 1 silver)

ALAN FONTELES CARDOSO OLIVEIRA

1 Born on August 21, 1992, Oliveira has already won four gold, four silver, and four bronze medals from Paralympic Games and world championships.

CALE YARBOROUGH

9 His career included 60 pole positions over 33 years of NASCAR competitions. His first NASCAR race was in his home state at the Bojangles Southern 500 in 1957.

Rusty Wallace's total pole positions: **36**

TOP 10

GREATEST NASCAR CHAMPIONS' TOTAL RACES

Of all the championship NASCAR events, these drivers took part in the most...

	NAME	FROM	CAREER RACES
1	RICHARD PETTY	NORTH CAROLINA	1,199
2	DARRELL WALTRIP	KENTUCKY	921
3	JEFF GORDON	CALIFORNIA	865
4	DALE EARNHARDT	NORTH CAROLINA	812
5	BOBBY ALLISON	FLORIDA	778
6	RUSTY WALLACE	MISSOURI	749
7	JIMMIE JOHNSON	CALIFORNIA	596
8	DAVID PEARSON	SOUTH CAROLINA	583
9	CALE YARBOROUGH	SOUTH CAROLINA	568
10	LEE PETTY	NORTH CAROLINA	427

DARRELL WALTRIP

2 These days, the former NASCAR champion is a broadcaster. He is Fox's lead race commentator, alongside veteran announcer Mike Joy and former NASCAR driver Jeff Gordon.

F1 CONSTRUCTOR NATIONS

Here's the below chart summarized by country...

UK
33

ITALY
16

AUSTRIA
4

FRANCE
3

GERMANY
2

Renault has been involved with F1 racing since

1977

MCLAREN

3 New Zealand engineer and car designer Bruce McLaren set up this company in 1963. Sadly, he died from a car accident in 1970 at age 32.

TOP 10

MOST SUCCESSFUL F1 CONSTRUCTORS

These are the engineering brains behind Formula One's most world championship wins...

FERRARI

1 This company began as Scuderia Ferrari in 1929. Ferrari is the only team that has participated in every F1 world championship.

	NAME	COUNTRY	TOTAL WORLD CONSTRUCTORS CHAMPIONSHIP WINS
1	FERRARI	ITALY	16
2	WILLIAMS	UK	9
3	MCLAREN	UK	8
4	LOTUS	UK	7
5	RED BULL	AUSTRIA	4
6	COOPER	UK	2
=	BRABHAM	UK	2
=	RENAULT	FRANCE	2
=	MERCEDES	GERMANY	2
10	MATRA/VANWELL, BRM, TYRELL, BENETTON & BRAWN	FRANCE/UK	1*

* Each team at the 10th spot has won one World Constructor Championship.

MIKE HAILWOOD

4

British biking legend Mike Hailwood also achieved 79 fastest laps. In the Sixties and Seventies, he had a Formula One career and raced in 50 Grand Prix events.

CASEY STONER

10

Choosing to retire from the sport in 2012 at age 27, Stoner notched up 39 pole positions during his six-year career. Then, in 2015, the Australian decided to return to the sport.

Giacomo Agostini's wins include

68

in the 500cc class

TOP 10

GRAND PRIX MOTORCYCLE MASTERS

These are the 10 bikers who have notched up more wins than their fellow riders...

	NAME	COUNTRY	TOTAL WINS
1	GIACOMO AGOSTINI	ITALY	122
2	VALENTINO ROSSI	ITALY	112
3	ÁNGEL NIETO	SPAIN	90
4	MIKE HAILWOOD	UK	76
5	JORGE LORENZO	SPAIN	60
6	MICHAEL DOOHAN	AUSTRALIA	54
7	PHIL READ	UK	52
8	DANI PEDROSA	SPAIN	50
=	MARC MÁRQUEZ	SPAIN	50
10	CASEY STONER/JIM REDMAN	AUSTRALIA/ RHODESIA	45

GIACOMO AGOSTINI

1

Known by his nickname of "Ago," in addition to his Grand Prix wins at the top of this chart, Agostini also triumphed at 15 Motorcycle World Championships.

MOST SUCCESSFUL MOTOCROSS NATIONS

TOP 10

Off-road motorcycle racing involves high speeds, leaps, and a lot of dirt...

	COUNTRY	TOTAL WORLD CHAMPIONSHIPS MEDALS
1	BELGIUM	135
2	SWEDEN	55
3	UK	47
4	ITALY	45
5	FRANCE	43
6	NETHERLANDS	36
7	USA	25
8	GERMANY	24
9	FINLAND	14
10	CZECH REPUBLIC	12

Stefan Everts has won the most World Championships:

10

RYAN DUNGEY

By the age of 24, American Ryan Dungey had already won every title the various Motocross events had to offer. Before his 25th birthday, he notched up 146 AMA Motocross/Supercross wins.

BELGIUM

1 The popularity of Motocross means Belgium has 13 courses available for training and racing.

FIVE FARTHEST CHALLENGES

Here's how the top 5 compare graphically...

TOUR DE FRANCE 3,569.8 MILES

GREAT DIVIDE MOUNTAIN BIKE ROUTE 2,745 MILES

FREEDOM TRAIL CHALLENGE 1,460.2 MILES

ULTRAMARATHON 1,000+ MILES

YUKON QUEST 1,000 MILES

The first Yukon Quest was in **1984**

TOP 10

LONGEST ENDURANCE SPORT EVENTS

These are the sports that push human stamina to its limit and way beyond...

	NAME	EVENTS INCLUDED	TOTAL DISTANCE COVERED (MILES)	(KM)
1	TOUR DE FRANCE*	CYCLING	3,569.8**	5,745**
2	GREAT DIVIDE MOUNTAIN BIKE ROUTE	MOUNTAIN BIKING	2,745**	4,418**
3	FREEDOM TRAIL CHALLENGE	MOUNTAIN BIKING	1,460.2**	2,350**
4	ULTRAMARATHON	RUNNING, WALKING	1,000+**	1,609+**
5	YUKON QUEST	DOG SLEDDING	1,000**	1,609**
6	MONGOL DERBY	HORSE RIDING (MULTIPLE HORSES USED)	621.37	1,000
7	IRON MAN TRIATHALON	SWIMMING (2.3 MI), CYCLING (112 MI), MARATHON (26.2 MI)	140.6	226.31
8	POWERMAN ZOFINGEN DUATHALON	HILL RUN (6.2 MI), HILL CYCLE (93.2 MI), HILL RUN (18.6 MI)	118.06	190
9	CANADIAN SKI MARATHON	SKIING	99.42	160
10	QUADRATHALON	SWIMMING (42.48 MI), KAYAKING (12.4 MI), CYCLING (62.1 MI), RUNNING (13 MI)	90.1	145

*Longest ever Tour de France, staged in 1926   ** Multiday event

TOUR DE FRANCE

1

The first ever Tour de France, staged July 1 to 19, 1903, was won by Maurice-Francois Garin. The course covered 1,509 miles (2,428 km) across six stages.

ELEKTRISCHE BMW i3

WILSON KIPSANG

3 At the 2014 London Marathon, Kipsang came in first place with a new course record of 2 hours 4 minutes and 29 seconds.

TOP 10

FASTEST MALE & FEMALE MARATHON RUNNERS

These 10 men and women are the masters of endurance racing...

	NAME	GENDER	COUNTRY	YEAR	TIME	AVERAGE SPEED (MPH)	(KPH)
1	DENNIS KIPRUTO KIMETTO	MALE	KENYA	2014	2:02.57	12.79	20.58
2	EMMANUEL MUTAI	MALE	KENYA	2014	2:03.13	12.77	20.55
▶ 3	WILSON KIPSANG	MALE	KENYA	2013	2:03.23	12.75	20.52
4	PATRICK MAKAU	MALE	KENYA	2011	2:03.38	12.72	20.47
5	HAILE GEBRSELASSIE	MALE	ETHIOPIA	2008	2:03.59	12.69	20.42
▶ 6	PAULA RADCLIFFE	FEMALE	UK	2003	2:15.25	11.62	18.70
7	MARY KEITANY	FEMALE	KENYA	2012	2:18.37	11.37	18.30
8	CATHERINE NDEREBA	FEMALE	KENYA	2001	2:18.47	11.36	18.28
9	TIKI GELANA	FEMALE	ETHIOPIA	2012	2:18.58	11.35	18.27
=	MIZUKI NOGUCHI	FEMALE	JAPAN	2005	2:19.12	11.31	18.20

PAULA RADCLIFFE

6 Paula Radcliffe retired after taking part in the London Marathon on April 26, 2015. Her career medals include 15 gold.

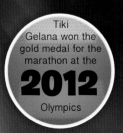

Tiki Gelana won the gold medal for the marathon at the **2012** Olympics

LONGEST LONG JUMPS

These 10 athletes have leapt the greatest distances into a soft sand landing pit...

	ATHLETE	COUNTRY	YEAR	DISTANCE (FEET)	(M)
1	MIKE POWELL	USA	1991	29.36	8.95
2	BOB BEAMON	USA	1968	29.20	8.9
3	CARL LEWIS	USA	1991	29.10	8.87
4	ROBERT EMMIYAN	USSR (NOW RUSSIA)	1987	29.06	8.86
5	LARRY MYRICKS	USA	1988	28.67	8.74
=	ERICK WALDER	USA	1994	28.67	8.74
=	DWIGHT PHILLIPS	USA	2009	28.67	8.74
8	IRVING SALADINO	PANAMA	2008	28.64	8.73
9	IVÁN PEDROSO	CUBA	1995	28.58	8.71
=	SEBASTIAN BAYER	GERMANY	2009	28.58	8.71

Irving Saladino was born on

JAN. 23, 1983

MIKE POWELL

1

His record was achieved at the World Championships in Athletics held in Tokyo, Japan, in 1991. Powell also won two silver long jump Olympic medals, in 1988 and 1992.

GALINA CHISTYAKOVA

Russian Galina Chistyakova may not be part of this Top 10, but she holds the unbeaten female long jump record. Her 24.67-foot (7.52-m) jump was achieved on June 11, 1988.

SEBASTIAN BAYER

9

Born in Aachen, Germany on June 11, 1986, Bayer landed the second-longest jump ever made in indoor competition. He has also won three European Championships.

SPORTS THAT PROPEL THE BALL THE FARTHEST

TOP 10

For all the sports where a ball is thrown or hit, these are the all-time distance records...

	SPORT	CHAMPION	COUNTRY	YEAR	DISTANCE (FEET)	(M)
1	LONG DRIVE GOLF	MIKE DOBBYN	USA	2007	1,653	503.83
2	GOLF	MIKE AUSTIN	USA	1974	1,545.3	471
3	BASEBALL (HOME RUN)	MICKEY MANTLE	USA	1960	634	193.24
4	CRICKET (HIT/SIX)	SHAHID KHAN AFRIDI	PAKISTAN	2013	518.37	158
5	BASEBALL (THROW)	GLEN GORBOUS	CANADA	1957	445.83	135.89
6	CRICKET (THROW)	ROALD BRADSTOCK	UK	2010	435.04	132.6
7	SOCCER (GOAL KICK)	ASMIR BEGOVIĆ	BOSNIA	2013	301.5	91.9
8	RUGBY	GERRY BRAND	SOUTH AFRICA	1932	254.92	77.7
9	FOOTBALL (FIELD GOAL)	CHING DO KIM	USA	1944	234	71.32
10	SOCCER (THROW IN)	THOMAS GRONNEMARK	DENMARK	2010	168.4	51.33

MIKE DOBBYN

1 This American Long Drive Golf competitor is 6.7 feet (2.01 m) tall. The World Long Drive Championship has been held annually since 1975.

ASMIR BEGOVIĆ

7 Born in Bosnia and Herzegovina, Begović scored his recording-breaking goal during a match between the UK teams Southampton FC and Stoke City (for whom he played 2010–15).

Mickey Mantle's total home runs:

536

199

Paris Saint-Germain FC has been a soccer club for more than **46** years

MOST POPULAR TEAMS ON FACEBOOK

In terms of "Likes," these are the sports teams that have the most fans...

FC BARCELONA

1 Its stadium, Camp Nou, can hold 99,354 people. Lionel Messi holds several records for the club, including the most goals scored at 447.

	TEAM	SPORT	"LIKES" (MILLIONS)
1	FC BARCELONA	SOCCER	87.3
2	REAL MADRID CF	SOCCER	84.8
3	MANCHESTER UNITED FC	SOCCER	66.7
4	CHELSEA FC	SOCCER	43.7
5	ARSENAL FC	SOCCER	33.7
6	FC BAYERN MÜNCHEN	SOCCER	32.7
7	LIVERPOOL FC	SOCCER	26.4
8	AC MILAN	SOCCER	24.5
9	PARIS SAINT-GERMAIN FC	SOCCER	21.3
10	LA LAKERS	BASKETBALL	21.2

FIVE SOCCER GIANTS

Here's how the top 5 compare visually...

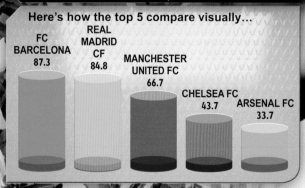

FC BARCELONA 87.3

REAL MADRID CF 84.8

MANCHESTER UNITED FC 66.7

CHELSEA FC 43.7

ARSENAL FC 33.7

LA LAKERS

10 The LA Lakers team has won the most consecutive games. The 33 wins took place between November 5, 1971 and January 9, 1972.

TOP 10

MOST POPULAR TEAMS ON TWITTER

On the social media micro-blog platform, these teams have the most followers...

	TEAM	SPORT	FOLLOWERS (MILLIONS)
1	REAL MADRID CF	SOCCER	17.3
2	FC BARCELONA	SOCCER	16.1
3	ARSENAL FC	SOCCER	6.4
4	MANCHESTER UNITED FC	SOCCER	6.2
5	CHELSEA FC	SOCCER	6.1
6	LIVERPOOL FC	SOCCER	4.9
7	LA LAKERS	BASKETBALL	4.5
8	MIAMI HEAT	BASKETBALL	3.1
9	AC MILAN	SOCCER	2.9
10	MANCHESTER CITY FC	SOCCER	2.7

MIAMI HEAT

8 Founded in 1988, the team got its current coach Erik Spoelstra in 2008. He is the sixth the team has had.

ARSENAL FC

3 This British soccer team dates back 130 years to 1886. Its global fanbase means Arsenal is valued at more than $1 billion. Its Emirates Stadium home has 152 executive suites.

Real Madrid CF was founded more than a century ago on **MARCH 6, 1902**

201

MUSIC

ZONE **8**

TOP 10

MOST DOWNLOADED SONGS EVER

Digital music sales have been the main contributor to the overall success of singles and albums for more than a decade...

	ARTIST(S)	SONG	YEAR RELEASED	TOTAL DOWNLOADS
1	THE BLACK EYED PEAS	I GOTTA FEELING	2009	8,770,000
2	ADELE	ROLLING IN THE DEEP	2010	8,508,000
3	LMFAO FT. LAUREN BENNETT & GOONROCK	PARTY ROCK ANTHEM	2001	8,096,000
4	GOTYE FT. KIMBRA	SOMEBODY THAT I USED TO KNOW	2011	7,941,000
5	IMAGINE DRAGONS	RADIOACTIVE	2012	7,902,000
6	MACKLEMORE & RYAN LEWIS FT. WANZ	THRIFT SHOP	2012	7,842,000
7	CARLY RAE JEPSEN	CALL ME MAYBE	2011	7,632,000
8	ROBIN THICKE FT. T.I. & PHARRELL	BLURRED LINES	2013	7,486,000
9	FLORIDA GEORGIA LINE	CRUISE	2012	7,440,000
10	FLO RIDA FT. T-PAIN	LOW	2007	7,297,000

CARLY RAE JEPSEN

7 The Canadian singer-songwriter drafted Oscar-winning actor Tom Hanks to star in the music video for her 2015 single "I Really Like You" (taken from her third album, E•MO•TION).

Total digital tracks sold in 2015:

964.8 MILLION

BY THE NUMBERS

Here's the above chart expressed by type of artist...

- SOLO ARTIST **2**
- COLLABORATIONS **5**
- BANDS **3**

ADELE

2 "Hello" (the first single from the 2015 album 25) has been played on American radio more than 270,000 times, and heard an estimated 1.56 billion times.

BEYONCÉ

8 The Super Bowl 50 halftime show (Feb. 7, 2016) saw Beyoncé perform alongside Coldplay and Bruno Mars. She also headlined the Super Bowl halftime show in 2013.

TAYLOR SWIFT

3 The singer-songwriter has won 248 international awards, including 22 Billboard Music Awards. She has played the guitar since she was 12 years old.

In its first week on sale, Adele's *25* was downloaded **1.1 MILLION** times

TOP 10

MOST DOWNLOADED ALBUMS EVER

From iTunes to Amazon to Bandcamp, there are numerous services that sell digital albums...

	ARTIST(S)	SONG	YEAR RELEASED	TOTAL DOWNLOADS
1	**ADELE**	21	2011	**3,225,000**
2	**ADELE**	25	2015	**2,466,000**
▶ **3**	**TAYLOR SWIFT**	1989	2014	**2,369,000**
4	**MUMFORD & SONS**	SIGH NO MORE	2009	**1,776,000**
5	**IMAGINE DRAGONS**	NIGHT VISIONS	2012	**1,588,000**
6	**VARIOUS**	FROZEN (ORIGINAL SOUNDTRACK)	2013	**1,566,000**
7	**MUMFORD & SONS**	BABEL	2012	**1,453,000**
▶ **8**	**BEYONCÉ**	BEYONCÉ	2013	**1,440,000**
9	**EMINEM**	RECOVERY	2010	**1,394,000**
10	**TAYLOR SWIFT**	RED	2012	**1,279,000**

Between 2014–15, music streaming increased **92.8%**

FETTY WAP

1 His debut single "Trap Queen" peaked at number 2 on the *Billboard* Hot 100 in May 2015. His self-titled debut album featured guest performances by Monty and M80.

MAJOR LAZER & DJ SNAKE FT. MØ

5 "Lean On" was taken from Major Lazer's third album, *Peace Is the Mission* (released June 1, 2015). They are pictured with Danish singer-songwriter Karen Marie Ørsted, also known as MØ (far right), and singer J. Balvin (center). DJ Snake is French producer William Grigahcine.

TOP 10

MOST STREAMED SONGS 2015

Streaming as a way to experience music is extremely popular. These are the songs that were played the most in 2015...

	ARTIST(S)	SONG	TOTAL STREAMS
1	FETTY WAP	TRAP QUEEN	214,842,000
2	THE WEEKND	THE HILLS	207,504,000
3	DRAKE	HOTLINE BLING	177,413,000
4	THE WEEKND	CAN'T FEEL MY FACE	174,451,000
5	MAJOR LAZER & DJ SNAKE FT. MØ	LEAN ON	167,819,000
6	MARK RONSON FT. BRUNO MARS	UPTOWN FUNK!	160,763,000
7	FETTY WAP FT. REMY BOYZ	679	155,994,000
8	JUSTIN BIEBER	WHAT DO YOU MEAN?	154,446,000
9	SKRILLEX & DIPLO FT. JUSTIN BIEBER	WHERE ARE Ü NOW	153,575,000
10	THE WEEKND	EARNED IT (FIFTY SHADES OF GREY)	151,941,000

The music video for Bruno Mars's "The Lazy Song" (2011) total streams:

885 MILLION

THE WEEKND

6 The Canadian artist (real name: Ab I Makkonen Tesfaye) has won 19 international music awards since 2012.

ED SHEERAN

7 "Thinking Out Loud" won two awards, Song of the Year and Best Pop Solo Performance, at the 58th Grammy Awards, held in Los Angeles on February 15, 2016.

TOP 10

MOST STREAMED VIDEOS 2015

People are watching music videos online more than ever, with figures that have more than doubled since last year's *Top 10 of Everything*...

	ARTIST(S)	SONG	TOTAL ON-DEMAND VIDEO STREAMS
1	SILENTÓ	WATCH ME (WHIP/NAE NAE)	487,490,000
2	FETTY WAP	TRAP QUEEN	401,621,000
3	MARK RONSON FT. BRUNO MARS	UPTOWN FUNK!	395,045,000
4	WIZ KHALIFA FT. CHARLIE PUTH	SEE YOU AGAIN	327,156,000
5	TAYLOR SWIFT	SHAKE IT OFF	237,745,000
6	THE WEEKND	THE HILLS	236,514,000
7	ED SHEERAN	THINKING OUT LOUD	204,804,000
8	ADELE	HELLO	198,963,000
9	TAYLOR SWIFT	BLANK SPACE	192,930,000
10	OMARION FT. CHRIS BROWN & JHENE AIKO	POST TO BE	192,681,000

TOP 10

BIGGEST-SELLING DIGITAL SONGS 2015

When you consider that the most downloaded song ever (The Black Eyed Peas' 2009 hit "I Gotta Feeling") has sold 8.77 million copies, these 2015 hits' sales are huge...

	ARTIST(S)	SONG	TOTAL SALES
1	MARK RONSON FT. BRUNO MARS	UPTOWN FUNK!	5,529,000
2	ED SHEERAN	THINKING OUT LOUD	3,976,000
3	WIZ KHALIFA FT. CHARLIE PUTH	SEE YOU AGAIN	3,801,000
4	ADELE	HELLO	3,712,000
5	MAROON 5	SUGAR	3,343,000
6	WALK THE MOON	SHUT UP AND DANCE	2,986,000
7	FETTY WAP	TRAP QUEEN	2,730,000
8	OMI	CHEERLEADER	2,698,000
9	THE WEEKND	THE HILLS	2,586,000
10	TAYLOR SWIFT FT. KENDRICK LAMAR	BAD BLOOD	2,580,000

WALK THE MOON

6 Electronic duo The Knocks invited Walk the Moon to appear on their song "Best for Last," taken from their 2016 album 55.

OMI

8 Jamaican singer OMI, also known as Omar Samuel Pasley, initially independently released "Cheerleader" in 2012. Its 2014 remix by German producer Felix Jaehn led to it being a worldwide hit the next year.

In 2015, individual digital tracks by Taylor Swift sold:

10,563,000

KENDRICK LAMAR

7 The artist, born in Compton, California, won five of his 11 Grammy Award nominations in 2016, including Best Rap Album for *To Pimp a Butterfly*.

CHRIS STAPLETON

10 Although *Traveller* is the country artist's debut album, he's written more than 150 songs for other artists over the past 15 years, including Alison Krauss and Adele.

ALBUMS OF 2015

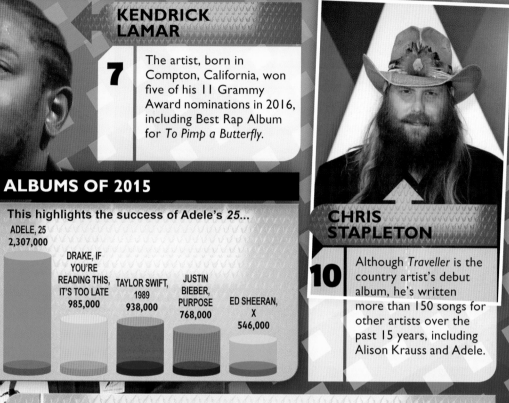

This highlights the success of Adele's *25*...

ADELE, 25
2,307,000

DRAKE, IF YOU'RE READING THIS, IT'S TOO LATE
985,000

TAYLOR SWIFT, 1989
938,000

JUSTIN BIEBER, PURPOSE
768,000

ED SHEERAN, X
546,000

Drake and Future's collaboration was released on **SEPT. 20, 2015**

TOP 10

BIGGEST-SELLING DIGITAL ALBUMS 2015

Even though Drake and Taylor Swift had a hugely successful 2015, the year really belonged to Adele...

	ARTIST(S)	ALBUM	TOTAL SALES
1	ADELE	25	2,307,000
2	DRAKE	IF YOU'RE READING THIS, IT'S TOO LATE	985,000
3	TAYLOR SWIFT	1989	938,000
4	JUSTIN BIEBER	PURPOSE	768,000
5	ED SHEERAN	X	546,000
6	VARIOUS	FIFTY SHADES OF GREY (SOUNDTRACK)	538,000
7	KENDRICK LAMAR	TO PIMP A BUTTERFLY	516,000
8	THE WEEKND	BEAUTY BEHIND THE MADNESS	514,000
9	DRAKE AND FUTURE	WHAT A TIME TO BE ALIVE	508,000
10	CHRIS STAPLETON	TRAVELLER	411,000

On Instagram, Taylor Swift follows just **82** accounts

SELENA GOMEZ

2 The Texan singer has crafted more than 1,100 Instagram posts. She follows 227 Instagram accounts. Music aside, Gomez also has 36 movie and television acting credits.

TOP 10

MOST INSTAGRAM FOLLOWERS

Since its launch on October 6, 2010, this platform for sharing photos and videos is more popular than ever...

	ARTIST	HANDLE	FOLLOWERS
1	**TAYLOR SWIFT**	@TAYLORSWIFT	**62 MILLION**
2	**SELENA GOMEZ**	@SELENAGOMEZ	**60 MILLION**
3	**BEYONCÉ**	@BEYONCÉ	**56 MILLION**
4	**ARIANA GRANDE**	@ARIANAGRANDE	**55 MILLION**
5	**JUSTIN BIEBER**	@JUSTINBIEBER	**53 MILLION**
6	**NICKI MINAJ**	@NICKIMINAJ	**44 MILLION**
7	**KATY PERRY**	@KATYPERRY	**37 MILLION**
8	**MILEY CYRUS**	@MILEYCYRUS	**34 MILLION**
9	**RIHANNA**	@BADGALRIRI	**32 MILLION**
10	**DEMI LOVATO**	@DDLOVATO	**31 MILLION**

DEMI LOVATO

10 Before being a pop star, Lovato's acting career began by playing Angela on children's TV show *Barney & Friends*, which also featured a young Selena Gomez.

Number of studio albums released by Prince: **39**

MOST STREAMED MUSIC GENRES

TOP 10

The order has changed since last year, but the top 3 genres remain the most streamed...

	GENRE	% OF TOTAL STREAMS
1	R&B/HIP-HOP	21.1
2	ROCK	17.5
3	POP	14.5
4	LATIN	8.5
5	DANCE/ELECTRONIC	4.7
6	COUNTRY	4.1
7	CHRISTIAN/GOSPEL	2.1
8	HOLIDAY/SEASONAL	0.8
9	CLASSICAL	0.7
10	CHILDREN/JAZZ	0.6

FIGHTSTAR (ROCK)

2 Members of this British band are involved with other bands including Gunship, Once Upon a Dead Man, and Busted, as well as the production company Horsie in the Hedge that created the lyric video for Kylie Minogue's "I Was Gonna Cancel."

ANDRÉ RIEU (CLASSICAL)

9 The highly acclaimed Dutch violinist and conductor (born October 1, 1949) has been playing the violin since he was five years old. He has also been involved with the recording of more than 50 albums.

211

JUSTIN TIMBERLAKE

6 Timberlake joined Twitter in March 2009. Since then he has tweeted more than 3,150 times. The singer also has 29 acting credits since his debut in *Model Behavior* (2000).

POP & GENDER

Of the 10 entries below, more than half are female...

- FEMALE **8**
- MALE **2**

Total tweets related to the 57th Grammy Awards during broadcast: **13,432,000**

TOP 10

MOST TWITTER FOLLOWERS (SOLO)

By a huge proportion, female pop stars remain the musical artists most followed on Twitter...

	ARTIST	HANDLE	FOLLOWERS
1	KATY PERRY	@KATYPERRY	80 MILLION
2	JUSTIN BIEBER	@JUSTINBIEBER	73 MILLION
3	TAYLOR SWIFT	@TAYLORSWIFT13	69 MILLION
4	RIHANNA	@RIHANNA	55 MILLION
5	LADY GAGA	@LADYGAGA	54 MILLION
6	JUSTIN TIMBERLAKE	@JTIMBERLAKE	51 MILLION
7	BRITNEY SPEARS	@BRITNEYSPEARS	43 MILLION
8	SELENA GOMEZ	@SELENAGOMEZ	37 MILLION
9	SHAKIRA	@SHAKIRA	36 MILLION
10	ARIANA GRANDE	@ARIANAGRANDE	35 MILLION

SHAKIRA

9 Tweeting from her official account since June 2009, the Colombian artist enjoys posting Vines (micro-video loops). Shakira's tweets include 315,000 Vines.

PARAMORE

9 Lead singer Hayley Williams (pictured below) dueted with her lifelong friend, fellow musical artist Joy Williams, in 2014. A re-recorded version of Paramore's "Hate to See Your Heart Break" was featured on the deluxe edition of the band's self-titled fourth album.

TOP 10

MOST TWITTER FOLLOWERS (BANDS/GROUPS)

Their number of followers (and the amount of accounts they're following) has changed since last year, but the order of artists has not...

	ARTIST(S)	HANDLE	FOLLOWERS
1	ONE DIRECTION	@ONEDIRECTION	26 MILLION
2	COLDPLAY	@COLDPLAY	16 MILLION
3	MAROON 5	@MAROON5	12 MILLION
4	LMFAO	@LMFAO	9 MILLION
5	5 SECONDS OF SUMMER	@5SOS	8 MILLION
6	THE BLACK EYED PEAS	@BEP	5 MILLION
7	LINKIN PARK	@LINKINPARK	4.9 MILLION
8	GREEN DAY	@GREENDAY	4 MILLION
9	PARAMORE	@PARAMORE	3.9 MILLION
10	ZOÉ	@ZOETHEBAND	3 MILLION

Percentage of people who discover new music via radio:

61%

COLDPLAY

2 The band, formed in England in 1996, has tweeted more than 5,250 times since January 2009. Their seventh studio album, *A Head Full of Dreams*, was released on December 4, 2015.

21

Total studio albums by the Jackson 5 and Michael Jackson:
28

MICHAEL JACKSON

4

Known around the world as the King of Pop, Michael Jackson was born on August 29, 1958, and died on June 25, 2009. His short film "Ghosts" (1996) is the longest music video ever made, at almost 40 minutes.

TOP 10

MOST FACEBOOK LIKES (SOLO)

Examining all of the official Facebook pages for music stars, these are the most "liked"...

	SOLO ARTISTS	"LIKES"
1	SHAKIRA	104 MILLION
2	EMINEM	92 MILLION
3	RIHANNA	81 MILLION
4	MICHAEL JACKSON	76 MILLION
5	JUSTIN BIEBER	75 MILLION
6	BOB MARLEY	74 MILLION
7	TAYLOR SWIFT	73 MILLION
8	KATY PERRY	71 MILLION
9	BEYONCÉ	64 MILLION
10	ADELE	63 MILLION

KATY PERRY

8

Combining Katy Perry's followers on Twitter, Facebook, Instagram, and YouTube, the singer's total social media reach exceeds 211 million.

THE BEATLES

3 What began as the Quarrymen (started by John Lennon) in 1956 became the Beatles by 1960. Bass guitar player Paul McCartney's career spans 60+ years and more than 60 studio albums.

Number of years Linkin Park has been a band:

21

MOST FACEBOOK LIKES (BANDS/ GROUPS)

This chart includes a very broad range of musical genres...

	BAND/GROUP	"LIKES"
1	LINKIN PARK	63 MILLION
2	THE BLACK EYED PEAS	45 MILLION
▶ 3	THE BEATLES	42 MILLION
4	MAROON 5	40 MILLION
5	ONE DIRECTION	39 MILLION
6	COLDPLAY	38 MILLION
7	METALLICA	37 MILLION
8	GREEN DAY	32 MILLION
9	LMFAO	31 MILLION
▶ 10	AC/DC	30 MILLION

AC/DC

10 Formed in 1973, the Australian rock band has sold more than 150 million albums worldwide. Their 17th album, *Rock or Bust*, was the latest, released on November 28, 2014.

MOST SUBSCRIBED MUSIC YOUTUBE CHANNELS

TOP 10

The subscribers of these channels receive alerts when their favorite artists upload new videos...

	ARTIST(S)	SUBSCRIBERS
1	ONE DIRECTION	18.4 MILLION
2	RIHANNA	18.2 MILLION
3	TAYLOR SWIFT	17.7 MILLION
4	KATY PERRY	17.6 MILLION
5	JUSTIN BIEBER	17.2 MILLION
6	EMINEM	17 MILLION
7	SKRILLEX	12 MILLION
8	DAVID GUETTA	11 MILLION
9	NICKI MINAJ	10 MILLION
10	PENTATONIX	9 MILLION

YouTube was founded on **FEB. 14, 2005**

SKRILLEX

7 Sonny John Moore (aka Skrillex) is most famous for making dubstep. He has collaborated with heavy rock band Korn on their 2011 album *The Path of Totality*, as well as hip-hop artist A$AP Rocky for his 2013 debut *LONG.LIVE.A$AP*.

RIHANNA

2 Born in Barbados on February 20, 1988, Rihanna has released eight studio albums since her 2005 debut, *Music of the Sun*. She has appeared in more than 50 music videos.

JUSTIN BIEBER

5 Born March 1, 1994, Bieber has released four studio albums since his 2010 debut, *My World*. In 2015 *Purpose* featured guest performances by Big Sean, Travis Scott, Halsey, and Skrillex.

MTV was launched
AUG. 1, 1981

MEGHAN TRAINOR

10 "All About That Bass" was released on June 30, 2014. It was the first single from Meghan Trainor's fourth album *Title* (2015). She won the Best New Artist award at the 2016 Grammys.

PSY'S BIG LEAD

Taylor Swift's "Blank Space" needs just 1.2 billion more views to take the top spot...

GANGNAM STYLE 2,493,009,939

BLANK SPACE 1,390,955,285

SEE YOU AGAIN 1,328,732,185

UPTOWN FUNK! 1,275,655,404

BABY 1,274,782,558

TOP 10

OFFICIAL MUSIC VIDEOS WITH THE MOST VIEWS

Although hundreds of music videos were released in 2015, only one was watched enough times to make it into this Top 10...

	SONG	ARTIST(S)	DATE UPLOADED	VIEWS
1	GANGNAM STYLE	PSY	JULY 15, 2012	2,493,009,939
2	BLANK SPACE	TAYLOR SWIFT	NOV. 10, 2014	1,390,955,285
3	SEE YOU AGAIN	WIZ KHALIFA FT. CHARLIE PUTH	APRIL 6, 2015	1,328,732,185
4	UPTOWN FUNK!	MARK RONSON FT. BRUNO MARS	NOV. 19, 2014	1,275,655,404
▶5	BABY	JUSTIN BIEBER FT. LUDACRIS	FEB. 19, 2010	1,274,782,558
6	SHAKE IT OFF	TAYLOR SWIFT	AUG. 18, 2014	1,256,908,141
7	DARK HORSE	KATY PERRY FT. JUICY J	FEB. 20, 2014	1,240,231,174
8	BAILANDO	ENRIQUE IGLESIAS FT. DESCEMER BUENO & GENTE DE ZONA	APRIL 11, 2014	1,236,121,125
9	ROAR	KATY PERRY	SEPT. 5, 2013	1,213,111,251
▶10	ALL ABOUT THAT BASS	MEGHAN TRAINOR	JUNE 1, 2014	1,202,513,937

In 2015 hip-hop increased in radio airplay by **12%**

ELLIE GOULDING

9 The British singer's debut release was the 2009 EP *An Introduction to Ellie Goulding*. Her third full-length album, *Delirium*, was released on November 6, 2015.

WIZ KHALIFA

6 "See You Again" (ft. Charlie Puth) was featured on the soundtrack to *Furious 7*. It was written to honor *Fast & Furious* star Paul Walker who died before the seventh movie was completed.

TOP 10

MOST RADIO IMPRESSIONS OF 2015

If you heard any of these hit songs played on a radio station, you experienced it clocking up another "impression" toward these enormous figures...

	ARTIST(S)	SONG	TOTAL RADIO IMPRESSIONS
1	MARK RONSON FT. BRUNO MARS	UPTOWN FUNK!	4,804,496,000
2	WALK THE MOON	SHUT UP AND DANCE	3,981,730,000
3	ED SHEERAN	THINKING OUT LOUD	3,586,173,000
4	MAROON 5	SUGAR	3,470,501,000
5	TAYLOR SWIFT	STYLE	3,163,189,000
▶ 6	WIZ KHALIFA FT. CHARLIE PUTH	SEE YOU AGAIN	3,140,899,000
7	JASON DERULO	WANT TO WANT ME	3,071,643,000
8	THE WEEKND	EARNED IT	2,928,354,000
▶ 9	ELLIE GOULDING	LOVE ME LIKE YOU DO	2,928,018,000
10	THE WEEKND	CAN'T FEEL MY FACE	2,900,066,000

Total tweets related to the 2015 MTV Video Music Awards during broadcast:
21,356,000

BEATS 1 WITH ZANE LOWE

Apple Music's radio station Beats 1 airs nonstop in more than 100 countries. New Zealander DJ Zane Lowe is one of the station's key curators.

TOP 10

TOP RADIO FORMATS OF 2015 (18-34)

Pop remains, by a great margin, the genre most people listen to on the radio...

	FORMAT	% MARKET SHARE (18- TO 34-YEAR-OLDS)
1	POP CONTEMPORARY HIT RADIO	12.4
2	COUNTRY	9.1
3	HOT ADULT CONTEMPORARY	7.6
4	URBAN CONTEMPORARY	6.5
5	ADULT CONTEMPORARY	6.4
6	RHYTHMIC CONTEMPORARY HIT RADIO	5.8
7	ALTERNATIVE	5
8	MEXICAN REGIONAL	4.6
9	CLASSIC ROCK	4.5
10	NEWS TALK	3.6

MADDIE & TAE (COUNTRY)

2 Taylor "Tae" Dye (above) is one half of country duo Maddie & Tae, with Madison Marlow. Their debut album *Start Here* was released August 28, 2015.

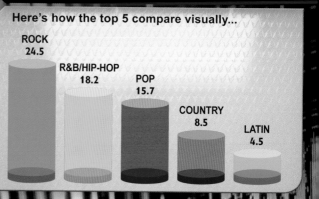

GALANTIS (DANCE/ELECTRONIC)

6 This Swedish duo is Linus Eklöw (also known by his moniker Style of Eye, pictured above right) and Christian Karlsson (above left) from Miike Snow. Their mascot character is called the Seafox.

SEVENDUST (ROCK)

1 Hailing from Atlanta, Georgia, Sevendust has released 11 studio albums since 1997. Their song "Thank You" (taken from 2015 album *Kill The Flaw*) was nominated Best Metal Performance for the 2016 Grammy Awards.

MOST POPULAR GENRES

TOP 10

The genre with guitar riffs and driving drum sections remains the most popular...

Of total music consumption, children's music represents

1.1%

	GENRE	% OF TOTAL CONSUMPTION
1	ROCK	24.5
2	R&B/HIP-HOP	18.2
3	POP	15.7
4	COUNTRY	8.5
5	LATIN	4.5
6	DANCE/ELECTRONIC	3.4
7	CHRISTIAN/GOSPEL	2.8
8	HOLIDAY/SEASONAL	1.7
9	JAZZ	1.3
=	CLASSICAL	1.3

GENRE BREAKDOWN

Here's how the top 5 compare visually...

ROCK 24.5

R&B/HIP-HOP 18.2

POP 15.7

COUNTRY 8.5

LATIN 4.5

BIGGEST-SELLING **ALBUMS** EVER

The accurate sales figures of albums and singles started in 1991 via SoundScan, and these are the 10 most successful sellers since then...

	ARTIST(S)	ALBUM	YEAR RELEASED	TOTAL SALES
1	METALLICA	METALLICA	1991	**16.2 MILLION**
2	SHANIA TWAIN	COME ON OVER	1997	**15.6 MILLION**
3	ALANIS MORISSETTE	JAGGED LITTLE PILL	1995	**15 MILLION**
4	THE BEATLES	1	2000	**12.6 MILLION**
5	BACKSTREET BOYS	MILLENNIUM	1999	**12.2 MILLION**
6	WHITNEY HOUSTON/VARIOUS	THE BODYGUARD (SOUNDTRACK)	1992	**12.1 MILLION**
7	BOB MARLEY & THE WAILERS	LEGEND	1984	**11.9 MILLION**
8	SANTANA	SUPERNATURAL	1999	**11.8 MILLION**
9	CREED	HUMAN CLAY	1999	**11.7 MILLION**
10	ADELE	21	2011	**11.4 MILLION**

Alanis Morissette has released

32

singles

SHANIA TWAIN

2 On March 3, 2015, Shania Twain released *Still the One: Live from Vegas*. The DVD edition includes 25 tracks and it celebrates the 105 shows she performed as part of her residency at The Colosseum in Caesar's Palace, Las Vegas, between 2012 and 2014.

THE BEATLES

4 In 2016 former Beatle Paul McCartney created instrumental tunes to accompany animated emojis for the communication application Skype.

Total CD, vinyl, cassette, and digital albums sold in 2015:

241.4
MILLION

LUKE BRYAN

10 Released August 7, 2015, Luke Bryan's fifth studio album *Kill The Lights* debuted at number 1 on the *Billboard* 200 chart. Little Big Town's Karen Fairchild guested on "Home Alone Tonight."

DRAKE

5 Alongside his solo studio albums, Drake has been releasing "mixtapes" since the 2006 debut *Room For Improvement*, which included 23 tracks. In 2015, mixtapes *If You're Reading This It's Too Late* and *What a Time to Be Alive* (a collaboration with Future) were released.

TOP 10

BIGGEST-SELLING ALBUMS (ALL FORMATS) 2015

Combining vinyl, CD, and digital downloads, these were the biggest albums of 2015...

	ARTIST(S)	ALBUM	TOTAL SALES
1	ADELE	25	7,441,000
2	TAYLOR SWIFT	1989	1,993,000
3	JUSTIN BIEBER	PURPOSE	1,269,000
4	ED SHEERAN	X	1,162,000
5	DRAKE	IF YOU'RE READING THIS, IT'S TOO LATE	1,142,000
6	SAM SMITH	IN THE LONELY HOUR	1,018,000
7	MEGHAN TRAINOR	TITLE	1,007,000
8	THE WEEKND	BEAUTY BEHIND THE MADNESS	862,000
9	VARIOUS	FIFTY SHADES OF GREY (SOUNDTRACK)	861,000
10	LUKE BRYAN	KILL THE LIGHTS	851,000

NINA SIMONE (JAZZ)

7 Iconic American singer-songwriter Nina Simone (February 21, 1933–April 21, 2003) featured on more than 50 live and studio albums. Her final studio album, *A Single Woman*, was released in 1993.

TOP 10

MOST POPULAR ALBUM GENRES 2015

Almost one-third of all albums sold in 2015 fall under the genre of rock...

	GENRE	% OF TOTAL ALBUMS SOLD
1	ROCK	32.6
2	R&B/HIP-HOP	15.1
3	POP	14.1
4	COUNTRY	11.2
5	CHRISTIAN/GOSPEL	3.4
6	HOLIDAY/SEASONAL	3.0
7	LATIN	2.1
=	JAZZ	2.1
=	CLASSICAL	2.1
10	DANCE/ELECTRONIC	1.8

Total studio albums released by Dance/Electronic group The Prodigy:

6

JOY WILLIAMS (POP)

3 The Grammy award-winning artist released 12 albums, including *Venus* on June 30, 2015. Her collaborations include songs with Chris Cornell, Taylor Swift, and Mike Einziger (Incubus).

The sales
of CDs declined
10.8%
in 2015

PENTATONIX

9 A capella group Pentatonix is comprised of (from left) Avi Kaplan, Kirstie Maldonado, Scott Hoying, Mitch Grassi, and Kevin Olusola. They formed in 2011.

TOP 10

BIGGEST-SELLING CD ALBUMS 2015 (USA)

Although CD sales are in decline, this didn't affect Adele's new album...

JOSH GROBAN

7 American operatic pop vocalist Josh Groban has released three live albums and seven studio albums. He was a guest star on an episode of *The Muppets* on September 29, 2015.

	ARTIST(S)	ALBUM	TOTAL SALES
1	ADELE	25	5,018,000
2	TAYLOR SWIFT	1989	981,000
3	LUKE BRYAN	KILL THE LIGHTS	623,000
4	SAM SMITH	IN THE LONELY HOUR	621,000
5	MEGHAN TRAINOR	TITLE	591,000
6	ED SHEERAN	X	579,000
7	JOSH GROBAN	STAGES	551,000
8	JUSTIN BIEBER	PURPOSE	492,000
9	PENTATONIX	THAT'S CHRISTMAS TO ME	435,000
10	ONE DIRECTION	MADE IN THE A.M.	426,000

ALABAMA SHAKES

8 Alabama Shakes enjoyed a double win at the 2016 Grammy Awards for Best Alternative Music Album (for their second album *Sound & Color*) and Best Rock Song for "Don't Wanna Fight."

TOP FIVE VINYLS

2015's most successful albums on vinyl...

ADELE, 25 116,000	TAYLOR SWIFT, 1989 74,000	PINK FLOYD, DARK SIDE OF THE MOON 50,000	THE BEATLES, ABBEY ROAD 49,800	MILES DAVIS, KIND OF BLUE 49,000

Total vinyl sales in 2015:

12 MILLION

HOZIER

9 Irish singer-songwriter Andrew Hozier-Byrne released his self-titled debut album September 19, 2014. It featured the global hit single "Take Me to Church."

TOP 10

BIGGEST-SELLING VINYL ALBUMS 2015 (USA)

Although a specialized format, vinyl records saw sales increase between 2014 and 2015...

	ARTIST(S)	ALBUM	TOTAL SALES
1	ADELE	25	116,000
2	TAYLOR SWIFT	1989	74,000
3	PINK FLOYD	DARK SIDE OF THE MOON	50,000
4	THE BEATLES	ABBEY ROAD	49,800
5	MILES DAVIS	KIND OF BLUE	49,000
6	ARCTIC MONKEYS	AM	48,000
7	SUFJAN STEVENS	CARRIE & LOWELL	44,900
8	ALABAMA SHAKES	SOUND & COLOR	44,600
9	HOZIER	HOZIER	43,000
10	VARIOUS	GUARDIANS OF THE GALAXY (SOUNDTRACK)	43,000

TOP 10

MOST POPULAR GENRE OF SONGS 2015

When it comes to individual songs (not albums), pop music rises to the top...

	GENRE	% OF TOTAL SONGS SOLD
1	POP	22.6
2	ROCK	19.8
3	R&B/HIP-HOP	19.7
4	COUNTRY	11.5
5	DANCE/ELECTRONIC	4.2
6	CHRISTIAN/GOSPEL	2.8
7	LATIN	1.7
8	HOLIDAY/SEASONAL	0.8
9	JAZZ	0.6
10	CLASSICAL	0.5

Over 28 years, iconic rock band Motörhead released

22

studio albums

DAVID BOWIE

The innovative David Bowie (January 8, 1947–January 10, 2016) had a musical output that defied genre classification. His 27 studio albums covered everything from pop and funk to jazz and electronica. Bowie's final album, *Blackstar*, was released on his 69 birthday, two days before he died.

JAMIE XX (DANCE/ELECTRONIC)

5 Also a member of the band The xx, Jamie xx has provided remixes for artists including Florence and the Machine, Adele, Radiohead, Jack Penate, Eliza Doolittle, and Rui de Silva.

BRUNO MARS & MARK RONSON

3 Taken from Mark Ronson's fourth album *Uptown Special* (2015), "Uptown Funk!" featured lead vocals from Bruno Mars. It reached the number 1 position in 31 different charts. It was released on November 10, 2014, on digital download, CD, and 12" vinyl.

During 2015 on-demand video streams increased
101.9 %

TOP 10

MOST ON-DEMAND STREAMS 2015 (AUDIO + VIDEO)

Rounding off the music zone, these were the most streamed songs, be it via audio or video...

	ARTIST(S)	ALBUM	TOTAL ON-DEMAND AUDIO + VIDEO STREAMS
1	**FETTY WAP**	TRAP QUEEN	**616,463,000**
2	**SILENTÓ**	WATCH ME (WHIP/NAE NAE)	**563,406,000**
3	**MARK RONSON FT. BRUNO MARS**	UPTOWN FUNK!	**555,808,000**
4	**WIZ KHALIFA FT. CHARLIE PUTH**	SEE YOU AGAIN	**472,264,000**
5	**THE WEEKND**	THE HILLS	**444,018,000**
6	**ED SHEERAN**	THINKING OUT LOUD	**350,579,000**
7	**ADELE**	HELLO	**334,799,000**
8	**OMI**	CHEERLEADER	**328,365,000**
9	**FETTY WAP FT. REMY BOYZ**	679	**322,176,000**
10	**THE WEEKND**	CAN'T FEEL MY FACE	**314,499,000**

SILENTÓ

2 Silentó (real name Richard Lamar Hawk) hails from Atlanta, Georgia. His debut single "Watch Me (Whip/ Nae Nae)," known for its accompanying dance moves, was released as a digital download only on June 25, 2015.

OUTER
SPACE

ZONE **9**

TOP 10

BIGGEST OBJECTS IN OUR SOLAR SYSTEM

Of all the things we know about in our solar system, these are the largest...

	OBJECT	TYPE	MASS (X 1021 KG)*
1	THE SUN	STAR	1,989,100,000
2	JUPITER	PLANET	1,898,130
3	SATURN	PLANET	568,319
4	NEPTUNE	PLANET	102,410
5	URANUS	PLANET	86,810.3
6	EARTH	PLANET	5,972.2
7	VENUS	PLANET	4,867.3
8	MARS	PLANET	641.69
9	MERCURY	PLANET	330.1
10	GANYMEDE	MOON	148.2

* For each mass, multiply it by another 1021 kg.

THE SUN

1 The Sun is so massive that it represents 99.8 percent of the total mass of our solar system. Scientists believe that it's 4.6 billion years old and is currently halfway through its life cycle.

NEPTUNE

4 Known as the "ice giant," Neptune experiences vicious winds. Its solid core (approximately the same size as Earth) is surrounded by dense ammonia, methane, and water. In 2013 a 14th moon (S/2004 N 1) was discovered from old Hubble Space Telescope photos.

Ganymede is the largest of Jupiter's

67

moons

Dwarf planet Haumea was discovered on **DECEMBER 28, 2004**

CERES

1 On March 6, 2015, NASA's space probe *Dawn* (launched on September 27, 2007) was caught in Ceres's gravity. It became the first man-made craft to successfully orbit a dwarf planet in our solar system.

TOP 10

SMALLEST PLANETS/DWARF PLANETS IN OUR SOLAR SYSTEM

There are only eight planets in our solar system, so dwarf planets are included in this Top 10...

	PLANET/ DWARF PLANET	DIAMETER (MILES)	(KM)
1	CERES	590	950
2	MAKEMAKE	883.59	1,422
3	HAUMEA	1,217	1,960
4	ERIS	1,445.3	2,326
5	PLUTO	1,471.4	2,368
6	MERCURY	3,031	4,878
7	MARS	4,220	6,792
8	VENUS	7,521	12,104
9	EARTH	7,904	12,720
10	NEPTUNE	30,775	49,528

TOP 5 SMALLEST

Here is how their diameters compare graphically...

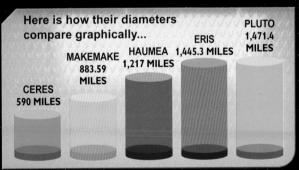

CERES 590 MILES

MAKEMAKE 883.59 MILES

HAUMEA 1,217 MILES

ERIS 1,445.3 MILES

PLUTO 1,471.4 MILES

MAKEMAKE

2 In Earth years, it takes dwarf planet Makemake 310 years to orbit the Sun. Makemake resides in the Kuiper Belt, an area of space just outside Neptune's orbit.

VENUS

2 Even though Mars is the planet we talk about the most, Venus is actually Earth's nearest neighbor. After the Sun and the Moon, it's the brightest thing in the sky.

TOP 10

FASTEST PLANETS/ DWARF PLANETS ORBITING THE SUN

If you consider that the time it takes Earth to orbit the Sun is called a "year," check out how long these "years" are...

	PLANET/DWARF PLANET	DAYS TO ORBIT THE SUN
1	MERCURY	87.97
2	VENUS	224.7
3	EARTH	365.26
4	MARS	686.98
5	CERES	1,680.19
6	JUPITER	4,332.82
7	SATURN	10,755.7
8	URANUS	30,687.15
9	NEPTUNE	60,190.03
10	PLUTO	90,553.02

Scientists estimate the Sun formed more than **4.6 BILLION** years ago

MERCURY

1 On March 6, 2013, NASA's robot spacecraft *MESSENGER* successfully completed a first full mapping of the planet. The findings: Mercury's surface looks a lot like our Moon's.

TOP 10

PLANETS/DWARF PLANETS FARTHEST FROM THE SUN

Dwarf planets Makemake and Eris were only discovered in 2005...

	NAME	TYPE	DISTANCE FROM THE SUN (MILES)	(KM)
1	ERIS	DWARF PLANET	6,344,199,872.7	10,210,000,000
2	MAKEMAKE	DWARF PLANET	4,256,392,666.8	6,850,000,000
3	HAUMEA	DWARF PLANET	4,028,970,810.5	6,484,000,000
4	PLUTO	DWARF PLANET	3,670,054,382.4	5,906,380,000
5	NEPTUNE	PLANET	2,795,084,767.5	4,498,252,900
6	URANUS	PLANET	1,783,939,418.8	2,870,972,200
7	SATURN	PLANET	886,526,062.8	1,426,725,400
8	JUPITER	PLANET	483,682,798.7	778,412,010
9	CERES	DWARF PLANET	257,061,262.2	413,700,000
10	MARS	PLANET	141,633,261.8	227,936,640

PLUTO

4 The most famous of the dwarf planets, Pluto has five moons: Charon (the largest), Hydra, Kerberos, Nix, and Styx.

Earth's population is approximately

7.3
BILLION

MARS

10 The red planet's Mariner Valley was discovered in 1972 and is 2,500 miles (4,023 km) long. There have been 44 missions to learn about Mars.

233

TOP 10

PLANETS/DWARF PLANETS WITH LONGEST DAYS

Counting from sunrise to night to the following sunrise, look at how long days are in the top 3...

	PLANET/DWARF PLANET	HOURS PER DAY
1	MERCURY	4,222.6
2	VENUS	2,802
3	PLUTO	153.28
4	ERIS	25.9
5	MARS	24.66
6	EARTH	23.93
7	URANUS	17.24
8	NEPTUNE	16.11
9	SATURN	10.66
10	JUPITER	9.93

SATURN

9 The second-largest planet in our solar system (behind Jupiter), Saturn has winds up to 1,118.5 mph (1,800 kph). That's five times faster than Earth's strongest winds.

DAYS COMPARED

As a bar chart, here's how the top 5 look...

MERCURY
4,222.6

VENUS
2,802

PLUTO
153.28

ERIS
25.9

MARS
24.66

EARTH

6 On October 24, 1946, a V-2 rocket captured the first photo of our planet from space. On November 5, 2013, an Earth-sized planet, Kepler-78b, was found outside our solar system.

From midnight to midnight on Mercury, you would experience **175.9** Earth days

TOP 10

PLANETS/DWARF PLANETS WITH THE **BIGGEST SURFACE AREA**

You could stretch Earth's surface around Jupiter 125 times...

	NAME	TYPE	SURFACE AREA (MILES^2)	(KM^2)
1	JUPITER	PLANET	24,710,538,146.7	64,000,000,000
2	SATURN	PLANET	16,988,494,975.8	44,000,000,000
3	URANUS	PLANET	3,127,427,484.2	8,100,000,000
4	NEPTUNE	PLANET	2,972,986,620.8	7,700,000,000
5	EARTH	PLANET	196,912,100.9	510,000,000
6	VENUS	PLANET	177,606,992.9	460,000,000
7	MARS	PLANET	54,054,302.2	140,000,000
8	MERCURY	PLANET	28,957,661.9	75,000,000
9	PLUTO	DWARF PLANET	6,834,008.2	17,700,000
10	ERIS	DWARF PLANET	6,563,736.7	17,000,000

URANUS

3 On January 24, 1986, NASA space probe *Voyager 2* captured close-up views of Uranus, including its clouds. Methane gas gives the planet its blue appearance.

JUPITER

1 The largest planet in our solar system is famous for its large red spot. This is not a mark on the surface. It's actually a huge swirling storm that's twice the width of Earth.

Dwarf planet Eris was discovered **JANUARY 5, 2005**

MAKEMAKE

Missing out on this Top 10, dwarf planet Makemake has a surface temperature of −398.2°F (239°C). Pronounced "mah-kee-mah-kee," it's named after the god of fertility worshipped by the natives of Easter Island.

VENUS

1 The highest point on Venus is Maxwell Montes, which is 6.8 miles (11 km) high. To date, there have been 41 missions to study more about Venus.

TOP 10

PLANETS/DWARF PLANETS WITH HOTTEST SURFACE TEMPERATURE

Humans would have to develop special technology to survive these brutal temperatures...

	NAME	TYPE	SURFACE TEMPERATURE (°F)	(°C)
1	VENUS	PLANET	863.6	462
2	MERCURY	PLANET	(−279.4 TO) 800.6	(−173 TO) 427
3	EARTH	PLANET	(−126.4 TO) 136.4	(−88 TO) 58
4	MARS	PLANET	(−124.6 TO) 23	(−87 TO) −5
5	CERES	DWARF PLANET	−157	−105
6	JUPITER	PLANET	−162.4	−108
7	SATURN	PLANET	−218.2	−139
8	URANUS	PLANET	−322.6	−197
9	NEPTUNE	PLANET	−329.8	−201
10	PLUTO	DWARF PLANET	−380.2	−229

Venus's diameter is only **403.89** MILES less than Earth's

MARS

7 This image of Mars was taken by NASA's *Mars Pathfinder*. The craft deployed a robotic rover called Sojourner, which explored the planet for 83 days in 1997.

Mars has

2

moons

TOP 10

PLANETS/DWARF PLANETS WITH STRONGEST GRAVITY

You would have great difficulty jumping high on Jupiter, and could float away on Pluto...

	NAME	TYPE	EQUATORIAL GRAVITY (M/S^2)
1	**JUPITER**	PLANET	23.12
2	**NEPTUNE**	PLANET	11
3	**SATURN**	PLANET	10.44
4	**EARTH**	PLANET	9.81
5	**VENUS**	PLANET	8.87
6	**URANUS**	PLANET	8.69
7	**MARS**	PLANET	3.71
8	**MERCURY**	PLANET	3.70
9	**HAUMEA**	DWARF PLANET	0.63
10	**PLUTO**	DWARF PLANET	0.62

NEPTUNE

2 In 1989 NASA's *Voyager 2* captured this image of Neptune's largest moon, Triton. Neptune has 13 confirmed moons, with a 14th waiting to be officially classified.

GRAVITY EXPLAINED

Gravity is a naturally occurring phenomenon. It causes the tidal cycles of the oceans, and it's what gives objects their different weights. The stronger the gravity is on a planet, the "heavier" objects feel.

Mariner 7's mission length:

3 YEARS
23 DAYS

MARS 3

6 After *Mars 3* successfully touched down on the surface of the red planet, it ceased functioning after 45 seconds. Only a single, distorted image was sent.

TOP 10

FIRST SUCCESSFUL FLYBY & ORBITER **MARS MISSIONS**

Before machines attempt to land on celestial bodies, probes get close to send key data back to Earth...

	MISSION NAME	SPACE AGENCY	LAUNCH DATE	ARRIVED ON MARS
1	**MARINER 4***	NASA	NOVEMBER 28, 1964	**JULY 14, 1965**
2	**MARINER 6***	NASA	FEBRUARY 25, 1969	**JULY 31, 1969**
3	**MARINER 7***	NASA	MARCH 27, 1969	**AUG. 5, 1969**
4	**MARINER 9**	NASA	MAY 30, 1971	**NOV. 13, 1971**
5	**MARS 2**	SOVIET SPACE PROGRAM	MAY 19, 1971	**NOV. 27, 1971**
6	**MARS 3**	SOVIET SPACE PROGRAM	MAY 28, 1971	**DEC. 2, 1971**
7	**MARS 4***	SOVIET SPACE PROGRAM	JULY 21, 1973	**FEB. 10, 1974**
8	**MARS 5**	SOVIET SPACE PROGRAM	JULY 25, 1973	**FEB. 12, 1974**
9	**MARS 7**	SOVIET SPACE PROGRAM	AUG. 9, 1973	**MAR. 9, 1974**
10	**MARS 6**	SOVIET SPACE PROGRAM	AUG. 5, 1973	**MAR. 12, 1974**

* Successful flybys, the rest are successful orbiter missions.

MARINER 4

1 A total of 21 complete images were captured by NASA's unmanned *Mariner 4* spacecraft from July 14–15, 1965.

TOP 10

FIRST LANDERS/ROVERS ON MARS

The first probe to successfully reach Mars got there 40 years ago...

	MISSION NAME	SPACE AGENCY	LAUNCH DATE	ARRIVED ON MARS
▷ 1	VIKING 1 LANDER	NASA	AUGUST 20, 1975	**JULY 20, 1976**
2	VIKING 2 LANDER	NASA	SEPTEMBER 9, 1975	**SEPT. 3, 1976**
▷ 3	MARS PATHFINDER LANDER*	NASA	DECEMBER 4, 1996	**JULY 4, 1997**
=	SOJOURNER ROVER*	NASA	DECEMBER 4, 1996	**JULY 4, 1997**
5	BEAGLE 2	ESA	JUNE 2, 2003	**DEC. 25, 2003**
6	SPIRIT ROVER	NASA	JUNE 10, 2003	**JAN. 4, 2004**
7	OPPORTUNITY ROVER	NASA	JULY 7, 2003	**JAN. 25, 2004**
8	PHOENIX MARS LANDER	NASA	AUGUST 4, 2007	**MAY 25, 2008**
9	MARS SCIENCE LABORATORY*	NASA	NOVEMBER 26, 2011	**AUG 6, 2012**
=	CURIOSITY ROVER*	NASA	NOVEMBER 26, 2011	**AUG. 6, 2012**

* 3 & 4, and 9 & 10, were paired units

Lost for 11 years, *Beagle 2* was found on Mars on

JANUARY 16, 2015

by NASA's Mars Reconnaissance Orbiter (MRO)

VIKING 1 LANDER

1 Until the Mars rover Opportunity came along, *Viking 1* held the Mars surface mission record of 2,307 days. Its orbit photography includes images of clouds on Mars.

MARS PATHFINDER LANDER

3 After 297 successful mission days, *Mars Pathfinder* (and its robot rover Sojourner) ceased to operate on September 27, 1997.

COMPARE THE SPACE AGENCIES

One country remains the leader of Mars missions...

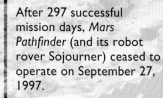

■ NASA (USA) **9**
■ ESA (EUROPE) **1**

TOP 10

MOST RECENT **SUCCESSFUL** MARS MISSIONS

Although humankind hasn't set foot on Mars yet, plenty of robots have...

NASA's Phoenix mission cost
$386 MILLION

	MISSION NAME	SPACE AGENCY	LAUNCH DATE	ARRIVED ON MARS
1	MARS ORBITER MISSION	ISRO (INDIA)	NOV. 5, 2013	**SEPT. 24, 2014**
2	MAVEN	NASA	NOV. 18, 2013	**SEPT. 22, 2014**
3	MSL CURIOSITY	NASA	NOV. 26, 2011	**AUG. 6, 2012**
4	PHOENIX	NASA	AUGUST 4, 2007	**MAY 25, 2008**
5	MARS RECONNAISSANCE ORBITER	NASA	AUGUST 12, 2005	**MAR. 10, 2006**
6	ROSETTA	ESA (EUROPE)	MARCH 2, 2004	**FEB. 25, 2007**
7	MER-B OPPORTUNITY	NASA	JULY 7, 2003	**JAN. 25, 2004**
8	MER-A SPIRIT	NASA	JUNE 10, 2003	**JAN. 4, 2004**
9	MARS EXPRESS	ESA (EUROPE)	JUNE 2, 2003	**DEC. 25, 2003**
10	2001 MARS ODYSSEY	NASA	APRIL 7, 2001	**OCT. 24, 2001**

MARS ORBITER MISSION

1 "MOM" cost $74 million. It marks the first space mission for India, and the first nation to achieve this success on a first attempt.

MARS EXPRESS

9 The ESA's *Mars Express* orbiter had its mission time extended until the end of 2016. In 2013 it mapped nearly all of Mars's surface.

TOP 10

MISSIONS TO HELP COLONIZE MARS*

Have you read the book or seen *The Martian*? Scientists are working to make Mars missions a reality...

	MISSION NAME	AGENCY	YEAR	MISSION
1	MARS ONE DEMO	MARS ONE & INTERPLANETARY MEDIA GROUP	2016	DEMONSTRATION/PREP
2	MARS ONE SUPPLIES	MARS ONE & INTERPLANETARY MEDIA GROUP	2016	SUPPLIES LAUNCHED TO MARS
3	MARS ONE COMSTAT	MARS ONE & INTERPLANETARY MEDIA GROUP	2020	LAUNCH COMMUNICATIONS SATELLITE
4	INSPIRATION MARS FOUNDATION	DENNIS TITO	2021	MANNED FLYBY TO MARS
5	MARTIAN MOON SAMPLE RETURN	JAXA (JAPAN)	2021	COLLECT AND RETURN SAMPLES
6	RED DRAGON	NASA	2022	TEST FOR HUMAN ENTRY TO ATMOSPHERE
7	FOOTPRINT	ESA (EUROPE)	2022	COLLECT AND RETURN SAMPLES
8	MARS ONE ROVER	MARS ONE & INTERPLANETARY MEDIA GROUP	2022	ROVER LANDS TO FIND COLONY LOCATION
9	MARS ONE ROVER II	MARS ONE & INTERPLANETARY MEDIA GROUP	2024	ROVER II LANDS WITH LIFE SUPPORT/SUPPLIES
10	MARS ONE TEAM ONE	MARS ONE & INTERPLANETARY MEDIA GROUP	2026	TEAM OF 4 ASTRONAUTS TO LAND ON MARS

* In date order

DENNIS TITO'S INSPIRATION MARS FOUNDATION PLAN

A 76-year-old American engineer and business mogul, Dennis Tito spent almost eight days in orbit when he visited the ISS (International Space Station) in 2001. Tito's nonprofit Inspiration Mars Foundation aims to achieve a manned Mars flyby by 2018.

If completed, Red Dragon could weigh more than **14,000** POUNDS

MARS ONE PROGRAM

This Dutch nonprofit organization hopes to achieve the first permanent human colony on Mars by 2027. The 39-year-old Dutch inventor Bas Lansdorp is the cofounder and CEO of the project.

YURI ROMANENKO

5 Romanenko was twice awarded his country's highest honor, the national Hero of the Soviet Union medal. His son, Roman, also an astronaut, won the medal in 2010.

Sergei Avdeyev's total time in space:

747 DAYS
14.23 HOURS

LONGEST HUMAN SPACE FLIGHTS

The record-making lengths of time on this chart are for single continuous missions...

	NAME	COUNTRY	CONSECUTIVE DAYS IN SPACE
1	VALERI POLYAKOV	RUSSIA	437.7
2	SERGEI AVDEYEV	RUSSIA	379.6
3	VLADIMIR TITOV	RUSSIA (SOVIET UNION ERA)	365
=	MUSA MANAROV	RUSSIA (SOVIET UNION ERA)	365
5	YURI ROMANENKO	RUSSIA (SOVIET UNION ERA)	326.5
6	SERGEI KRIKALEV	RUSSIA (INCL. SOVIET UNION ERA)	311.8
7	VALERI POLYAKOV	RUSSIA (SOVIET UNION ERA)	240.9
8	LEONID KIZIM	RUSSIA (SOVIET UNION ERA)	237
=	VLADIMIR SOLOVYOV	RUSSIA (SOVIET UNION ERA)	237
=	OLEG ATKOV	RUSSIA (SOVIET UNION ERA)	237

OLEG ATKOV

8 The former cosmonaut and trained doctor currently works for the EU's European Commission. He's a telemedicine specialist, delivering healthcare to remote areas.

NATIONS WITH THE
MOST SPACEWALKERS

Astronauts often leave their spacecraft to perform
tasks in space, which is called a spacewalk...

	NATION	TOTAL SPACEWALKERS
1	USA	126
2	RUSSIA (INCL. SOVIET UNION ERA)	63
3	CANADA	3
=	JAPAN	3
=	FRANCE	3
6	CHINA	2
=	GERMANY	2
8	SWEDEN	1
=	ITALY	1
=	SWITZERLAND	1

CHINA

6 The CNSA (China
National Space
Administration)
was established in
1993, but other
forms of the
country's space
agency have existed
since 1956.

USA

1 NASA TV provides archival and
live footage of a variety of NASA
missions. The channel has won
two Emmy Awards and can be
watched online.

SPACEWALKING NATIONS

This is how the above chart's top 5 compare...

USA
126

RUSSIA
63

The CSA
(Canadian
Space Agency)
was formed on

**MARCH 1,
1989**

CANADA
3

JAPAN
3

FRANCE
3

USA

1

More than 62 percent of all manned space missions have been American. A total of 40 different countries have ventured into outer space.

MOST ASTRONAUTS
LAUNCHED BY A NATION

There may be 10 countries in this chart, but two lead the race by a substantial number...

NATION	TOTAL PEOPLE SENT INTO SPACE
1 **USA**	**335**
2 **RUSSIA (INCLUDING SOVIET UNION ERA)**	**120**
3 **GERMANY**	**11**
4 **CHINA**	**10**
= **JAPAN**	**10**
6 **CANADA**	**9**
= **FRANCE**	**9**
8 **ITALY**	**7**
9 **BELGIUM**	**2**
= **NETHERLANDS**	**2**

ISS HISTORY

The first parts of the ISS (International Space Station) were launched into space on November 20, 1988. It's a collaborative project by Canadian, Japanese, and European space agencies.

Russian space station Mir was deorbited (controlled destruction/ reentry) on **MARCH 23, 2001**

CCCP

AŤ ŽIJE PRVNÍ KOSMONAUTKA SVĚTA!

ISS-6A ★ STS-100

ROBOTICS SCIENCE LOGISTICS

ISS FUTURE PLANS

American manufacturer Boeing continues to be the main ISS contractor. At this stage, there are plans to extend the maintenance and development of the ISS through 2028.

ISS width:

356
FEET

TOP 10

MOST ISS VISITS BY NATION

For more than 15 years, space agencies have been sending astronauts to the International Space Station...

	NATION	INDIVIDUAL(S)	ISS CREW MEMBER(S)
1	USA	141	47
2	RUSSIA	44	37
3	JAPAN	7	5
4	ITALY	5	3
5	CANADA	7	2
6	GERMANY	3	2
7	FRANCE	3	1
8	BELGIUM	1	1
=	NETHERLANDS	1	1
10	SWEDEN	1	0

JAPAN

3 JAXA (Japan Aerospace eXploration Agency) aims to "Explore to Realize." It's also working on developing next generation supersonic air travel.

LONGEST AMOUNT OF TIME SPENT IN SPACE

Russian astronauts' total mission time in space exceeds 68 years...

	COUNTRY	TOTAL HUMAN DAYS IN SPACE
1	RUSSIA (INCL. SOVIET UNION ERA)	25,123.74
2	USA	17,786.40
3	JAPAN	1,031.06
4	GERMANY	658.97
5	ITALY	627.22
6	CANADA	506.15
7	FRANCE	432.19
8	NETHERLANDS	210.69
9	BELGIUM	207.66
10	CHINA	100.81

USA

2 American astronaut Sunita Williams holds the record for the second-longest single spaceflight by a woman. Her 195 days on the ISS is just eclipsed by Italian Samantha Cristoforetti's 199.6 days.

PEOPLE IN SPACE

The nations that have explored space most are...

RUSSIA 25,123.74

USA 17,786.40

Lodewijk van den Berg was the first Dutch astronaut sent into space, on **APRIL 29, 1985**

JAPAN 1,031.06

GERMANY 658.97

ITALY 627.22

CANADA

6 Marc Garneau was the first Canadian in space. He was a Payload Specialist for the STS-41-G Space Shuttle mission, which launched on October 5, 1984.

TOP 10

LONGEST RUNNING
OPERATIONAL SPACE AGENCIES

The space race continues to be expensive and competitive, with these nations as the longest participants...

	AGENCY	COUNTRY	YEAR FOUNDED
1	INSTITUTO NACIONAL DE TÉCNICA AEROESPACIAL (INTA)	SPAIN	1942
2	NATIONAL AERONAUTICS & SPACE ADMINISTRATION (NASA)	USA	1958
3	NATIONAL CENTER OF SPACE RESEARCH (CNES)	FRANCE	1961
=	SPACE AND UPPER ATMOSPHERE RESEARCH COMMISSION (SUPARCO)	PAKISTAN	1961
5	GERMAN AEROSPACE CENTER (DLR)	GERMANY	1969
=	INDIAN SPACE RESEARCH ORGANIZATION (ISRO)	INDIA	1969
7	SWEDISH NATIONAL SPACE BOARD (SNSB)	SWEDEN	1972
8	EUROPEAN SPACE AGENCY (ESA)	(EUROPEAN SYNDICATE)	1975
9	ITALIAN SPACE AGENCY (ASI)	ITALY	1988
10	CANADIAN SPACE AGENCY (CSA)	CANADA	1989

Russian astronaut Valentina Tereshkova was the first woman sent into space:

JUNE 16, 1963

KARI (KOREA AEROSPACE RESEARCH INSTITUTE)

Founded October 10, 1989, KARI missed out on a place in the above Top 10 chart by just seven months. The agency plans to launch its second rocket, KSLV-2, by 2020.

NASA

2 This is a 1989 team of NASA astronauts. The 9th Administrator of NASA, Daniel S. Goldin, holds the record for the longest term. He served for 3,517 days between April 1, 1992, and November 17, 2001.

247

MICE

9 This photo shows American Colonel John P. Stapp and engineer Charles Wade inspecting the "Mousenick" space capsule before its space mission in 1959.

NASA sent two bullfrogs into space on **NOVEMBER 9, 1970**

FIRST LIVING THINGS IN SPACE

TOP 10

The original heroes for providing scientists key intel about space? This array of creatures...

DOG

5 Laika was a stray dog that made history by being the first dog in space. She died within hours, but this wasn't revealed to the public until 2002. There's a monument in Moscow in her honor.

	ORGANISM	ROCKET	DATE
1	FRUIT FLIES	V2	FEBRUARY 20, 1947
2	MOSS	V2	VARIOUS, 1947
3	RHESUS MONKEY (ALBERT II)	V2	JUNE 14, 1949
4	MOUSE	V2	AUGUST 31, 1950
5	DOG (LAIKA)	SPUTNIK 2	NOVEMBER 3, 1957
6	SQUIRREL MONKEY (GORDO)	JUPITER IRBM AM-13	DEC. 13, 1958
7	RABBIT (MARFUSA)	R2	JULY 2, 1959
8	CHIMPANZEE (HAM)	REDSTONE	JANUARY 31, 1961
9	GUINEA PIGS, FROGS & MICE	VOSTOK 3A	MARCH 1961
10	TORTOISE	ZOND 5	SEPTEMBER 18, 1968

MOST **TIME SPENT IN** SPACE (MULTIPLE MISSIONS)

TOP 10

All of these astronauts have spent at least 18 months in space, and some nearly 2.5 years...

NAME	COUNTRY	FLIGHTS	TOTAL TIME IN SPACE (DAYS)
1 GENNADY PADALKA	RUSSIA	5	**879.5**
2 SERGEI KRIKALEV	RUSSIA*	6	**803.4**
3 ALEXANDR KALERI	RUSSIA	5	**769.3**
4 SERGEI AVDEYEV	RUSSIA*	3	**747.6**
5 VALERI POLYAKOV	RUSSIA*	2	**678.7**
6 ANATOLY SOLOVYEV	RUSSIA*	5	**651.1**
7 YURI MALENCHENKO	RUSSIA	5	**641.5**
8 VIKTOR AFANASYEV	RUSSIA*	4	**555.8**
9 YURY USACHEV	RUSSIA	4	**552.8**
10 PAVEL VINOGRADOV	RUSSIA	3	**546.9**

* Includes mission(s) during Soviet Union era

GENNADY PADALKA

1 During his time in space, Padalka worked on both the ISS and the Mir space station. He also performed 10 EVA (Extra-vehicular Activity) tasks.

ANATOLY SOLOVYEV

6 The photo above captures the moment just before Anatoly Solovyev and Pavel Vinogradov boarded the Soyuz TM-26 spacecraft on August 5, 1997.

PAVEL VINOGRADOV

10 The Russian Soyuz TM-26 spacecraft that took Vinogradov and Solovyev to Mir was the 32nd mission to the space station. The mission was completed on February 19, 1998.

Yuri Malenchenko married Texan Ekaterina Dmitrieva via satellite from the ISS on **AUGUST 10, 2003**

EXPLORATION

CHARLES DUKE

10 Born October 3, 1935, Charles Duke holds the record for being the youngest astronaut to walk on the Moon. He was 36 years old.

BUZZ ALDRIN

2 The second man to walk on the Moon has published two autobiographies, *Return To Earth* (1973) and *Magnificent Desolation: The Long Journey Home from the Moon* (2009).

Retired astronaut Edgar Mitchell's total time in space:

9 DAYS
1 MINUTE

FIRST HUMANS TO WALK ON THE MOON

Our moon is the only celestial body that humankind has made physical contact with, for now...

	NAME	COUNTRY	MISSION	DATE(S) OF MOON WALKS
1	NEIL ARMSTRONG	USA	APOLLO 11	JULY 21, 1969
2	BUZZ ALDRIN	USA	APOLLO 11	JULY 21, 1969
3	PETE CONRAD	USA	APOLLO 12	NOVEMBER 19–20, 1969
4	ALAN BEAN	USA	APOLLO 12	NOVEMBER 19–20, 1969
5	ALAN SHEPARD	USA	APOLLO 14	FEBRUARY 5–6, 1971
6	EDGAR MITCHELL	USA	APOLLO 14	FEBRUARY 5–6, 1971
7	DAVID SCOTT	USA	APOLLO 15	JULY 31–AUGUST 2, 1971
8	JAMES IRWIN	USA	APOLLO 15	JULY 31–AUGUST 2, 1971
9	JOHN W. YOUNG	USA	APOLLO 16	APRIL 21–23, 1972
10	CHARLES DUKE	USA	APOLLO 16	APRIL 21–23, 1972

NASA

1

The first iteration of the U.S. space agency was NACA (National Advisory Committee for Aeronautics), founded March 3, 1915.

TOP 10

BIGGEST **SPACE PROGRAMS**

Adventures into the black vastness of space are a high priority for these nations' agencies...

	AGENCY	COUNTRY	BUDGET ($ MILLIONS)
1	**NASA** (NATIONAL AERONAUTICS & SPACE ADMINISTRATION)	USA	18,500
2	**ROSCOSMOS** (RUSSIAN FEDERAL SPACE AGENCY)	RUSSIA	5,600
3	**ESA** (EUROPEAN SPACE AGENCY)	EUROPEAN NATIONS	5,510
4	**CNES** (NATIONAL CENTER OF SPACE RESEARCH)	FRANCE	2,500
5	**JAXA** (JAPAN AEROSPACE EXPLORATION AGENCY)	JAPAN	2,460
6	**DLR** (GERMAN AEROSPACE CENTER)	GERMANY	2,000
7	**ASI** (ITALIAN SPACE AGENCY)	ITALY	1,800
8	**CNSA** (CHINA NATIONAL SPACE ADMINISTRATION)	CHINA	1,780
9	**ISRO** (INDIAN SPACE RESEARCH ORGANIZATION)	INDIA	1,200
10	**CSA** (CANADIAN SPACE AGENCY)	CANADA	488.7

ROSCOSMOS

2

Founded on February 25, 1992, this Russian space agency took over from the Soviet Space Program, which had been operational for 60 years from 1931 to 1991.

AGENCIES SIDE BY SIDE

Here's how the biggest 5 compare...

NASA
$18,500 MILLION

ROSCOSMOS
$5,600 MILLION

ESA
$5,510 MILLION

CNES
$2,500 MILLION

JAXA
$2,460 MILLION

Total ESA member states:

22

Total *Space Invaders* games across all platforms:

46

ASTEROIDS

7 The highest score ever achieved playing *Asteroids* is 41,338,740 by John McAllister on April 6, 2010. The previous world record had not been beaten for over 27 years.

ATARI

ASTEROIDS™

• Explosive rapid-fire space action • 1 or 2 players are challenged to destroy asteroids and enemy spacecraft • New Atari-designed QuadraScan™ display system • New personal high score table display • Optional "Hyperspace" • Optional coinage including Susan B. Anthony coin slot • Bonus play at 10,000 points.

TOP 10

OLDEST ARCADE GAMES SET IN SPACE

The multibillion-dollar video game industry has its roots in simple, but highly effective, arcade classics...

	NAME	DEVELOPED BY	RELEASE DATE
1	GALAXY GAME	BILL PITTS & HUGH TUCK	**SEPT. 1971**
2	COMPUTER SPACE	NOLAN BUSHNELL & TED DABNEY	**NOV. 1971**
3	ASTRO RACE	TAITO	**JULY 1973**
4	SPACE WARS	CINEMATRONICS	**OCT. 1977**
5	SPACE INVADERS	TAITO	**JULY 1978**
6	GALAXIAN	NAMCO	**OCT. 1979**
7	ASTEROIDS	ATARI	**NOV. 1979**
=	TAIL GUNNER	VECTORBEAM	**NOV. 1979**
9	DEFENDER	WILLIAMS ELECTRONICS	**FEB. 1981**
10	ELIMINATOR	SEGA	**DEC. 1981**

Sonic

SPACE WARS

SPACE WARS

4 Unlike other arcade games of the 1970s, *Space Wars* could not be played as a solo game. It was designed for two players to battle each other.

STAR WARS BATTLEFRONT

3 More than two years in the making, this third game in the series was released on November 17, 2015, for PS4, Xbox One, and PC platforms.

TOP 10

MOST GROSSING **STAR WARS** VIDEO GAMES

The Force awakened in 2015, but it's been strong with video gamers for decades...

	NAME	GENRE	PLATFORM	RELEASED	UNIT SALES ($MILLIONS)
1	LEGO STAR WARS: THE COMPLETE SAGA	ACTION	WII	2007	**5.57**
2	LEGO STAR WARS: THE COMPLETE SAGA	ACTION	DS	2007	**4.73**
3	STAR WARS BATTLEFRONT	SHOOTER	PS2	2004	**3.61**
4	STAR WARS BATTLEFRONT II	SHOOTER	PS2	2005	**3.59**
5	LEGO STAR WARS: THE VIDEO GAME	ACTION	PS2	2005	**3.53**
6	STAR WARS: EPISODE III—REVENGE OF THE SITH	ACTION	PS2	2005	**3.32**
7	STAR WARS: EPISODE I RACER	RACING	N64	1999	**3.12**
8	STAR WARS: THE FORCE UNLEASHED	ACTION	XBOX 360	2008	**2.71**
9	LEGO STAR WARS II: THE ORIGINAL TRILOGY	ACTION	PS2	2006	**2.69**
10	STAR WARS: SHADOWS OF THE EMPIRE	ACTION	N64	1996	**2.65**

Across all gaming platforms, **230** Star Wars games have been made

LEGO STAR WARS: THE COMPLETE SAGA

1 Released across eight platforms between 2007 and 2015, this 2012 Kids' Choice Award-winning game features LEGO spins on the *Star Wars* movies, *Episodes I* to *VI*.

MOVIES & TV

ZONE 10

BIGGEST MOVIES OF ALL TIME

Comparing every movie ever made from around the world, these are the most successful...

	MOVIE	YEAR OF RELEASE	BOX OFFICE ($ WORLDWIDE)
1	AVATAR	2009	2,787,965,087
2	TITANIC	1997	2,186,772,302
▶ 3	STAR WARS: EPISODE VII—THE FORCE AWAKENS	2015	2,028,057,964
▶ 4	JURASSIC WORLD	2015	1,670,400,637
5	THE AVENGERS	2012	1,519,557,910
6	FURIOUS 7	2015	1,514,827,481
7	AVENGERS: AGE OF ULTRON	2015	1,405,413,868
8	HARRY POTTER AND THE DEATHLY HALLOWS: PART 2	2011	1,341,511,219
9	FROZEN	2013	1,276,480,335
10	IRON MAN 3	2013	1,215,439,994

James Spader (who played Ultron in the *Avengers* sequel) has **55** acting credits

JURASSIC WORLD

4 The fourth *Jurassic Park* movie holds the record for the biggest opening weekend for a summer movie. The website *JurassicWorld.com* is created as an in-world experience, as though the park is real.

STAR WARS: EPISODE VII— THE FORCE AWAKENS

3 *Episode VII* broke dozens of box office records around the world. In the United States, it's the most successful movie of all time. It also holds the U.S. record for the biggest opening day, weekend, and first week.

Francis Lawrence (director of the last three *Hunger Games* movies) total box office: **$3,204,946,658**

STEVEN SPIELBERG

1 This filmmaker directed many of the most popular and influential movies of all time, including *Jaws* (1975), the *Indiana Jones* series, and *Jurassic Park* (1993). Spielberg has also won two Academy Awards for Best Director.

DIRECTORS BY COUNTRY

Here's how the below list breaks down by nation...

- USA **6**
- UK **2**
- CANADA **1**
- NZ **1**

J.J. ABRAMS

The 11th most successful movie director of all time is J. J. Abrams. His five films total $3,539,065,992 at the worldwide box office. He also has a further 44 producer credits and 21 writing credits.

TOP 10

MOST SUCCESSFUL DIRECTORS OF ALL TIME

Behind every hit blockbuster is a team of thousands of people, all led by the movie's director...

	NAME	COUNTRY	TOTAL MOVIES DIRECTED (THEATRICALLY RELEASED)	BOX OFFICE ($ WORLDWIDE)
1	STEVEN SPIELBERG	USA	29	9,508,961,476
2	PETER JACKSON	NEW ZEALAND	14	6,530,713,297
3	JAMES CAMERON	CANADA	10	6,207,806,867
4	MICHAEL BAY	USA	12	5,775,726,013
5	CHRISTOPHER NOLAN	UK	9	4,227,531,716
6	DAVID YATES	UK	6	4,176,096,940
7	ROBERT ZEMECKIS	USA	17	4,139,921,474
8	CHRIS COLUMBUS	USA	15	4,099,031,132
9	GEORGE LUCAS	USA	6	3,997,678,795
10	TIM BURTON	USA	18	3,803,729,658

257

DANCES WITH WOLVES

5 Kevin Costner starred in and directed this winner of seven Oscars. Michael Blake wrote the screenplay based on his own novel.

Peter *"Lord of the Rings"* Jackson's debut feature film, *Bad Taste* (an alien invasion horror comedy), was made in

1987

BIGGEST BEST PICTURE OSCAR WINNERS

Of all the movies that were awarded Best Picture, these made the most at the box office...

	MOVIE	YEAR WON ACADEMY AWARD FOR BEST PICTURE	BOX OFFICE ($ WORLDWIDE)
1	TITANIC	1997	2,186,772,302
2	THE LORD OF THE RINGS: THE RETURN OF THE KING	2003	1,119,929,521
3	FORREST GUMP	1994	677,945,399
4	GLADIATOR	2000	457,640,427
5	DANCES WITH WOLVES	1990	424,208,848
6	THE KING'S SPEECH	2010	414,211,549
7	SLUMDOG MILLIONAIRE	2008	377,910,544
8	AMERICAN BEAUTY	1999	356,296,601
9	RAIN MAN	1988	354,825,435
10	SCHINDLER'S LIST	1993	321,306,305

SLUMDOG MILLIONAIRE

7 Dev Patel and Freida Pinto both made their feature film acting debuts in this movie. It won eight Academy Awards and was based on Vikas Sawrup's 2005 novel *Q & A*.

THE LAST EMPEROR

6 Italian filmmaker Bernardo Bertolucci's tale of China's final emperor is one of 25 movies he directed.

WEST SIDE STORY

4 This musical was inspired by William Shakespeare's *Romeo and Juliet*. In December 2015, one of its stars, Rita Moreno, was honored with a Lifetime Artistic Achievement Award at The Kennedy Center Honors.

From *Here to Eternity*'s total international award wins:

22

TOP 10

MOVIES WITH THE MOST OSCAR WINS & NOMINATIONS

Dramatic performances and epic landscapes are very popular with the Academy Awards...

	MOVIE	YEAR	NOMINATIONS	WON
1	TITANIC	1997	14	11
2	THE LORD OF THE RINGS: THE RETURN OF THE KING	2003	12	11
3	BEN-HUR	1959	11	11
4	WEST SIDE STORY	1961	11	10
5	THE ENGLISH PATIENT	1996	12	9
6	GIGI	1958	9	9
=	THE LAST EMPEROR	1987	9	9
8	AMADEUS	1984	11	8
9	GONE WITH THE WIND	1939	13	8 (+2 HON.)*
10	FROM HERE TO ETERNITY	1953	13	8

* 2 posthumous honorary wins

259

Star Wars:
The Clone Wars
(2008) box office
total:
$68,282,844

STAR WARS: EPISODE V—THE EMPIRE STRIKES BACK

7 Lawrence Kasdan cowrote the screenplay for this, the second *Star Wars* movie made, and also cowrote *The Force Awakens*. Kasdan's 17 other writing credits include *Raiders of the Lost Ark* (1981).

STAR WARS: EPISODE VII—THE FORCE AWAKENS

1 Kylo Ren was played by Adam Driver. The role marked his 24th acting credit. He returns in *Star Wars: Episode VIII* in 2017.

TOP 10

BIGGEST STAR WARS MOVIES

The adventures of Rey, Finn, and BB-8 truly are a box-office Force to be reckoned with...

	MOVIE	YEAR OF RELEASE	BOX OFFICE ($ WORLDWIDE)
1	STAR WARS: EPISODE VII—THE FORCE AWAKENS	2015	2,028,057,964
2	STAR WARS: EPISODE I—THE PHANTOM MENACE	2009	1,027,044,677
3	STAR WARS: EPISODE III—REVENGE OF THE SITH	2005	848,754,768
4	STAR WARS: EPISODE IV—A NEW HOPE	1977	775,398,007
5	STAR WARS: EPISODE II—ATTACK OF THE CLONES	2002	649,398,328
6	STAR WARS: EPISODE IV—A NEW HOPE (SPECIAL EDITION)	1997	579,646,015
7	STAR WARS: EPISODE V—THE EMPIRE STRIKES BACK	1980	538,375,067
8	STAR WARS: EPISODE VI—RETURN OF THE JEDI	1983	475,106,177
9	STAR WARS: EPISODE VI—RETURN OF THE JEDI (SPECIAL EDITION)	1997	353,096,720
10	STAR WARS: EPISODE V—THE EMPIRE STRIKES BACK (SPECIAL EDITION)	1997	347,689,833

LONGEST-RUNNING TV SHOWS SET IN SPACE

Beloved outer-space series feature a Time Lord and even a beer-drinking robot...

	TV SHOW	YEARS ON AIR	TOTAL EPISODES
1	SPACE PATROL	1950–55	1,110
2	DOCTOR WHO	1963–89; 2005–PRESENT	825+
3	STARGATE SG-1	1997–2007	214
4	MYSTERY SCIENCE THEATER 3000	1988–99	197
5	STAR TREK: THE NEXT GENERATION	1987–94	178
6	STAR TREK: DEEP SPACE NINE	1993–99	176
7	STAR TREK: VOYAGER	1995–2001	172
8	THUNDERCATS	1985–89; 2011	156
9	FUTURAMA	1999–2003; 2008–13	141
10	VOLTRON	1984–85	124

SPACE PATROL

1

Creator Mike Moser's sci-fi saga began as a radio show on March 9, 1950. In addition to its TV episodes, 129 radio episodes were made.

The first episode of *Voltron* aired in the U.S. on

SEPTEMBER 10, 1984

TOP 5 TV IN SPACE

Here's how the most popular compare visually...

SPACE PATROL
1,110 EPISODES

DOCTOR WHO
825 EPISODES

STARGATE SG-1
214 EPISODES

MYSTERY SCIENCE THEATER 3000
197 EPISODES

STAR TREK: THE NEXT GENERATION
178 EPISODES

FUTURAMA

9

Billy West performed dozens of characters' voices for *Futurama*, including Professor Hubert J. Farnsworth, Philip J. Fry, Dr. Zoidberg, and Zapp Brannigan.

BIGGEST HUMAN/ALIEN ENCOUNTER MOVIES

If the movie featured an alien organism having contact with a human, it qualified for this Top 10...

	MOVIE	ALIENS ENCOUNTERED	YEAR OF RELEASE	BOX OFFICE ($ WORLDWIDE)
1	AVATAR	PANDORANS	2009	2,787,965,087
2	THE AVENGERS	CHITAURI, ASGARDIANS	2012	1,519,557,910
3	TRANSFORMERS: DARK OF THE MOON	AUTOBOTS & DECEPTICONS	2011	1,123,794,079
4	TRANSFORMERS: AGE OF EXTINCTION	AUTOBOTS & DECEPTICONS	2014	1,104,054,072
5	SPIDER-MAN 3	EXTRATERRESTRIAL SYMBIOTE	2007	890,871,626
6	TRANSFORMERS: REVENGE OF THE FALLEN	AUTOBOTS & DECEPTICONS	2009	836,303,693
7	INDEPENDENCE DAY	UNNAMED ALIENS	1996	817,400,891
8	E.T. THE EXTRA-TERRESTRIAL	E.T.	1982	792,910,554
9	GUARDIANS OF THE GALAXY	SEVERAL	2014	773,312,399
10	TRANSFORMERS	AUTOBOTS & DECEPTICONS	2007	709,709,780

GUARDIANS OF THE GALAXY

9 Director James Gunn's previous movies include the horror-comedy *Slither* (2006) and vigilante superhero tale *Super* (2010).

SPIDER-MAN 3

5 Spidey's alien symbiote costume debuted in *The Amazing Spider-Man* #252 (May 1984). The symbiote with Eddy Brock as its host, became Venom in issue #300 (May 1988).

E.T. was director Steven Spielberg's

6TH

theatrically-released movie

Shane Black's *Predator* sequel is due for release in

2018

ALIEN 3

4 Sigourney Weaver's 78 acting credits feature several iconic sci-fi movies: four *Alien* movies, *Avatar* (2009), the *Ghostbusters* movies, and *Chappie* (2015).

TOP 10

BIGGEST ALIEN & PREDATOR MOVIES

These terrifying and iconic creatures share the same movie universe...

	MOVIE	YEAR OF RELEASE	BOX OFFICE ($ WORLDWIDE)
1	PROMETHEUS	2012	403,354,469
2	ALIEN VS. PREDATOR	2004	172,544,654
3	ALIEN: RESURRECTION	1997	161,376,068
4	ALIEN 3	1992	159,814,498
5	ALIENS	1986	131,060,248
6	ALIEN VS. PREDATOR: REQUIEM	2007	128,884,494
7	PREDATORS	2010	127,233,108
8	ALIEN	1979	104,931,801
9	PREDATOR	1987	98,267,558
10	PREDATOR 2	1990	57,120,318

ALIEN VS. PREDATOR

2 Long before the *Alien* franchise's xenomorph organisms battled the Predators on the big screen, they did so in the pages of Dark Horse Comics in 1990.

STAR TREK INTO DARKNESS

1

This was the 12th feature film adventure for characters in the *Star Trek* universe. Zachary Quinto has played Spock (originated by Leonard Nimoy) in the three most recent movies, including 2016's *Star Trek Beyond*.

Star Trek Beyond was released on

JULY 7, 2016

TOP 10

BIGGEST STAR TREK MOVIES

Since the first big-screen adventure in 1979, *Star Trek* has continued to warp into movie theaters...

	MOVIE	YEAR OF RELEASE	BOX OFFICE ($ WORLDWIDE)
1	STAR TREK INTO DARKNESS	2013	467,381,584
2	STAR TREK	2009	385,680,446
3	STAR TREK: FIRST CONTACT	1996	146,027,888
4	STAR TREK: GENERATIONS	1994	118,071,125
5	STAR TREK: INSURRECTION	1998	112,587,658
6	STAR TREK IV: THE VOYAGE HOME	1986	109,713,132
7	STAR TREK VI: THE UNDISCOVERED COUNTRY	1991	96,888,996
8	STAR TREK: THE MOTION PICTURE	1979	82,258,456
9	STAR TREK II: THE WRATH OF KHAN	1982	78,912,963
10	STAR TREK III: THE SEARCH FOR SPOCK	1984	76,471,046

STAR TREK: FIRST CONTACT

3

The second movie to feature the *Star Trek: Next Generation* characters, this focused on villains known as the "Borg." Alice Krige played the Borg Queen who grappled with Captain Jean-Luc Picard (Patrick Stewart).

THE MARTIAN

3 Drew Goddard adapted this screenplay from Andy Weir's novel of the same name. Goddard also wrote *Cloverfield* (2008), and cowrote with Joss Whedon *The Cabin in the Woods* (2012), which he also directed.

APOLLO 13

5 This was based on the real-life story of how the crew of *Apollo 13* was almost lost in space in 1970. It won two Academy Awards.

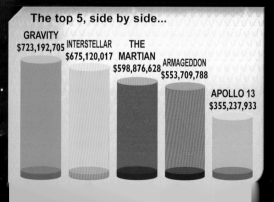

Duncan Jones's indie movie *Moon* (2009) total box office:

$9,760,104

TOP 10

BIGGEST ASTRONAUT MOVIES

Of all the movies to feature traditional human astronauts, these are the 10 huge successes...

	MOVIE	YEAR OF RELEASE	BOX OFFICE ($ WORLDWIDE)
1	GRAVITY	2013	723,192,705
2	INTERSTELLAR	2014	675,120,017
▶ 3	THE MARTIAN	2015	598,876,628
4	ARMAGEDDON	1998	553,709,788
▶ 5	APOLLO 13	1995	355,237,933
6	MOONRAKER	1979	210,308,099
7	2001: A SPACE ODYSSEY	1968	190,700,000
8	SPACE COWBOYS	2000	128,884,132
9	MISSION TO MARS	2000	110,983,407
10	2010	1984	40,400,657

SPACE COMPARISONS

The top 5, side by side...

GRAVITY
$723,192,705

INTERSTELLAR
$675,120,017

THE MARTIAN
$598,876,628

ARMAGEDDON
$553,709,788

APOLLO 13
$355,237,933

The TV series adaptation of *iZombie* premiered on

MAR. 17, 2015

ARROW

7 Based on the DC comic *Green Arrow*, this show exists in the same TV universe as *The Flash* (2014–present), *Supergirl* (2015–present), and *Legends of Tomorrow* (2016–present).

SMALLVILLE

1 Its 10-year run charted the early years of Clark Kent/Superman (played by Tom Welling). He finally donned a cape and flew in the series finale that aired May 13, 2011.

TOP 10

LONGEST-RUNNING COMIC BOOK TV SHOWS (LIVE ACTION)

If it was based on a comic book, it qualified for a chance to be in this Top 10...

	TV SHOW	YEARS ON AIR	TOTAL EPISODES
1	SMALLVILLE	2001–11	218
2	SABRINA THE TEENAGE WITCH	1996–2003	163
3	BATMAN	1966–68	120
4	ADVENTURES OF SUPERMAN	1952–58	104
5	SUPERBOY	1988–92	100
6	TALES FROM THE CRYPT	1986–96	93
7	ARROW	2012–PRESENT	92+
8	LOIS & CLARK: THE NEW ADVENTURES OF SUPERMAN	1993–97	88
9	THE INCREDIBLE HULK	1978–82	86 *
10	THE WALKING DEAD	2010–PRESENT	83+

* including 3 TV movies

LONGEST-RUNNING COMIC BOOK TV SHOWS (ANIMATED)

Countless cartoons have been made about comic-book characters, but these have the greatest legacies...

	TV SHOW	YEARS ON AIR	TOTAL EPISODES
1	TEENAGE MUTANT NINJA TURTLES	1987–96	193
2	TMNT	2003–10	158
3	TEEN TITANS GO!	2013–PRESENT	156+
4	HERGÉ'S ADVENTURES OF TINTIN	1957–64; 1991–92	141
5	DENNIS THE MENACE & GNASHER	1996–98; 2009–10; 2013	120
6	CAPTAIN PUGWASH	1957–66; 1974–75	107
7	DUCK TALES	1987–90; 2015–PRESENT	100+
8	BATMAN: THE ANIMATED SERIES	1992–95	85
9	TEENAGE MUTANT NINJA TURTLES	2012–PRESENT	78+
10	X-MEN	1992–97	76

Tintin's first published appearance was in

1929

SPAWN

With 18 episodes over three seasons (1997–99), HBO's *Spawn* won two Emmys for animation achievements. Keith David (*The Thing*) voiced Spawn/Al Simmons, with John Rafter Lee (*Aeon Flux*) voicing antagonist Jason Wynn.

TEENAGE MUTANT NINJA TURTLES

9 The origins of the heroes in a half-shell date back to a black-and-white comic book. The first issue was published in May 1984 by Mirage Studios.

TOP 10

BIGGEST SUPERHERO MOVIES

These 10 comic-book movies also rank among the 80 most successful movies ever made...

	MOVIE	YEAR OF RELEASE	BOX OFFICE ($ WORLDWIDE)
1	THE AVENGERS	2012	1,519,557,910
2	AVENGERS: AGE OF ULTRON	2015	1,405,035,767
3	IRON MAN 3	2013	1,215,439,994
4	THE DARK KNIGHT RISES	2012	1,084,939,099
5	THE DARK KNIGHT	2008	1,004,558,444
6	SPIDER-MAN 3	2007	890,871,626
7	SPIDER-MAN	2002	821,708,551
8	SPIDER-MAN 2	2004	783,766,341
9	GUARDIANS OF THE GALAXY	2014	773,312,399
10	THE AMAZING SPIDER-MAN	2012	757,930,663

CAP SALUTES YOU!

for Buying WAR BONDS

SEE YOUR LOCAL POST OFFICE

Guardians of the Galaxy's international award wins:

44

from 85 nominations

THE DARK KNIGHT RISES

4 The conclusion of British filmmaker Christopher Nolan's *Dark Knight* trilogy won 44 international movie awards. The trilogy took in a total of $2,463,716,216 at the box office.

CAPTAIN AMERICA: CIVIL WAR

Chris Evans debuted as Steve Rogers in *Captain America: The First Avenger* (2011), which was his 28th acting credit. *Captain America: Civil War* was released April 27, 2016. Evans made his directorial debut with the romantic comedy *Before We Go* in 2014.

MOST **MARVEL/DC** **CHARACTER** MOVIE APPEARANCES

Find out where your favorite movie/comic-book character ranks below...

	CHARACTER	NO. OF MOVIE APPEARANCES
1	BATMAN	10
2	WOLVERINE	8
=	PROFESSOR X	8
=	SUPERMAN	8
5	CAPTAIN AMERICA	7
=	IRON MAN	7
=	SPIDER-MAN	7
=	MAGNETO	7
9	JEAN GREY	6
=	MYSTIQUE	6

Along with her Jean Grey/*X-Men* movies, Famke Janssen has

57

acting credits

WOLVERINE

2 Australian actor Hugh Jackman will don the claws for a final time in the 2017 *Wolverine* movie, directed by James Mangold.

OFF-THE-CHART ENTRIES

Let's not forget these three key characters...

BLACK WIDOW
5

STORM
5

PEGGY CARTER
4

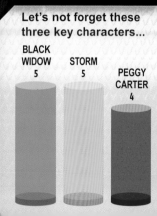

MYSTIQUE

9 *The Hunger Games* saga's Jennifer Lawrence has portrayed the younger iteration of Raven Darkholme/Mystique three times. Rebecca Romijn has played her four times.

NICK FURY

Samuel L. Jackson has appeared as Nick Fury in eight Marvel productions (seven movies and the TV series *Agents of S.H.I.E.L.D.*). The actor, born in Washington, D.C., has appeared in more than 160 productions.

TOP 10

BIGGEST MARVEL MOVIES

Of all the comic-book adaptions, characters and stories from Marvel publications rule the box office...

	MOVIE	YEAR OF RELEASE	BOX OFFICE ($ WORLDWIDE)
1	THE AVENGERS	2012	1,519,557,910
2	AVENGERS: AGE OF ULTRON	2015	1,405,035,767
3	IRON MAN 3	2013	1,215,439,994
4	SPIDER-MAN 3	2007	890,871,626
5	SPIDER-MAN	2002	821,708,551
6	SPIDER-MAN 2	2004	783,766,341
7	GUARDIANS OF THE GALAXY	2014	773,312,399
8	THE AMAZING SPIDER-MAN	2012	757,930,663
9	X-MEN: DAYS OF FUTURE PAST	2014	747,862,775
10	CAPTAIN AMERICA: THE WINTER SOLDIER	2014	714,421,503

X-Men Apocalypse was released

MAY 1, 2016

THE AVENGERS

1 The fifth most successful movie of all time, *The Avengers* is one of only 24 movies to make more than $1 billion at the box office worldwide. It was director Joss Whedon's second feature film of the four he's made.

THE DARK KNIGHT

2 Australian actor Heath Ledger posthumously won the 2009 Oscar for Best Supporting Actor for his portrayal of the Joker in the second movie of the *Dark Knight* trilogy.

Batman (1989) was composer Danny Elfman's **11TH** feature film score of his 100 credits

MAN OF STEEL

3 Including voice artists, 11 different actors have played Superman. Henry Cavill made his Clark Kent debut in *Man of Steel*, and reprised the role in *Batman v Superman: Dawn of Justice* (2016).

TOP 10

BIGGEST DC MOVIES

Prior to 2016's *Batman v Superman: Dawn of Justice*, these are the most lucrative DC movies...

	MOVIE	YEAR OF RELEASE	BOX OFFICE ($ WORLDWIDE)
1	THE DARK KNIGHT RISES	2012	1,084,939,099
2	THE DARK KNIGHT	2008	1,004,558,444
3	MAN OF STEEL	2013	668,045,518
4	BATMAN	1989	411,348,924
5	SUPERMAN RETURNS	2006	391,081,192
6	BATMAN BEGINS	2005	374,218,673
7	BATMAN FOREVER	1995	336,529,144
8	SUPERMAN	1978	300,218,018
9	BATMAN RETURNS	1992	266,822,354
10	BATMAN AND ROBIN	1997	238,207,122

BIGGEST INDEPENDENT CREATOR-OWNED MOVIES

A "creator-owned" comic features stories wholly produced/ owned by an independent publisher...

	MOVIE	PUBLISHER(S)	YEAR OF RELEASE	BOX OFFICE ($ WORLDWIDE)
1	TEENAGE MUTANT NINJA TURTLES	MIRAGE STUDIOS/IDW	2014	493,333,584
2	THE MASK	DARK HORSE	1994	351,583,407
3	WANTED	TOP COW	2008	341,433,252
4	THE GREEN HORNET	DYNAMITE	2011	227,817,248
5	TEENAGE MUTANT NINJA TURTLES	MIRAGE STUDIOS/IDW	1990	201,965,915
6	HELLBOY II: THE GOLDEN ARMY	DARK HORSE	2008	160,388,063
7	JUDGE DREDD	FLEETWAY/REBELLION	1995	113,493,481
8	HELLBOY	DARK HORSE	2004	99,318,987
9	TMNT	MIRAGE STUDIOS/IDW	2007	95,608,995
10	SPAWN	IMAGE	1997	87,840,042

Dredd (2012) starred Karl Urban and Lena Headey and made

$35,626,525

THE MASK

2 The comic was first published in 1987. Jim Carrey portrayed the character for the 1994 movie, which also marked the acting debut of Cameron Diaz.

30 DAYS OF NIGHT

Just off the chart is director David Slade's adaptation of the vampire comic *30 Days Of Night* (2002) by Steve Niles and Ben Templesmith. Released in 2007, it made $75,505,973 at the box office.

WATCHMEN

5 Zack Snyder (*Batman v Superman: Dawn of Justice*) directed this movie adaptation of the graphic novel by Alan Moore and Dave Gibbons.

PUBLISHING COMPARISON

More DC creator-owned titles have become successful movies...

- DC **7**
- MARVEL **3**

TOP 10

BIGGEST CREATOR-OWNED MOVIES (BASED ON MARVEL OR DC COMIC/IMPRINT)

These creator-owned comics (turned movies) had Marvel/DC publishing support...

	MOVIE	PUBLISHER(S)	YEAR OF RELEASE	BOX OFFICE ($ WORLDWIDE)
1	MIB 3	AIRCEL/MALIBU/MARVEL	2012	624,026,776
2	MEN IN BLACK	AIRCEL/MALIBU/MARVEL	1997	589,390,539
3	MEN IN BLACK II	AIRCEL/MALIBU/MARVEL	2002	441,818,803
4	RED	HOMAGE/WILDSTORM/DC	2010	199,006,387
5	WATCHMEN	DC	2009	185,258,983
6	ROAD TO PERDITION	PARADOX PRESS/DC	2002	181,001,478
7	THE LEAGUE OF EXTRAORDINARY GENTLEMEN	ABC/WILDSTORM/DC	2003	179,265,204
8	RED 2	HOMAGE/WILDSTORM/DC	2013	148,075,565
9	STARDUST	VERTIGO/DC	2007	135,560,026
10	V FOR VENDETTA	VERTIGO/DC	2006	132,511,035

V FOR VENDETTA

10 The comic was published in different forms from 1982–89. The movie's screenplay was written by the Wachowskis, the siblings behind *The Matrix* franchise.

The first issue of *Red* (by Warren Ellis and artist Cully Hamner) was published in

2003

INSIDE OUT

10 The 15th Disney/Pixar movie, this won 47 international film awards. It was released five months before their 16th film, *The Good Dinosaur*.

Minions + Despicable Me 1 & 2 total box office: **$2,672,970,113**

ICE AGE: CONTINENTAL DRIFT

9 The fourth *Ice Age* movie was the most successful animated film of 2012. Its sequel, *Ice Age: Collision Course*, was released on June 30, 2016.

TOP 10

BIGGEST ANIMATED MOVIES

Examining all of the different kinds of animated movies ever made, these are the 10 box-office smashes...

	MOVIE	YEAR OF RELEASE	BOX OFFICE ($ WORLDWIDE)
1	FROZEN	2013	1,276,480,335
2	MINIONS	2015	1,159,094,243
3	TOY STORY 3	2010	1,063,171,911
4	THE LION KING	1994	987,483,777
5	DESPICABLE ME 2	2013	970,761,885
6	FINDING NEMO	2003	936,743,261
7	SHREK 2	2004	919,838,758
8	ICE AGE: DAWN OF THE DINOSAURS	2009	886,686,817
9	ICE AGE: CONTINENTAL DRIFT	2012	877,244,782
10	INSIDE OUT	2015	856,809,711

BIGGEST TRADITIONALLY ANIMATED MOVIES

Making animated tales with hand-drawn/painted images predates CGI (computer-generated imagery)...

	MOVIE	YEAR OF RELEASE	BOX OFFICE ($ WORLDWIDE)
1	THE LION KING	1994	987,483,777
2	THE SIMPSONS MOVIE	2007	527,071,022
3	ALADDIN	1992	504,050,219
4	TARZAN	1999	448,191,819
5	BEAUTY AND THE BEAST	1991	424,967,620
6	POCAHONTAS	1995	346,079,773
7	WHO FRAMED ROGER RABBIT?	1988	329,803,958
8	THE HUNCHBACK OF NOTRE DAME	1996	325,338,851
9	MULAN	1998	304,320,254
10	SPIRITED AWAY	2002	274,925,095

WHO FRAMED ROGER RABBIT?

7 Filmmaker Robert Zemeckis followed up *Back to the Future* (1985) with this fusion of live-action and cell animation. Both movies starred Christopher Lloyd.

SPIRITED AWAY

10 Studio Ghibli's 12th feature is its most successful movie. It won the 2003 Academy Award for Best Animated Feature, and another 53 international movie awards.

The *Emperor's New Groove* (2000) total box office: **$169,327,687**

275

LONGEST-RUNNING ANIMATED TV SERIES

These popular animated shows also count among some of the most successful TV shows of all time...

	TV SHOW	YEARS ON AIR	TOTAL EPISODES
1	THE SIMPSONS	1989–PRESENT	595+
2	FAMILY GUY	1999–2003; 2005–PRESENT	274+
3	SOUTH PARK	1997–PRESENT	267+
4	KING OF THE HILL	1997–2010	259
5	ARTHUR	1996–PRESENT	227+
6	BEAVIS AND BUTT-HEAD	1993–97; 2011	222
7	ADVENTURE TIME	2007; 2010–PRESENT	219+
8	AMERICAN DAD!	2005–PRESENT	210+
9	SPONGEBOB SQUAREPANTS	1999–PRESENT	200+
10	TEENAGE MUTANT NINJA TURTLES	1987–96	193

SOUTH PARK

3 Matt Stone and Trey Parker's TV show also spawned the animated feature film *South Park: Bigger, Longer & Uncut.* It made $83,137,603 at the box office worldwide.

THE SIMPSONS

1 This franchise's spin-off video games have sold more than 21 million units. Universal Studios Hollywood features a re-creation of the town of Springfield.

4 MORE HITS

Here's how 4 other popular cartoons compare to the top 10...

FUTURAMA
1999–2003; 2008–13
141 EPISODES

DORA THE EXPLORER
1999; 2000–13
172 EPISODES

RUGRATS
1991–2003
172 EPISODES

THE FLINTSTONES
1999–2003; 2008–13
141 EPISODES

Number of *Adventure Time* seasons to date:

7

DORAEMON

2 Aside from the hit TV show, the time-traveling robotic cat Doraemon has also starred in 37 feature films and more than 80 video games.

SAZAE-SAN

6 Created, written, and illustrated by Japanese artist Machiko Hasegawa in 1946, the manga comic became an animated TV series in October 1969.

A live-action feature film of *Nintama Rantarō* was released in

2011

TOP 10

LONGEST-RUNNING ANIME TV SERIES

Japanese animation is a popular art form and industry the world over, as these stats prove...

	TV SHOW	YEARS ON AIR	TOTAL EPISODES
1	SAZAE-SAN	1969–PRESENT	7,332+
2	DORAEMON	1973; 1978; 1979–2005; 2005–PRESENT	2,561+
3	NINTAMA RANTARŌ	1993–PRESENT	1,878+
4	OYAKO CLUB	1994–2013	1,818
5	KIRIN NO MONOSHIRI YAKATA	1975–79	1,565
6	OJARUMARU	1998–PRESENT	1,551+
7	KIRIN ASHITA NO CALENDAR	1980–84	1,498
8	MANGA NIPPON MUKASHI BANASHI	1975–85	1,488
9	HOKA HOKA KAZOKU	1976–82	1,428
10	SOREIKE! ANPANMAN	1988–PRESENT	1,315+

CORPSE BRIDE

5 Oscar-nominated actress Helena Bonham-Carter provided the voice for the Corpse Bride in this stop-motion feature. Her love interest, Victor Van Dort, was voiced by fellow Oscar-nominee Johnny Depp.

Wallace & Gromit's first adventure was *A Grand Day Out*, which debuted on **DEC. 24, 1990**

TOP 10

BIGGEST STOP-MOTION ANIMATED MOVIES

This style of animation incorporates numerous still photos, edited to create movement...

	MOVIE	YEAR OF RELEASE	BOX OFFICE ($ WORLDWIDE)
1	CHICKEN RUN	2000	224,834,564
2	WALLACE & GROMIT: THE CURSE OF THE WERE-RABBIT	2005	192,610,372
3	CORALINE	2009	124,596,398
4	THE PIRATES! IN AN ADVENTURE WITH SCIENTISTS!	2012	123,054,041
5	CORPSE BRIDE	2005	117,195,061
6	THE BOXTROLLS	2014	109,285,033
7	PARANORMAN	2012	107,139,399
8	SHAUN THE SHEEP MOVIE	2015	83,475,982
9	FRANKENWEENIE	2012	81,491,068
10	THE NIGHTMARE BEFORE CHRISTMAS	1993	75,082,668

THE BOXTROLLS

6 This is based on British novelist Alan Snow's book *Here Be Monsters!* (2005). It was produced by Laika, the studio behind *ParaNorman* and *Coraline*.

TOP 10

BIGGEST ANIME MOVIES

Japan's Studio Ghibli is responsible for six of the movies in this Top 10...

	MOVIE	YEAR OF RELEASE	BOX OFFICE ($ WORLDWIDE)
1	SPIRITED AWAY	2002	274,925,095
2	HOWL'S MOVING CASTLE	2005	235,184,110
3	PONYO	2009	201,750,937
4	POKÉMON: THE FIRST MOVIE	1999	163,644,662
5	PRINCESS MONONOKE	1999	159,375,308
6	THE SECRET WORLD OF ARRIETTY	2012	145,570,827
7	POKÉMON: THE MOVIE 2000	2000	133,949,270
8	THE WIND RISES	2013	117,932,401
9	STAND BY ME, DORAEMON	2014	105,100,000
10	ONE PIECE FILM: Z	2012	72,822,122

THE WIND RISES

8 The 19th Studio Ghibli animated feature film debuted in Japan on July 20, 2013. The American release included the vocal talents of Emily Blunt.

Since 2007, the *Shaun the Sheep* TV series has aired

140

episodes

PONYO

3 This was written and directed by Studio Ghibli cofounder Hayao Miyazaki. It won 11 international movie awards, including Animation of the Year at the 2009 Tokyo Anime Awards.

FIRST MOVIES EVER BASED ON VIDEO GAMES

Long before the 2016 adaptation of *Assassin's Creed*, these video game movies pioneered the way...

	MOVIE	BASED ON GAME FRANCHISE	RELEASED
1	SUPER MARIO BROS.: THE GREAT MISSION TO RESCUE PRINCESS PEACH!	SUPER MARIO BROS.	JULY 20, 1986
=	RUNNING BOY STAR SOLDIER	STAR SOLDIER	JULY 20, 1986
3	SUPER MARIO BROS.	SUPER MARIO BROS.	MAY 28, 1993
4	FATAL FURY: THE MOTION PICTURE	FATAL FURY	JULY 16, 1994
5	STREET FIGHTER II: THE ANIMATED MOVIE	STREET FIGHTER II	AUGUST 8, 1994
6	DOUBLE DRAGON	DOUBLE DRAGON	NOV. 4, 1994
7	STREET FIGHTER	STREET FIGHTER	DEC. 23, 1994
8	MORTAL KOMBAT	MORTAL KOMBAT	AUGUST 18, 1995
9	MORTAL KOMBAT: ANNIHILATION	MORTAL KOMBAT	NOV. 21, 1997
10	POKÉMON: THE FIRST MOVIE	POKÉMON	JULY 18, 1998

MORTAL KOMBAT: ANNIHILATION

9

The first *Mortal Kombat* video game was released in 1992. After the initial movie adaptation made $122,195,920 at the box office, the 1997 sequel achieved $51,376,861.

STREET FIGHTER

Number of *Pokémon* movies made:

18

7

Street Fighter (1999) starred Jean-Claude Van Damme as Guile. It took $99,423,521 at the box office worldwide. *Street Fighter: The Legend of Chun-Li* (2009) made $12,764,201.

MEGA MAN STAR FORCE

6 One of Capcom's most famous characters was designed by Akira Kitamura and Keiji Inafune. Mega Man is the star of more than 100 games across all major platforms.

KIRBY: RIGHT BACK AT YA!

3 Created by Japanese game designer Masahiro Sakurai, the Kirby franchise has sold 36.2 million copies of games worldwide.

Number of *Digimon* movies made:

9

GAMES ON TV

This bar chart reflects the popularity of each gaming franchise...

POKÉMON
940+
EPISODES

DIGIMON
332
EPISODES

KIRBY:
RIGHT
BACK AT
YA!
100
EPISODES

SATURDAY
SUPERCADE
97
EPISODES

SONIC X
78
EPISODES

LONGEST-RUNNING TV SHOWS BASED ON VIDEO GAMES

TOP 10

The *Pokémon* brand is a force to be reckoned with in the TV industry, as well as in the gaming world...

	TV SHOW	BASED ON GAME FRANCHISE	YEARS ON AIR	TOTAL EPISODES
1	POKÉMON	POKÉMON	18 (1997–PRESENT)	940+
2	DIGIMON	DIGIMON	12 (1999–2011)	332
3	KIRBY: RIGHT BACK AT YA!	KIRBY	2 (2001–3)	100
4	SATURDAY SUPERCADE	VARIOUS	2 (1983–85)	97
5	SONIC X	SONIC THE HEDGEHOG	2 (2003–5)	78
6	MEGA MAN STAR FORCE	MEGA MAN	2 (2006–8)	76
7	MONSTER RANCHER	MONSTER RANCHER	2 (1999–2001)	73
8	ADVENTURES OF SONIC THE HEDGEHOG	SONIC THE HEDGEHOG	3 (1993–96)	67
9	THE SUPER MARIO BROS. SUPER SHOW!	SUPER MARIO BROS.	1 (1989)	65
10	BOMBERMAN JETTERS	BOMBERMAN	1 (2002–3)	52

WRECK-IT RALPH

1 The cast of this Disney movie features comedic actors from acclaimed movies and TV shows, including John C. Reilly (*Step Brothers*), Sarah Silverman (*Bob's Burgers*), Jack McBrayer (*30 Rock*), and Jane Lynch (*Glee*).

The Angry Birds Movie was released on

MAY 11, 2016

SPY KIDS 3D: GAME OVER

4 Filmmaker Robert Rodriguez, the man behind *Sin City* (2005) and its sequel, wrote and directed four *Spy Kids* movies between 2001 and 2011. They grossed a box-office total of $550,233,830.

TOP 10

BIGGEST MOVIES ABOUT VIDEO GAMING

These original stories all took inspiration from the technology and tales of the video game industry...

	MOVIE	YEAR OF RELEASE	BOX OFFICE ($ WORLDWIDE)
1	WRECK-IT RALPH	2012	471,222,889
2	TRON LEGACY	2010	400,062,763
3	PIXELS	2015	244,150,128
4	SPY KIDS 3D: GAME OVER	2003	197,011,982
5	WARGAMES	1983	79,567,667
6	SCOTT PILGRIM VS. THE WORLD	2010	47,664,559
7	TRON	1982	33,000,000
8	THE LAST STARFIGHTER	1984	28,733,290
9	STAY ALIVE	2006	27,105,095
10	AVALON	2001	15,740,796

TOP 10

BIGGEST VIDEO GAME MOVIE ADAPTATIONS

Dozens of popular gaming series have been made into big-screen adventures, and these are the box-office hits...

	MOVIE	YEAR OF RELEASE	BASED ON GAME FRANCHISE	BOX OFFICE ($ WORLDWIDE)
1	PRINCE OF PERSIA: THE SANDS OF TIME	2010	PRINCE OF PERSIA	336,365,676
2	RESIDENT EVIL: AFTERLIFE	2010	RESIDENT EVIL	296,221,663
3	LARA CROFT: TOMB RAIDER	2001	TOMB RAIDER	274,703,340
4	RESIDENT EVIL: RETRIBUTION	2012	RESIDENT EVIL	240,159,255
5	NEED FOR SPEED	2014	NEED FOR SPEED	203,277,636
6	POKÉMON: THE FIRST MOVIE	1998	POKÉMON	163,644,662
7	LARA CROFT TOMB RAIDER: THE CRADLE OF LIFE	2003	TOMB RAIDER	156,505,388
8	RESIDENT EVIL: EXTINCTION	2007	RESIDENT EVIL	147,717,833
9	POKÉMON: THE MOVIE 2000	1999	POKÉMON	133,949,270
10	RESIDENT EVIL: APOCALYPSE	2004	RESIDENT EVIL	129,394,835

Hitman: Agent 47 (2015) total box office: **$82,347,656**

PRINCE OF PERSIA: THE SANDS OF TIME

1 It's inspired by the 2003 video game of the same name, and Jake Gyllenhaal plays Prince Dastan. His first movie role was as the son of Billy Crystal's character in *City Slickers* (1991).

RESIDENT EVIL: RETRIBUTION

4 This is the fifth movie in the series. The sixth, *Resident Evil: The Final Chapter*, is set for a 2017 release.

283

BIGGEST WESTERNS

In the past 30 years, there have been more than 80 movies made in the western genre...

	MOVIE	YEAR OF RELEASE	BOX OFFICE ($ WORLDWIDE)
1	DJANGO UNCHAINED	2012	425,368,238
2	DANCES WITH WOLVES	1990	424,208,848
3	THE LONE RANGER	2013	260,502,115
4	TRUE GRIT	2010	252,276,927
5	RANGO	2011	245,724,603
6	BACK TO THE FUTURE PART III	1990	244,527,583
7	WILD WILD WEST	1999	222,104,681
8	MAVERICK	1994	183,031,272
9	BROKEBACK MOUNTAIN	2005	178,062,759
10	COWBOYS & ALIENS	2011	174,822,325

Quentin Tarantino's western *The Hateful Eight* (2015) is his

10TH
movie

DJANGO UNCHAINED

1

Jamie Foxx plays the titular Django, who battles Leonardo DiCaprio's villainous Calvin Candie. The film's cinematographer, Robert Richardson, won Academy Awards for his work on *JFK* (1991), *The Aviator* (2004), and *Hugo* (2011).

RANGO

5

This movie's director, Gore Verbinski, was the man behind the first three *Pirates of the Caribbean* movies. Their star, Johnny Depp, also voices Rango the chameleon.

TOP 5 SHOWDOWN

It's a close call between the two biggest westerns...

DJANGO UNCHAINED $425,368,238   DANCES WITH WOLVES $424,208,848   THE LONE RANGER $260,502,115   TRUE GRIT $252,276,927   RANGO $245,724,603

Titanic was director James Cameron's **7TH** movie

THE PASSION OF THE CHRIST

3 Jim Caviezel (from the TV series *Person of Interest*), played Jesus in this movie, and also played Edmond Dantes in the 2002 adaptation of Alexandre Dumas's 1844 novel *The Count of Monte Cristo*.

THE LAST SAMURAI

5 Tom Cruise's 26th movie role was as Nathan Algren in *The Last Samurai*. It was scored by Hanz Zimmer, the composer of Christopher Nolan's *Dark Knight* trilogy, *Inception*, and *Interstellar*.

TOP 10

BIGGEST DRAMAS

This genre focuses on personal stories and relationships, often with a historical or biographic leaning...

	MOVIE	YEAR OF RELEASE	BOX OFFICE ($ WORLDWIDE)
1	TITANIC	1997	2,186,772,302
2	FORREST GUMP	1994	677,945,399
3	THE PASSION OF THE CHRIST	2004	611,899,420
4	SAVING PRIVATE RYAN	1998	481,840,909
5	THE LAST SAMURAI	2003	456,758,981
6	PEARL HARBOR	2001	449,220,945
7	AMERICAN SNIPER	2014	433,008,447
8	CAST AWAY	2000	429,632,142
9	THE KING'S SPEECH	2010	414,211,549
10	GONE WITH THE WIND	1939	400,176,459

BIGGEST JAMES BOND MOVIES

Sean Connery was the first actor to play Secret Agent 007, in the 1962 adaptation of Ian Fleming's novel *Dr. No*...

	MOVIE	YEAR OF RELEASE	BOX OFFICE ($ WORLDWIDE)
1	SKYFALL	2012	1,108,561,013
2	SPECTRE	2015	877,853,952
3	CASINO ROYALE	2006	599,045,960
4	QUANTUM OF SOLACE	2008	586,090,727
5	DIE ANOTHER DAY	2002	431,971,116
6	THE WORLD IS NOT ENOUGH	1999	361,832,400
7	GOLDENEYE	1995	352,194,034
8	TOMORROW NEVER DIES	1997	333,011,068
9	MOONRAKER	1979	210,308,099
10	LICENCE TO KILL	1989	156,167,015

SPECTRE

2 Daniel Craig plays 007 in all four of the most successful Bond movies. He also played him in two short films— *XXX Summer Olympics Opening Ceremony* (2012) and *James Bond Supports International Women's Day* (2011)—and two 007 video games.

LICENCE TO KILL

10 Carey Lowell and Timothy Dalton starred as Pam Bouvier and James Bond in Dalton's second and final 007 movie. Its director, John Glen, helmed four other Bond movies, including *The Living Daylights* (1987), also starring Dalton.

Daniel Craig's Bond movies' total box office:

$3,114,719,956

LUCY

5 For her 46th acting role (of 53 to date), Scarlett Johansson played a woman accidentally given enhanced physical and mental abilities. She also played a woman with mysterious powers in *Under the Skin* (2014).

MISSION: IMPOSSIBLE—GHOST PROTOCOL

2 Brad Bird, best known for directing acclaimed animated movies like *The Iron Giant* (1999) and *The Incredibles* (2004), helmed this, his first live-action movie. It is the most successful of all five *Mission: Impossible* movies, all starring Tom Cruise as Ethan Hunt.

TOP 10

BIGGEST (NON-BOND) CRIME ACTION MOVIES

Action-packed, crime-based movies can make hundreds of millions at the box office...

	MOVIE	YEAR OF RELEASE	BOX OFFICE ($ WORLDWIDE)
1	INCEPTION	2010	825,532,764
▶ 2	MISSION: IMPOSSIBLE—GHOST PROTOCOL	2011	694,713,380
3	MISSION: IMPOSSIBLE—ROGUE NATION	2015	682,330,139
4	MISSION: IMPOSSIBLE II	2000	546,388,105
▶ 5	LUCY	2014	463,360,063
6	MISSION: IMPOSSIBLE	1996	457,696,359
7	THE BOURNE ULTIMATUM	2007	442,824,138
8	KINGSMAN: THE SECRET SERVICE	2015	414,351,546
9	MISSION: IMPOSSIBLE III	2006	397,850,012
10	LIVE FREE OR DIE HARD	2007	383,531,464

Total number of *Die Hard* movies:

5

BACK TO THE FUTURE PART II

10 To honor the date that Marty McFly and Doc Brown time-traveled to, the October 21, 2015, edition of *USA Today* re-created the cover story of Martin McFly Jr.'s arrest shown in the movie.

Total number of *Terminator* movies:

5

GET BACK IN TIME

Here's the top 5 compared visually...

X-MEN: DAYS OF FUTURE PAST
$747,862,775

INTERSTELLAR
$675,120,017

MIB 3
$624,026,776

TERMINATOR 2: JUDGMENT DAY
$519,843,345

TERMINATOR: GENISYS
$440,603,537

TOP 10

BIGGEST TIME-TRAVEL MOVIES

From cyborgs and mutants to DeLoreans and sharp suits, time-travel movies are as eclectic as they are popular...

	MOVIE	YEAR OF RELEASE	BOX OFFICE ($ WORLDWIDE)
1	X-MEN: DAYS OF FUTURE PAST	2014	747,862,775
2	INTERSTELLAR	2014	675,120,017
3	MIB 3	2012	624,026,776
4	TERMINATOR 2: JUDGMENT DAY	1991	519,843,345
5	TERMINATOR: GENISYS	2015	440,603,537
6	TERMINATOR 3: RISE OF THE MACHINES	2003	433,371,112
7	STAR TREK	2009	385,680,446
8	BACK TO THE FUTURE	1985	381,109,762
9	EDGE OF TOMORROW	2014	370,541,256
10	BACK TO THE FUTURE PART II	1989	331,950,002

MIB 3

3 Will Smith starred in all three *Men in Black* movies (1997, 2002, and 2012). He has two Academy Award nominations for his lead roles in *The Pursuit of Happyness* (2007) and *Ali* (2002).

INDIANA JONES AND THE KINGDOM OF THE CRYSTAL SKULL

4 Harrison Ford played Indiana Jones for the fifth time in 2008. He'd last played the character in 1993 in an episode of *The Young Indiana Jones Chronicles* TV series.

Pirates franchise star Johnny Depp was born on

JUNE 9, 1963

THE CHRONICLES OF NARNIA: THE LION, THE WITCH & THE WARDROBE

5 Anna Popplewell starred as Susan Pevensie in all three Narnia movies, including *The Chronicles of Narnia: Prince Caspian* (2008) and *The Chronicles of Narnia: The Voyage of the Dawn Treader* (2010).

TOP 10

BIGGEST PERIOD ADVENTURE MOVIES

Adventures that take place in the past make for a successful movie-making formula...

	MOVIE	YEAR OF RELEASE	BOX OFFICE ($ WORLDWIDE)
1	PIRATES OF THE CARIBBEAN: DEAD MAN'S CHEST	2006	1,066,179,725
2	PIRATES OF THE CARIBBEAN: ON STRANGER TIDES	2011	1,045,713,802
3	PIRATES OF THE CARIBBEAN: AT WORLD'S END	2007	963,420,425
4	INDIANA JONES AND THE KINGDOM OF THE CRYSTAL SKULL	2008	786,636,033
5	THE CHRONICLES OF NARNIA: THE LION, THE WITCH & THE WARDROBE	2005	745,013,115
6	PIRATES OF THE CARIBBEAN: THE CURSE OF THE BLACK PEARL	2003	654,264,015
7	KING KONG	2005	550,517,357
8	SHERLOCK HOLMES: A GAME OF SHADOWS	2011	545,448,418
9	SHERLOCK HOLMES	2009	524,028,679
10	TROY	2004	497,409,852

MAMMA MIA!

1 Catherine Johnson wrote the screenplay for this big-screen adaptation of her own hit stage musical, which created a narrative from ABBA lyrics. It won the Golden Reel for Best Sound Editing: Music in a Feature Film in 2009.

SEX AND THE CITY

3 Kim Cattrall played *Sex and the City*'s Samantha Jones in 94 episodes and two movies. Her 85 other acting credits include *Big Trouble in Little China* (1986), *Mannequin* (1987), and *Police Academy* (1984).

TOP 10

BIGGEST ROMANTIC COMEDIES

Singing and dancing, weddings, and the calamities of dating all feature in these hit romcoms...

	MOVIE	YEAR OF RELEASE	BOX OFFICE ($ WORLDWIDE)
1	MAMMA MIA!	2008	609,841,637
2	PRETTY WOMAN	1990	463,406,268
3	SEX AND THE CITY	2008	415,253,641
4	GREASE	1978	394,955,690
5	WHAT WOMEN WANT	2000	374,111,707
6	THERE'S SOMETHING ABOUT MARY	1998	369,884,651
7	MY BIG FAT GREEK WEDDING	2002	368,744,044
8	HITCH	2005	368,100,420
9	NOTTING HILL	1999	363,889,678
10	ENCHANTED	2007	340,487,652

Of its 136 international nominations, *Enchanted* won

47

BOWLING FOR COLUMBINE

Total Michael Moore feature documentaries:

8

7 The investigation by American filmmaker Michael Moore (left) into gun violence in the USA won 39 international movie awards, including the 2003 Academy Award for Best Documentary and 55th Anniversary Prize at the 2002 Cannes Film Festival.

MOST SUCCESSFUL DOCUMENTARIES

The filmmakers behind these productions aim to convey the human condition through a variety of means...

A BRAVE HEART: THE LIZZIE VELASQUEZ STORY

The 2015 documentary about the life of Texas-born motivational speaker, author, and filmmaker Lizzie Velasquez (left) has won five awards, including the 2015 SXSWFilm Festival Audience Award for Best Documentary.

	MOVIE	YEAR OF RELEASE	BOX OFFICE ($ WORLDWIDE)
1	FAHRENHEIT 9/11	2004	222,446,882
2	MARCH OF THE PENGUINS	2005	127,392,693
3	EARTH	2007	108,975,160
4	JUSTIN BIEBER: NEVER SAY NEVER	2011	99,036,827
5	OCEANS	2010	82,651,439
6	ONE DIRECTION: THIS IS US	2013	68,532,898
7	BOWLING FOR COLUMBINE	2002	58,008,423
8	AN INCONVENIENT TRUTH	2006	49,756,507
9	SICKO	2007	36,088,109
10	CHIMPANZEE	2012	34,823,764

THE NIGHTMARE BEFORE CHRISTMAS

5 Over two nights (October 31–November 1, 2015), in a live performance at the Hollywood Bowl composer Danny Elfman, a full orchestra, and cast performed the music to a screening of this movie.

Total movies made in the *Halloween* horror franchise:

10

HALLOWEEN WINNERS

Big differences between the Top 5...

E.T. THE EXTRA-TERRESTRIAL
$792,910,554

CASPER
$287,928,194

MONSTER HOUSE
$140,175,006

HALLOWEEN
$80,253,908

THE NIGHTMARE BEFORE CHRISTMAS
$75,082,668

CASPER

2 Casper the Friendly Ghost first appeared in comic books in 1939. His cartoon debut came in 1945. This 1995 movie starred Christina Ricci and Bill Pullman.

TOP 10

BIGGEST HALLOWEEN MOVIES

As this Top 10 reveals, it's not just horror movies that are set during the Halloween season...

	MOVIE	YEAR OF RELEASE	BOX OFFICE ($ WORLDWIDE)
1	E.T. THE EXTRA-TERRESTRIAL	1982	792,910,554
2	CASPER	1995	287,928,194
3	MONSTER HOUSE	2006	140,175,006
4	HALLOWEEN	2007	80,253,908
5	THE NIGHTMARE BEFORE CHRISTMAS	1993	75,082,668
6	HALLOWEEN: H20	1998	55,041,738
7	THE CROW	1994	50,693,129
8	HALLOWEEN	1978	47,000,000
9	HOCUS POCUS	1993	39,514,713
10	HALLOWEEN II	2009	39,421,467

ELF

7

Will Ferrell has 95 acting credits, including Buddy the Elf (shown here). The stop-motion sequences were a homage to Larry Roemer's 1964 animated TV special *Rudolph the Red-nosed Reindeer*.

Another movie with a Christmas-time setting, *Lethal Weapon* (1987) made **$120,207,127** at the box office

HOW THE GRINCH STOLE CHRISTMAS

2

Prior to Jim Carrey portraying the Grinch, horror icon Boris Karloff (1887–1969) voiced him in the 1966 cartoon animated by Chuck Jones.

BIGGEST CHRISTMAS MOVIES

TOP 10

Similarly to the Top 10 on the left, the wide range of movies set during Christmas may surprise you...

	MOVIE	YEAR OF RELEASE	BOX OFFICE ($ WORLDWIDE)
1	IRON MAN 3	2013	1,215,439,994
2	HOW THE GRINCH STOLE CHRISTMAS	2000	345,141,403
3	A CHRISTMAS CAROL	2009	325,286,646
4	THE POLAR EXPRESS	2004	307,514,317
5	ROCKY IV	1985	300,473,716
6	BATMAN RETURNS	1992	266,822,354
7	ELF	2003	220,443,451
8	GHOSTBUSTERS II	1989	215,394,738
9	THE SANTA CLAUSE	1994	189,833,357
10	WHILE YOU WERE SLEEPING	1995	182,057,016

Alice Through the Looking Glass was released

MAY 27, 2015

HARRY POTTER AND THE ORDER OF THE PHOENIX

9

Award-winning actor Alan Rickman (February 21, 1946–January 14, 2016) played Severus Snape in all eight Harry Potter movies that were released between 2001 and 2011. Aside from his 69 acting credits, he directed two films, including *A Little Chaos* (2014) starring Kate Winslet.

THE HOBBIT: AN UNEXPECTED JOURNEY

4

This was the 12th movie that Peter Jackson directed. Bilbo Baggins was played by British actor Martin Freeman. He also starred in *Captain America: Civil War* (2016) and season one of *Fargo* (2014–present).

TOP 10

BIGGEST FANTASY MOVIES

Adaptations of J. K. Rowling's *Harry Potter* saga and J. R. R. Tolkien's Middle Earth books rule this Top 10...

	MOVIE	YEAR OF RELEASE	BOX OFFICE ($ WORLDWIDE)
1	HARRY POTTER AND THE DEATHLY HALLOWS: PART 2	2011	1,341,511,219
2	THE LORD OF THE RINGS: THE RETURN OF THE KING	2003	1,119,929,521
3	ALICE IN WONDERLAND	2010	1,025,467,110
4	THE HOBBIT: AN UNEXPECTED JOURNEY	2012	1,021,103,568
5	HARRY POTTER AND THE PHILOSOPHER'S STONE	2001	974,755,371
6	THE HOBBIT: THE DESOLATION OF SMAUG	2013	960,366,855
7	HARRY POTTER AND THE DEATHLY HALLOWS: PART 1	2010	960,283,305
8	THE HOBBIT: THE BATTLE OF THE FIVE ARMIES	2014	956,019,788
9	HARRY POTTER AND THE ORDER OF THE PHOENIX	2007	939,885,929
10	HARRY POTTER AND THE HALF-BLOOD PRINCE	2009	934,416,487

THE CONJURING

6 Its director, Malaysian filmmaker James Wan, also helmed *Furious 7* (2015), *Dead Silence* (2007), and *Saw* (2004). In 2016 Wan directed the sequel *The Conjuring 2*, in which Vera Farmiga and Patrick Wilson reprised their paranormal investigator roles.

The Visit (2015), directed by M. Night Shyamalan (who helmed 1, 5, and 6 in this chart), made **$98,440,807**

TOP 10

BIGGEST HORROR MOVIES

Ghostly apparitions and hellish creatures continue to make fright nights very popular...

	MOVIE	YEAR OF RELEASE	BOX OFFICE ($ WORLDWIDE)
1	THE SIXTH SENSE	1999	672,806,292
2	I AM LEGEND	2007	585,349,010
3	JAWS	1975	470,653,000
4	THE EXORCIST	1973	441,306,145
5	SIGNS	2002	408,247,917
6	THE CONJURING	2013	318,000,141
7	RESIDENT EVIL: AFTERLIFE	2010	296,221,663
8	WHAT LIES BENEATH	2000	291,420,351
9	ANNABELLE	2014	256,873,813
10	THE VILLAGE	2004	256,697,520

THE VILLAGE

10 M. Night Shyamalan's sixth movie features several multi-award-winning actors, such as Sigourney Weaver, Joaquin Phoenix, Bryce Dallas Howard, Adrien Brody, William Hurt, and Brendan Gleeson.

TOP 10

BIGGEST SCI-FI MOVIES

Movie fans clearly love advanced robotics, spacecraft that achieve the speed of light, and resurrected dinosaurs...

	MOVIE	YEAR OF RELEASE	BOX OFFICE ($ WORLDWIDE)
1	AVATAR	2009	2,787,965,087
2	STAR WARS: EPISODE VII—THE FORCE AWAKENS	2015	2,028,057,964
3	JURASSIC WORLD	2015	1,670,400,637
4	THE AVENGERS	2012	1,519,557,910
5	AVENGERS: AGE OF ULTRON	2015	1,405,413,868
6	IRON MAN 3	2013	1,215,439,994
7	TRANSFORMERS: DARK OF THE MOON	2011	1,123,794,079
8	TRANSFORMERS: AGE OF EXTINCTION	2014	1,104,054,072
9	JURASSIC PARK	1993	1,029,153,882
10	STAR WARS: EPISODE I—THE PHANTOM MENACE	2009	1,027,044,677

THE AVENGERS

4 Long before his big-screen debut in 2008, Iron Man first appeared in a comic called *Tales of Suspense* #39. It was published by Marvel Comics back in March 1963.

AVATAR

1 Canadian filmmaker James Cameron's *Avatar* won 76 of its 114 international award nominations. These included three Academy Awards for Cinematography, Visual Effects, and Art Direction.

SCI-FI FRANCHISES

Here's the Top 10 ranked by their brands...

- MARVEL **3**
- STAR WARS **2**
- TRANSFORMERS **2**
- JURASSIC PARK **2**
- AVATAR **1**

The next Avengers movie, *Infinity War Part 1*, is planned for a **2018** release

Into the *Woods* received **60** international award nominations

GREASE

3 In the 1978 movie Olivia Newton-John played Sandy (above left). In the 2016 TV movie *Grease: Live*, American actress Julianne Hough played Sandy, and Canadian singer-songwriter Carly Rae Jepsen played the role of Frenchy.

ENCHANTED

4 Amy Adams, who plays lead character Giselle, has been nominated for an Academy Award five times. Her 53 acting credits include Lois Lane in *Batman v Superman: Dawn of Justice* (2016).

TOP 10

MOST SUCCESSFUL MUSICALS

The 10 biggest musical movies cover everything from colleges and puppets to magic....

	MOVIE	YEAR OF RELEASE	BOX OFFICE ($ WORLDWIDE)
1	MAMMA MIA!	2008	609,841,637
2	LES MISÉRABLES	2012	441,809,770
3	GREASE	1978	394,955,690
4	ENCHANTED	2007	340,487,652
5	CHICAGO	2002	306,776,732
6	HIGH SCHOOL MUSICAL 3: SENIOR YEAR	2008	252,909,177
7	INTO THE WOODS	2014	213,116,401
8	HAIRSPRAY	2007	202,548,575
9	MOULIN ROUGE!	2001	179,213,434
10	THE MUPPETS	2011	165,184,237

JURASSIC WORLD

1 The mock-real *Jurassic World* website describes its genetic creation the Indominus Rex as 40 feet (12.2 m) long. It states its roar reaches 160 decibels, which matches the sound of a 747 plane taking off.

Classic Eighties dinosaur movie *Baby: Secret of the Lost Legend* (1985) total box office: **$14,972,297**

TOP 10

BIGGEST PREHISTORIC MOVIES

All four of the *Jurassic Park* franchise movies feature here, totaling $3,686,974,327...

	MOVIE	YEAR OF RELEASE	BOX OFFICE ($ WORLDWIDE)
1	JURASSIC WORLD	2015	1,670,400,637
2	JURASSIC PARK	1993	1,029,153,882
3	ICE AGE: DAWN OF THE DINOSAURS	2009	886,686,817
4	THE LOST WORLD: JURASSIC PARK	1997	618,638,999
5	JURASSIC PARK III	2001	368,780,809
6	DINOSAUR	2000	349,822,765
7	THE GOOD DINOSAUR	2015	294,191,192
8	THE LAND BEFORE TIME	1988	84,460,846
9	LAND OF THE LOST	2009	68,777,554
10	WALKING WITH DINOSAURS	2013	61,021,593

THE GOOD DINOSAUR

7 The Disney/Pixar film won three Animated Feature awards at the 2016 VES (Visual Effects Society) for Visual Effects, Effects Simulations, and Created Environment.

KILLER SPIDER

Greg Grunberg (below right) and Lombardo Boyar (below left) both feature in the 2013 film *Big Ass Spider!*

The original Universal Studios *The Wolf Man* was released **DEC. 9, 1941**

TOP 10

MOST SUCCESSFUL CREATURE FEATURES (NON-DINO AND NON-ALIEN/ PREDATOR FRANCHISES)

Not counting the Jurassic Park movies or the *Alien* and *Predator* franchises, these creature movies are the 10 biggest...

	MOVIE	YEAR OF RELEASE	BOX OFFICE ($ WORLDWIDE)
1	KING KONG	2005	550,517,357
2	GODZILLA	2014	529,076,069
3	JAWS	1977	470,653,000
4	PACIFIC RIM	2013	411,002,906
5	GODZILLA	1998	379,014,294
6	SUPER 8	2011	260,095,986
7	CLOVERFIELD	2008	170,764,026
8	DEEP BLUE SEA	1999	164,648,142
9	GREMLINS	1985	153,083,102
10	THE WOLFMAN	2010	139,789,765

OFF-THE-CHART ENTRIES

Here are the next 10 most successful monster movies...

ANACONDA
$136,885,767

SPECIES
$113,374,103

THE HOST
$89,431,890

PIRANHA 3D
$83,188,165

ANACONDAS: THE HUNT FOR THE BLOOD ORCHID
$70,992,898

JEEPERS CREEPERS 2
$63,102,666

SNAKES ON A PLANE
$62,022,014

THE FLY
$60,629,159

JEEPERS CREEPERS
$59,217,789

THE MIST
$57,293,715

DEEP BLUE SEA

8 Beyond the sharks in this movie, actor Thomas Jane has faced a gigantic bear in *Into the Grizzly Maze* (2015) and interdimensional creatures in *The Mist* (2007).

INDEX BY A–Z

PICTURE CREDITS

T: top **B:** bottom **L:** left **C:** center **R:** right **BG:** background

---

ACKNOWLEDGMENTS

Paul Terry would like to thank: all of the contributing sources, especially paleobiologists Luke Hauser and David Martill, Anna Loynes and Nielsen for the music intel, and the brilliant IMDb and VGChartz teams; my Editor extraordinaire Polly Poulter for knocking another T-10 book out of the park; my brilliant Editorial Director Trevor Davies for the ongoing support (and film recommendations); Team T-10's designer, picture researchers, sub-editors, proofreaders, and marketeers for all their hard work; all at Octopus Books and Readerlink; and as always, a massive thank you to my frequent collaborator Tara Bennett for all the support and encouragement while I juggled these facts and stats alongside our other creature-filled projects.

DATA SOURCES:

Pages: 11, 16, 17, 24, 25, 32, 33 – data sourced from Luke Hauser and David Martill, paleobiologists. Pages: 98, 100–127, 253 – data sourced from VGChartz.com Pages: 152–154, 156, 158–163 – data sourced from the Council on Tall Buildings and Urban Habitat. Pages: 204–209, 211, 218–227 – data sourced from Copyright © 2016 The Nielsen Company. All rights reserved. Nielsen and the Nielsen logo are trademarks or registered trademarks of CZT/ACN Trademarks, L.L.C. Other product and service names are trademarks or registered trademarks of their respective companies.15/9032. Pages: 230–237 – data sourced from NASA (https://solarsystem. nasa.gov). Pages: 256, 260, 262–265, 268, 270–275, 278–279, 282–300 – data sourced from IMDB.com. Box office information courtesy of The Internet Movie Database (http://www.imdb.com). Used with permission.

The Top 10 team collects data on a rolling basis. All data in this book is the most recent data available at time of going to press.